Praise for *The Silver Waterfall*

"The battle of Midway in June 1942 has rightly held a commanding place in the history of the Second World War. And this great and significant new book by Professor Brendan Simms and veteran Steve McGregor not only reminds us of Midway's importance and drama, but also clearly establishes that the US victory was not just luck, despite common views to the contrary. Simms and McGregor relate a riveting story of migration, innovation, and skill that takes us from 1920s California to the climactic five minutes that doomed the Japanese strike force to destruction—and from there to the lessons of a climactic battle for a United States that once more faces a rising power in the Pacific. *The Silver Waterfall* is a story of authentic American characters, settings, issues, and heroism that will stay with readers long after they put the book down."

—GENERAL DAVID PETRAEUS, US Army (ret.); former commander of the surge in Iraq, US Central Command, and US/Coalition Forces in Afghanistan; and former director of the CIA

"While the Battle of Midway was decided by a margin of just five minutes, this was a critical difference made possible by the US Navy's relentless, painstaking effort. Numerous books have been written on this monumental battle to prove this point, but none shed better light on the battle-winning weapon, the Dauntless, than *The Silver Waterfall*. With extensive research on the technologies, tactics, and people behind the battle's aerial warfare, this book stands out among the literature, skillfully elucidating the ultimate causes of US naval victory."

—TSUKAMOTO KATSUYA, head of the security and economy division, National Institute for Defense Studies, Japan

"The Silver Waterfall provides a top-to-bottom description of the epic Battle of Midway."

—BARRETT TILLMAN, author of *Enterprise: America's Fightingest Ship*

"*The Silver Waterfall* is a splendidly written account of America's greatest naval battle. Simms and McGregor capture the grand sweep of history and strategy while bringing to life the skill, luck, and heroism of the men who turned the tide. An elegant tribute to the past with sobering reflections for our own time."

—A. WESS MITCHELL, former assistant secretary of state, European and Eurasian Affairs

"From aeronautical drawing boards in Southern California to Pacific waters aflame with spilled oil from twisted steel hulks, *The Silver Waterfall* is a unique new telling of one of history's greatest battles. Written by one of the world's leading historians and by a US Army combat veteran, *The Silver Waterfall* reveals in detail how advanced technology, intelligence gathering, planning, and unimaginable heroism turned the tide of the Pacific War in a single, blood-soaked day. As America faces a geopolitical challenge in Asia potentially equal to that of the 1940s, Simms and McGregor remind us why history remains a critical guide to thinking about the future. All policymakers should read the lessons in this book."

—MICHAEL R. AUSLIN, Hoover Institution, Stanford University,
and author of *Asia's New Geopolitics: Essays on Reshaping the Indo-Pacific*

"A vividly told and compelling history of one of history's most remarkable battles. While the Americans famously had much luck on their side, Simms and McGregor make clear that fortune favored the prepared—the Americans brought not only luck but also determination, skill, intrepidity, and professionalism. As the American Pacific primacy Midway helped gain is now under challenge from a rising China, this book serves as a timely and stirring reminder of the qualities it will take to sustain it."

—ELBRIDGE COLBY, former deputy assistant secretary of defense,
Strategy and Force Development, US Department of Defense; and author
of *Strategy of Denial: American Defense in an Age of Great Power Conflict*

"In *The Silver Waterfall*, authors Simms and McGregor focus on how the pivotal 1942 Battle of Midway was equally a result of technology and solid training as it was good fortune in catching Admiral Nagumo's Japanese carrier fleet at such an inopportune moment. In their original presentation, the authors build up to the climax by focusing on dive-bomber engineer Ed Heinemann, military strategist Chester Nimitz, and SBD Dauntless dive-bomber pilot Norman 'Dusty' Kleiss, a skilled aviator who epitomized American performance on June 4.

The book is rich with gripping drama during its lengthy coverage of the key five-minute span where Nimitz's carrier-air groups assault the Japanese carrier fleet. Simms and McGregor offer excellent Japanese perspectives of the chaos and destruction as carriers Kaga, Akagi, and Soryu are blasted apart. This fresh look at the Battle of Midway belongs on the bookshelf of any serious student of the Pacific War."

—STEPHEN L. MOORE, author of *Battle Stations:
How the USS Yorktown Helped Turn the Tide at Coral Sea and Midway*

"If you only read one book of history this year, make it *The Silver Waterfall*. Nobody better conjures military history into view. We need urgently to understand their conclusion that 'unless the United States wakes up to the steady erosion of its naval power, it risks another Pearl Harbor—without any guarantee of another Midway.'"

—KORI SCHAKE, director of foreign and defense policy,
American Enterprise Institute

THE SILVER WATERFALL

HOW AMERICA WON THE WAR IN THE PACIFIC AT MIDWAY

BRENDAN SIMMS
AND STEVEN McGREGOR

PUBLICAFFAIRS

New York

PublicAffairs
Hachette Book Group
1290 Avenue of the Americas, New York, NY 10104
www.publicaffairsbooks.com
@Public_Affairs

Printed in the United States of America

First Edition: May 2022

Published by PublicAffairs, an imprint of Perseus Books, LLC, a subsidiary of Hachette Book Group, Inc. The PublicAffairs name and logo is a trademark of the Hachette Book Group.

The Hachette Speakers Bureau provides a wide range of authors for speaking events. To find out more, go to www.hachettespeakersbureau.com or call (866) 376-6591.

The publisher is not responsible for websites (or their content) that are not owned by the publisher.

Print book interior design by Jeff Williams.

Library of Congress Cataloging-in-Publication Data

Names: Simms, Brendan, author. | McGregor, Steve, 1981– author.
Title: The silver waterfall : how America won the war in the Pacific at Midway / Brendan Simms and Steve McGregor.
Other titles: How America won the war in the Pacific at Midway
Description: First edition. | New York : PublicAffairs, [2022] | Includes bibliographical references and index.
Identifiers: LCCN 2021041953 | ISBN 9781541701373 (hardcover) | ISBN 9781541701397 (ebook)
Subjects: LCSH: Midway, Battle of, 1942.
Classification: LCC D774.M5 S54 2022 | DDC 940.54/26699—dc23/eng/20211027

LC record available at https://lccn.loc.gov/2021041953

ISBNs: 9781541701373 (hardcover) 9781541701397 (ebook)

LSC-C

Printing 1, 2022

Five minutes! Who would have dreamed
that the tide of battle would shift completely
in that brief interval of time?

—MITSUO FUCHIDA, *captain,*
Imperial Japanese Navy, eyewitness

— Furthest extent of Japanese control in World War II

SOVIET UNION

Lake Baikal

Sakhalin

Attu
Kiska
Aleutian Is.

MANCHUKUO
(Manchuria)

Vladivostok

Kurile Islands

MONGOLIA

Peking

KOREA

Sea of
Japan

JAPAN

Tokyo

PACIFIC OCEAN

CHINA

Yellow
Nanking Sea
Shanghai

Ryukyu
Islands

Midway

Iwo Jima

Okinawa
Formosa

Hong
Hanoi Kong

Saipan

Wake

Hawaiian Islands

Rangoon
THAILAND
(Siam)
Hainan
INDOCHINA
Bangkok
Saigon

Manila

Mariana Islands

Guam

PHILIPPINES

Marshall
Is.

MALAYA
Singapore

Caroline Islands

Bismarck
Arch.

Gilbert Is.

Sumatra
INDONESIA (Netherlands India)
Jakarta
Dutch East Indies
Java

Borneo

New
Guinea

Solomon Is.

Guadalcanal

0   1000 Miles

0   1000 Kilometers

AUSTRALIA

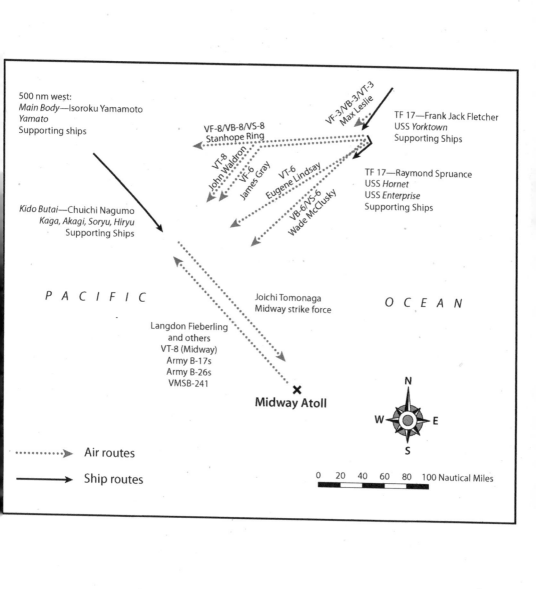

500 nm west:
Main Body—Isoroku Yamamoto
Yamato
Supporting ships

VF-8/VB-8/VS-8
Stanhope Ring

VF-3/VB-3/VT-3
Max Leslie

TF 17—Frank Jack Fletcher
USS *Yorktown*
Supporting Ships

VT-8
John Waldron

VF-6
James Gray

VT-6
Eugene Lindsay

TF 17—Raymond Spruance
USS *Hornet*
USS *Enterprise*
Supporting Ships

Kido Butai—Chuichi Nagumo
Kaga, Akagi, Soryu, Hiryu
Supporting Ships

VB-6/VS-6
Wade McClusky

P A C I F I C

Joichi Tomonaga
Midway strike force

O C E A N

Langdon Fieberling
and others
VT-8 (Midway)
Army B-17s
Army B-26s
VMSB-241

✕
Midway Atoll

N
W   E
S

┈┈┈► Air routes

───► Ship routes

0   20   40   60   80   100 Nautical Miles

CONTENTS

AUTHORS' NOTE

Brendan Simms

I was first introduced to the Battle of Midway at the birthday party of a school friend in 1976. We had gone to the cinema to see the new blockbuster film on the subject starring Henry Fonda, Charlton Heston, and Glenn Ford. I enjoyed the first half of the film, with its strategic backgrounding and personal drama, and became engrossed by the initial battle scenes. Soon, however, the tender eight-year-old was overwhelmed by the blood and burns of injured Wildcat and Devastator pilots. I left the theater and watched the last hour or so of the film intermittently over the shoulder of an usher at the exit. I could not see much, but I did register the spectacular detonations that rocked the doomed Japanese aircraft carriers, their purple glow unmistakable even from my vantage point in the hallway.

I took four things away from that day. The first was an abiding squeamishness about the physical costs of war in terms of death, pain, and burned flesh, which coexisted with the second, a new and profound interest in all things military, and the third, an (indefensibly) undimmed enthusiasm for "action" movies (so long as they were not too violent). Ten years passed before I dared to watch the film again, on television, though I have subsequently seen it on DVD many times. The fourth takeaway was an enduring fascination with the battle itself that has remained with me to this day, and to which this book is a testament.

Steven McGregor

I learned about Midway in 2019. I had been an infantry officer in the 101st Airborne Division, deployed to Iraq at the tail end of the surge. Originally commissioned at the United States Air Force Academy and having received a pilot slot, I requested a transfer to the infantry. The army needed officers. I had to read an article about it in the *New Yorker* of all places. After graduating from Infantry Officer School, Ranger School, and Air Assault School, I took my first platoon in Charlie Company of the 3rd Battalion of the 3rd Brigade of the 101st.

Several years after my return from Iraq, I became a historian. I met Brendan, and we began to talk about the Battle of Midway. I came across the memoir of Dusty Kleiss, one of the most important of the Dauntless dive-bomber pilots. He recalled his thoughts on the night before the famous battle: "Would I die tomorrow?" he asked himself. His fear was sickeningly familiar to me: "I fretted I might not make it home to marry Jean," he wrote. "My earlier reluctance gnawed away at me guiltily." It was my experience all over again. Like Kleiss, I had gone to war without proposing, thinking it would be more responsible to wait. And, also like Kleiss, I found myself far from home, wondering what I'd been thinking, convinced I'd made a mistake. Like Kleiss, I survived. Also like Kleiss, the girl I had sorely missed became my wife. But my sense of war as definitional, as a force that brings out the essence in men and women and in nations, has only strengthened.

PROLOGUE

IT WAS IN THE MIDDLE OF THE WAR, IN THE MIDDLE OF THE Pacific Ocean, and to Lieutenant Commander Clarence "Wade" McClusky, who was leading the Dauntless dive bombers from the aircraft carrier USS *Enterprise*, it seemed as if they were in the middle of nowhere, running dangerously short on fuel. Then the clouds opened and the main Japanese fleet appeared before him. McClusky's planes adopted attack formation, and he led his men into the dive maneuver they had practiced so often. To one observer, the descending dive bombers, the sun reflecting from their wingtips, looked like a "beautiful silver waterfall."

INTRODUCTION

THE BATTLE OF MIDWAY, IN WHICH AMERICA BROKE THE BACK of the Imperial Japanese Navy, has long been recognized as one of the turning points of World War II. It captured the imagination of the American public as an astonishing victory and has been celebrated in two major feature films, one released in 1976 and the other in 2019. The Japanese, it was said, had a clear numerical advantage in ships and aircraft. They were also widely believed to be more skilled than their American counterparts. The historian Walter Lord titled his book on the subject *Incredible Victory*. "They had no right to win," he wrote of the Americans, attributing victory to "Lady Luck." In the same vein, Gordon Prange titled his classic account *Miracle of Midway*. America's victory became a matter of divine intervention.

Luck and chance played a large role in the 1976 film, simply called *Midway*. A Japanese commander, desperate to find the US fleet, orders his scout plane to fly to the last reported position of the Americans and then "trust to luck." An American officer does the same. "Were we better than the Japanese," Admiral Chester Nimitz asks toward the end of the film, "or just luckier?"

Our book advances a very different argument. Unlike Allied war efforts in most other theaters in World War II, where, broadly speaking, the initial incompetence of professionals slowly gave way to the mass firepower of an amateur citizen army, the tide in

3

the Pacific was turned quickly by a peacetime navy. The Battle of Midway was decided by the skill of the dive-bomber pilots and the effectiveness of their equipment. If the Americans were lucky, they made their own luck.

Moreover, the navy, like the other service branches, could draw on the skills of a wide variety of emigrants or descendants of emigrants—especially from Germany, the principal hostile power. The engineer who designed the plane that decided the battle was Ed Heinemann; the strategist who decided that America would defend Midway was Admiral Nimitz; and the pilot who epitomized American performance on the day of battle was Norman Jack "Dusty" Kleiss. All three were German Americans. Without these men, America could not have designed and planned its strategy or done what was needed to win.

The Battle of Midway has been written about at length, and debates about it have been an argument without end, as the study of history should be. We do not purport to offer a definitive account, only a distinctive one. The first three chapters adopt a wide-angle view, locating the battle not just in the context of the deterioration of US-Japanese relations and the development of carrier warfare, but also in the broader sweep of American history. We begin with a story of innovation: how Heinemann created the battle-winning Douglas Dauntless dive bomber. This is followed by a chapter on Nimitz, the military strategist who put the Dauntless planes in the right place at the right time. We round out this first part of the book with a chapter on the pilot, Kleiss, whose intense training prepared him for the day that would define his life. Without the skill he and his comrades demonstrated that day, all the technological wizardry and strategic acumen in the world would have been to no avail.

In the second part of the book we steadily narrow the focus. One chapter explains how Admiral Isoroku Yamamoto planned to lure the Americans into a trap near Midway in the Pacific, and how Nimitz, thanks to superior military intelligence, was able to lay a snare of his own. It describes the sense of drama and foreboding as the confrontation drew near. We follow this up with a detailed account of the opening salvos of the battle as American land-based bombers and torpedo planes grappled with the Japanese fleet in vain. The book culminates with a chapter covering just five minutes—the crucial moments when the American dive bombers struck and crippled their opponent. Good fortune played a role, of course, but the key factors were superior training and technology. Professionals, not amateurs, won the day. The US victory at Midway was not inevitable, to be sure, but neither was it accidental.

This was war as pure as it could be. Not pure in the sense that it was beautiful or clean, but in the sense that it was fought only between men who had sailed thousands of miles to be there. Naval dive bombing was similarly intentional. In dive bombing, unlike in high-altitude bombing, a pilot brought his plane down below 3,000 feet to release his ordnance. He could see what he was about to destroy. The target was discrete, identifiable. It also bore the flag of his enemy. Naval dive bombing was designed to break ships, not a people's will. No civilians were killed at Midway. Even so, the battle was brutal, and sometimes criminal.

We hope our account does justice to the color and drama of this iconic juncture in world history without sensationalizing it. We tried to show that the protagonists were not only warriors but men with pasts and, in the case of the survivors, futures. Some of them were deeply moral people who thought hard about the act of killing. In the penultimate chapter, we chronicle the agony of their victims, the crewmen of the Japanese fleet, as they battled to save their burning carriers and their comrades, many of whom suffered terrible wounds. In the final section, we zoom back out to look at the legacy of this epic battle, and at what it means for a world in which the possibility of armed conflict in the Pacific is once again a terrifying reality.

PART I

BEFORE

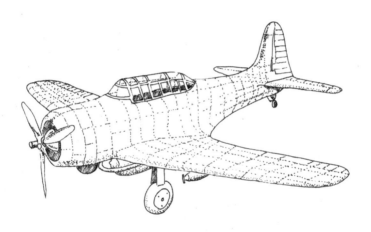

1

THE ENGINEER

IN THE BEGINNING WAS THE PLANE. WITHOUT THE DOUGLAS Dauntless dive bomber, the US Navy would never have won the Battle of Midway. Its designer, Ed Heinemann, a German American, went on to become one of the country's greatest aerospace engineers. Though slow and drafty, the sturdy Dauntless could dive straight down, remain controllable, and survive enormous stresses as it regained stable flight. It could also carry a bomb load of more than 1,000 pounds. The Dauntless was mass-produced at the Douglas plant in El Segundo, California, near Los Angeles. At one point during the war, Adolf Hitler asserted that the conflict was a "war of engineers" and lamented that German Americans were working on the side of the Allies.[1] On that count, he knew what he was talking about.

✪

EDWARD HEINEMANN WAS BORN Gustave Henry Edward Heinemann in Saginaw, Michigan, in 1908. His mother had emigrated from German-speaking Switzerland as a young girl.[2] His father was American-born but of German ancestry. Germans, in fact, were the single largest national group in the United States at that time.[3] The young Edward—he lost the "Gustave" early on—grew up with German spoken all around him. He clearly had an artistic and mechanical streak from the start, because his grandfather, observing Edward's homemade toys, said that "der Eduard ist aber ein Künstler" (Edward really is an artist).[4]

When Heinemann was about seven, the family moved to California, settling in Germantown at the northern end of the Sacramento Valley. His father's lemon trees did not prosper, and it was not long before the Heinemanns wound up in San Francisco.

There, in 1915, the young Edward was first exposed to the world of aviation. It was only twelve years since the Wright brothers had made their pioneering flight at Kitty Hawk on the other side of the United States.[5] San Francisco was buzzing with excitement about the Panama-Pacific International Exposition, which featured some of the new airplanes. The young Heinemann was mesmerized by these Heath-Robinson constructions of bamboo, spruce, and fabric. Looking at the concluding aerial display in early December of that year, he exclaimed, "Wunderbar!" (Wonderful!). A man standing nearby was so impressed that he turned to Edward's mother and remarked, "Madam, I would give one hundred dollars if I could speak German as well as your son."

The following year, 1916, Heinemann Sr. took a job in Los Angeles. Edward gravitated toward the Ascot Park Speedway, a racetrack at which aircraft landed and airships moored. As the huge Goodyear blimps loomed toward earth, he and several other boys would seize the guy lines to draw them in. In high winds they could be yanked high above the ground, and one day, Edward found himself 30 feet up, hanging on for dear life. The rush, the danger, and the technology itself, which made humanity seem both small and great at once—this was the world of early aviation.

A year later, the United States and the German Reich were at war. As Heinemann later recalled, that "pretty much ended our speaking the German language."[6] Germantown was renamed "Artois," after the series of World War I battles fought in the French province of that name. Not that Heinemann was in any doubt about his identity and loyalties. He may have been half German and half German-Swiss, but his home was in America.

After attending a grammar school in a Los Angeles suburb, Heinemann enrolled in Manual Arts High, which taught mechanical skills to young men. He was a diligent student and impressed his drafting teacher, August Flam, who helped him build up a portfolio of mechanical drawings. In his spare time, Heinemann read anything to do with airplanes and boats: "mathematics, mechanics, aerodynamics, physics, chemistry, meteorology." He had little formal training in these subjects but acquired a knowledge and "feel" for them that would stand him in good stead later.[7]

Heinemann continued to hang around the Ascot Park Speedway. He was particularly struck by Mary Anita "Neta" Snook, a kindly redhead who had taught another female pioneer aviator, Amelia Earhart, how to fly. This redoubtable lady had her first application for flight training stamped "no females allowed."[8] Undaunted, she had single-handedly reassembled a wrecked aircraft over the course of two years and taught herself to fly it. Heinemann helped her push her plane in and out of the hangar. Snook never actually delivered on her promise to give him a ride, but she did give the youngster early experience in handling aircraft.[9] As an old man, he would remember that magnificent woman and her flying machine with great affection.

In 1925, aged seventeen, Heinemann left school before completing his high school diploma. He knocked around for a while doing various jobs and attended night courses in aircraft design. Then Heinemann had his chance. In 1926, he was invited to apply for a training job as a tracer and draftsman at the Douglas Aircraft Company, which was then operating out of an old film studio in Santa Monica.

"My first impression," remembered Heinemann about arriving for his interview, "was the smell of banana oil or dope." Dope in this case was a kind of varnish used to stiffen aircraft fabric. The odor hung about the office, where some twenty draftsmen worked at large drafting tables. At the largest table was a shaggy-haired man in plus fours and a pair of argyle green-and-brown golf socks. This was James Howard "Dutch" Kindelberger, Douglas's chief engineer ("Dutch" was shorthand *Deutsch*, "German"). He was so impressed by Heinemann's portfolio that he offered him a job on the spot.[10]

When we speak of California today, we instinctively think of film and technology. In the 1920s, Hollywood was already a phenomenon, but the South Bay of San Francisco, what is now Silicon Valley, was still filled with plum and orange trees. The engineers and designers were in Los Angeles working in aviation. To be sure, aircraft were being built in other parts of the United States as well: in New York by Grumman, Curtiss, and Brewster; in Connecticut by Chance Vought; in Ohio by Great Lakes Aircraft. But it was in Los Angeles that three of aviation's greatest designers—Dutch Kindelberger, John K. "Jack" Northrop, and Donald Douglas—were to be found. Heinemann worked with all three men, later describing them as "healthy rivals and the best designers of their time."[11]

California attracted the aviation industry. Unlike other parts of the country, the state enjoyed the kind of climate that allowed for comfortable flying and maintenance all year round. In those days Californians experimented with aircraft in the same way as they do with software today. Designers, engineers, and pilots were constantly switching between jobs, tinkering with their machines far into the night. It was exciting, innovative, and often hazardous work.[12]

German Americans were especially prominent in this world. That was not surprising, because, as legend has it, Germans make good engineers. In the 1920s, Heinemann worked with many metalsmiths and engineers of a similar background. Along with Kindelberger, these men included Shorty Kaisar, Elmer "Weity" Weitekamp,[13] Fred Herman, Karl Peter "Pop" Grube, H. A. Speer, Art Goebel,[14] and Harry Wetzel.[15] He does not seem to have known the larger-than-life pilot and aircraft manufacturer Otto Timm, who operated out of Glendale, California, and later built gliders for the D-Day landings. Amelia Earhart was also of part-German ancestry, as her name (Americanized from "Ehrhardt") suggests. Her associate Wilmer Stultz, a Pennsylvania "Dutchman," made the first nonstop flight from New York to Havana. The list is endless. Years later, long after World War II, the National Air and Space Museum honored the contributions of German Americans to US aviation with a special exhibition.[16]

California was no paradise. Even before the Depression, many lived a precarious existence. There were severe racial tensions, especially between people of European, Asian, and Latino descent. The desire to limit Asian immigration into California was part of the background to the notorious 1924 Immigration Act. The large Japanese community in particular resisted discrimination fiercely, and this led to tension between the United States and the Japanese Empire before World War I.

If Heinemann was aware of this controversy, which continued to simmer throughout the 1920s, he left no record of it. His sister Helen married a native Hawaiian, which does not seem to have been an issue for him.[17] In time, though, the racial tensions of the age were ultimately to have a major bearing on Heinemann's life as well as the lives of millions of others.

✪

AMERICAN AVIATION EPITOMIZED AMERICAN capitalism. In the 1920s, the industry was a frenetic start-up sector recovering from the boom of World War I. Creative but also chaotic destruction ensued as firms chased contracts and profit margins. Many of these aircraft manufacturers were no more than sheds beside a makeshift airstrip.

Heinemann instantly took to this world. He moved from one company to another, and sometimes back again. In February 1927, he was laid off from Douglas, but the chief draftsman gave him a glowing recommendation, calling him a "fast and willing worker."[18] After seven months at the somewhat grandiosely named International Corporation (which said it built aircraft "to a standard not to a price"), in Long Beach, near Los Angeles, he garnered similar praise from the company's chief engineer.[19] In October 1929, the day before the stock market crash, Heinemann left Moreland Aircraft of Inglewood, California, with a letter of recommendation from its president.[20] In between, he would go back to work for Douglas, which served as a kind of "lender of last resort" when times were rough for the aviation sector in the state.[21]

Heinemann excelled at solving technical problems. When a friend at a small aircraft firm described the severity of landing on the structure of an airplane, the eighteen-year-old Heinemann drafted and manufactured a solution. The result was a pneumatic landing-gear strut, which later became a common feature in aircraft and is still used today. Weight was another aspect of aircraft design that was always under consideration. Along with the metalsmith Shorty Kaisar, Heinemann reduced the weight of a racing plane by replacing the fuel tank with a lighter aluminum design and by rearranging the cabin seating.[22] As Pop Grube, who first met Heinemann in the late 1920s, recalled, it was an exciting time. "We were young," he wrote, "full of ambition and thought we knew the answer to everything."[23]

In 1929, Heinemann designed his first aircraft "from drawing to flight" at the age of just twenty-one.[24] Known as the Moreland M-1, it sported a single fabric-covered wing that ran above the cabin. Fully loaded it weighed 2,750 pounds. Heinemann designed the Moreland to carry a pilot and one passenger, but the four that were manufactured ended up being used as crop dusters.[25] It was certainly an achievement of technical skill, but for Heinemann it was also very much a matter of artistry. "Show me a good design," Heinemann later recalled, "and I will show you the 'art' that went into it." "Designing," he continued, "is[,] in my opinion, a high order of specialized art."[26] In their symmetry and clean lines there is an unmistakable beauty to airplanes, their silhouettes as awesome as weapons, as distinctive as faces. Heinemann was, indeed, already an artist.

In the meantime, he learned to fly, taking lessons at twenty dollars an hour.[27] He also learned to use a parachute. As he spent time with aviators, he gained the respect of many test pilots, including the skilled Vance Breese. Later these were the men who would put their lives in Heinemann's hands each time they took off in one of his designs.

Heinemann seems to have weathered the Wall Street crash quite well, moving to the Northrop Corporation in Burbank, California. When the company planned to move to Kansas in 1931, he chose to stay in California. The corporation's legendary vice president, Jack Northrop, added more praise for Heinemann's abilities as an engineer.[28] The following year, Heinemann turned up at Northrop's plant in El Segundo, the place where he would spend most of his working life.

Unsurprisingly for a Californian, Heinemann also had a passion for boats. At seventeen he built his first: a 16-foot sloop with a motor. In the right weather, he would ride it along the coast of Los Angeles and out to Catalina, one of the Channel Islands, just over twenty miles away. He also designed racing boats and toyed with the idea of a maritime career. Heinemann, in short, was comfortable designing for both sea and air.[29]

✪

IT WAS IN FACT at the intersection of the two worlds, naval aviation, that Heinemann was to earn his place in history. America quickly grasped the significance of aircraft for controlling the sea and pursued naval aviation along with powered flight itself. The first aircraft to take off from a ship flew from the USS *Birmingham*, in Hampton Roads, Virginia, in November 1910. Then, during World War I, seaplanes demonstrated their value by conducting reconnaissance and harassing the enemy. Their cumbersome design, however, made them less suited for combat than land-based aircraft. Toward the end of the conflict, the British converted a liner into a ship capable of both launching and landing aircraft with undercarriages, and the aircraft carrier was born as HMS *Argus*. In 1922, the US Navy converted a large collier into its first carrier, the USS *Langley*, and soon keels were being laid for the first purpose-built carriers of the Lexington class.

Aviation is a difficult skill—naval aviation even more so. The most challenging maneuver is landing the plane, which is achieved through what is essentially a controlled crash. The pilot must bring the aircraft to a safe halt while monitoring altitude, speed, heading, pitch, and level, a task made all the more dangerous on the deck of a ship. The flight deck is always in motion: normally in or close to the wind, surging up or down according to the sea-state, and yawing from one side to another. The pilot must align himself with the center of the flight deck to avoid veering off into the sea, and must touch down within a certain area in order for the tailhook of his plane to catch one of the arrestor wires stretched across the deck. Otherwise, before the introduction of the angled flight deck in 1955, the plane could not be stopped before plowing into other aircraft if they were parked on the forward end.

Initially, carrier-borne aircraft were armed with torpedoes or bombs that would be dropped while in level flight. During World War I, however, pilots experimented with dive bombing. The plane would dive at the target and then, at the last possible moment, release its bomb and pull up. The bomb was essentially hurled where the pilot wanted it to go. What level bombing achieved by chance, if at all, dive bombing accomplished through skill. The difference was a vast improvement in accuracy. As early as 1918, a British pilot used the technique: diving on target before releasing his bomb. In the US Navy, the technique was first used in an exercise off Long Beach in October 1926; several battleships were surprised before they could even sound general quarters. The man who led the attack, Frank Dechant Wagner, recalled that the subsequent reports all agreed "there was no defence" against dive bombing.[30] Then, in 1928, US Marine aviators operating in Nicaragua developed what is now considered "the first combat-tested dive-bombing techniques." Within a decade, dive bombers and torpedo bombers constituted the main strike capability of US aircraft carriers.[31]

There were important differences between the two forms of aerial attack. Torpedo bombing, which was the preferred method of the British and the Japanese, was intended to sink a ship by flooding it with water. The torpedo traveled at a depth of some 30 feet and detonated upon hitting the ship, breaching the hull. Dive bombing was different. The ordnance rained down from above, puncturing a ship's deck, and then, with a delayed fuse, traveled through several decks before igniting a fire within the ship's guts. Because the hull remained intact, effective dive bombing transformed a ship into a floating pyre. The advantage of dive bombing—indeed, of any sort of bombing—was that damage to the flight deck could stop a carrier from launching or landing aircraft, rendering it temporarily useless, while a carrier that had suffered several torpedo hits might be able to continue air operations.

Dive bombing was a particularly demanding form of warfare. It placed huge strain on pilots. A steep dive meant a near-vertical descent from 15,000 to 1,000 feet in less than a minute. The rise in air pressure hurt the sinuses, and the acceleration turned the stomach. Then came the most grueling moment, when the pilot would release his bomb and pull up. Momentum shifted as the plane, which had been diving toward the ocean, changed direction to fly parallel to its surface. The perceived force of gravity intensified to seven, eight, or even nine times its normal force. The pilot felt the blood in his body rush into his seat, draining from his brain. His vision grayed around the edges, and, if the dive recovery was too quick, he might lose consciousness. Stanhope Ring, one of the Dauntless pilots at Midway, said dive bombing was like "hitting yourself in the head with a baseball bat."[32] This kind of self-harm required judgment. "The whole of the dive is really an aiming period," remembered another pilot. "You are pointing the plane." But the pointing was counterintuitive. It meant deliberately hurtling toward the target, plunging down as if intending to crash. For as long as the pilot endangered himself, he could steer the bomb toward the enemy. During this time, unsecured items of equipment floated about the cockpit and the rear-seat gunner shouted the altitude on the intercom while the pilot, secured only by a single lap belt, peered into a telescopic sight and attempted to concentrate: one hand wrestled the control stick, and the other waited to release the bomb. Pull up too soon, and the bomb might miss; too late, and the plane would crash. This was a task requiring immense skill and daring.

One of the first men to master it was Clarence "Wade" Mc-Clusky. Born in Buffalo, New York, of Protestant (probably Presbyterian) Scotch Irish and Irish Catholic stock at a time when these distinctions mattered intensely, he attempted to compromise by becoming an Episcopalian. After officer training at the United States Naval Academy in Annapolis, Maryland, McClusky learned to fly at the Naval Air Station in Pensacola, Florida. He was a talented pilot, earning a place in the navy's "High Hats" aerobatics squadron in the late 1920s, during which time he made his first landing on an aircraft carrier. This skill served him well when he took up dive bombing. McClusky made his first dive in 1930 and went on to log about four hundred hours' worth of time in similar aircraft before switching to fighters.[33]

What dive bombing did to man it also did to machine. Many planes could not withstand the speed of a steep dive or the stress of pulling up from one. In those days planes were composites of wood, fabric, and metal. In a 1929 test flight, one pilot experienced severe vibration after entering a dive. Recovering, he realized that "portions of the fabric covering the right wing surface had been torn off the ribs and were tattering in the slip stream." The vibrations produced by the speed of the air over the wing had pulled the plane apart. Fortunately, he managed a safe landing.[34]

Other pilots were not so lucky. The most dangerous moment in dive bombing was the recovery from the dive. Flight is possible because an aircraft's wings generate more lift than its weight. When pulling up from a dive, however, an aircraft's effective weight is increased in proportion to the angle of its recovery. A shallow recovery, when the pilot eases back on the stick, gradually introduces weight onto the wings. But a sharp recovery, caused by jerking the stick back, was required if a pilot wanted to release his bomb at the last possible moment. "You had to execute a 90-degree turn that low," remembered Heinemann.[35] This dramatically increased the effective weight of the aircraft—a weight that the wings needed to counteract by producing an equal or greater amount of lift; otherwise, the plane would stall. As with landing, the low altitude meant little room for error. When the stress of recovery overwhelmed one plane in 1931, the crash that ensued obliterated the pilot: "All that was recovered" was his "helmet and a part of his brain."[36]

While pilots waited for more rugged planes, they adjusted their tactics. This meant shallower dives and deeper recoveries— essentially, glide bombing instead of dive bombing. The adjustment made sense from an engineering standpoint, but it came with risks of its own. When approaching in a shallow dive, the pilot usually lost the element of surprise because his plane would be detected as it descended toward its target. The enemy had time to adjust antiaircraft fire and to prepare for attack. Moreover, as with level bombing, in glide bombing the horizontal motion of the plane made aiming more difficult, and this same motion was transferred to the bomb, requiring the pilot to release it in advance of the target. In a sense, the pilot was pitching the bomb, rather than flying it into the target. Another issue was the weight of the bomb itself. If a pilot dived on a target but decided not to release his bomb, its weight added to the load placed on his wings when recovering. Lighter payloads were therefore another means of lessening the stress of dive bombing.[37]

Despite the obvious efficacy of dive bombing, the advocates of level bombing did not give up. Partly, this resulted from the fact that the US Army had developed level bombers that could carry a greater number of bombs. These same planes had larger fuel tanks than dive bombers and could strike the enemy from farther away. But some of the risks of dive bombing, such as equipment failure and pilot error, encouraged strategists to look elsewhere, and by comparison, level bombing appeared to be a safe alternative. Supporters of this technique, known as the "Bomber Mafia," believed that with the right equipment they could be accurate while taking fewer risks. They envisioned a war that was, in a manner of speaking, clean. From an altitude of nearly 6 miles above the Earth, pilots would be relatively safe from attack. Believers in this idea put their faith in the colossally expensive Norden Bombsight, an analog computer that, according to its advocates, could "drop a bomb into a pickle barrel from six miles up." Pilots would be able to pick and choose their targets, destroying enemy forces or factories rather than, as often happened during area bombing runs, homes or hospitals. Supposedly, the same advantage would apply at sea. Curtis LeMay, a lieutenant and one of the leading members of the Bomber Mafia, proved the point in August 1937, when he and a squadron of B-17s hit the USS *Utah* with practice bombs in an exercise off the California coast.[38]

✪

MEANWHILE, THE JAPANESE WERE blazing their own path in the world and especially in naval aviation. They were latecomers to empire and modern warfare, but they caught up with astonishing speed. It was only a few decades after Commodore Matthew C. Perry had forced open the country in 1853 that the empire began a surge of rapid expansion. Japan first bested China, in 1894–1895, and then Russia, in 1904–1905. It sided with the Allies during World War I and was one of the victor powers in 1918. Japan, though, felt slighted by the refusal of the Western powers to accept the principle of racial equality at Versailles in 1919.[39]

The problem was compounded by the Washington Naval Treaty of 1922, which institutionalized Japanese naval inferiority in relation to the British Empire and the United States. The treaty stipulated that the navies of the United States, the United Kingdom, Japan, Italy, and France would abide by set limits in regard to the tonnage of certain ships and their navies as a whole. Proportionally, the United States and the United Kingdom would be equal in size, setting the benchmark for other powers. Japan would be smaller by 40 percent, and Italy and France smaller by about 60 percent. Signatories of the treaty claimed that these limitations would "contribute to the maintenance of the general peace, and . . . reduce the burdens of competition in armament."[40] Indeed, prior to the treaty, Japan was on track to spend 60 percent of its total budget on the construction of a vast naval fleet. Supporters of the Washington Naval Treaty, which included Isoroku Yamamoto, then a young Imperial Japanese naval officer, made this point. Yamamoto had traveled extensively in the United States, witnessing the automotive industry in Detroit and the oil resources in Texas. Hence, in the words of his biographer, he warned his country against "an unrestricted shipbuilding race" with the United States. But detractors thought the treaty was an insult and a hindrance. The Imperial Japanese Navy split into two factions: the "treaty faction" favored an agreement with America, and the "fleet faction" did not. Both groups, however, agreed that the United States was Japan's preeminent strategic rival.[41]

As part of its naval strategy and development, Japan also invested in aviation, starting with a great deal of foreign acquisition. Since Japan had not been part of the European arms race during World War I, it needed to catch up to other world powers. Once the war had finished, this was easily accomplished by purchasing stockpiled weaponry or hiring experienced engineers. Japan collaborated with many of aviation's leading experts—Sopwith in Britain, Heinkel in Germany, SPAD in France—in order to develop its own manufacturing and design capabilities. An early culmination of this strategy was the launch of the *Hosho*, commissioned in 1922 as the world's first purpose-built aircraft carrier. Its planes were designed by an engineer from Britain, but, like the carrier itself, built in Japan.[42]

If the first phase of Japanese naval aviation was characterized by acquisition and partnership, the second was one of independent production. In 1930, Yamamoto became head of the Technical Division of the Technical Aviation Department. A veteran of Admiral Togo Heihachiro's victory at the Battle of Tsushima Strait, Yamamoto was a significant national figure. He was also an early supporter of naval aviation and had argued in favor of developing long-range bombers. Then, when he was promoted, becoming head of the entire department, he took a stronger line: the future of naval warfare, he said, was aviation. "The practical value of battleships has declined," Yamamoto told a group of young pilots in 1935. These increasingly large ships still held symbolic value but only as "decoration for our [navy's] living room." The decisive weapon at sea was the plane.[43]

In a process similar to military procurement in the United States, private firms in Japan competed for government contracts. The heavyweights are still familiar names today: Mitsubishi, Kawasaki, and Nakajima (now Subaru). But unlike the US practice, once a contract was awarded, more than one Japanese firm was allowed to manufacture the winning design for government purchase. This ensured competition while protecting a relatively fragile industry.[44] By the mid-1930s, Japan was independently producing aircraft that rivaled those of any manufactured in the United States or Europe.[45] In 1937, when war broke out with China, all the planes in the Japanese arsenal were Japanese made.[46]

The Japanese Navy's numerical inferiority put a premium on quality and innovation. By 1940, its air arm was roughly half the size of the US Navy's, but it was arguably the strongest in the world.[47] The fighter, the Mitsubishi A6M "Zero," was remarkably fast and long ranged. It could turn sharper and climb faster than any other fighter then in production. The torpedo bomber, the Nakajima B5N "Kate," was another fast aircraft and could carry ordnance that was heavier and far more accurate than its US counterpart could. More importantly, its hit-rate was effectively between 70 and 80 percent. The dive bomber, the Aichi D3A "Val," was also a sturdy and effective platform. It would go on to sink more Allied warships than any other type of Axis aircraft.[48]

Japan not only built a formidable arsenal of ships and planes but also nurtured a particularly talented and innovative generation of naval aviators and air-minded sailors. Yamamoto, in other words, was not alone. His generation included men such as Minoru Genda and Mitsuo Fuchida, who, as we shall see, were virtuosos in their field. They were also profoundly political, intensely patriotic, and even chauvinistic. Their love of country mingled with insecurity and wounded pride. They smarted under the restrictions of the Washington Treaty and burned with indignation at the treatment of Japanese immigrants in the United States. They wanted recognition of their own space and of their independent role in the world—which included the right to colonize others. Their main enemies were the United States and—to a lesser extent—the British Empire, which had divided up the world to the exclusion of Japan. They looked forward to the day when they would show their supremacy.

By the mid-1930s, the Japanese Empire was on the march. First, it seized Manchuria from China in 1931, drawing considerable international, and especially Anglo-American, attention. Further moves were in the offing, driven partly by imperial ambition and partly by resource shortage, especially of oil. Second, Japan developed a powerful military striking force and became the world leader in naval aviation. Third, while the immediate enemies were the Soviet Union and the Nationalist Chinese regime of Chiang Kai-shek, the ultimate enemies, both in China and more generally, were the British and the Americans. It was their perceived arrogance, their presumed right to dictate to the rest of the world, that was most offensive to the Japanese. War in the Far East, even as the democracies steeled themselves to face Germany and Italy in Europe, became a distinct possibility.

This was the backdrop for the US Navy's search for new aircraft. In 1934 the navy's Bureau of Aeronautics invited the aerospace industry to submit proposals for a dive bomber that adhered to specific requirements. As Ed Heinemann remembered it, "the plane had to take off from a pitching carrier deck with a full load of fuel and a 1,000-pound bomb, [and] be capable of performing a stable, vertical, zero-lift dive at an airspeed of less than 250 knots [287 miles per hour]." The dive would be initiated at about 20,000 feet and maintained until the bomb release point of 3,000 feet, at which point the pilot would immediately recover. The airplane also had to be capable of completing this maneuver even if the bomb was not released. Aside from these guidelines, which largely involved the strength and load-bearing abilities of the aircraft, there were two further requirements. First, the plane needed to use a special crutch to deliver the bomb: in flight it held the bomb against the fuselage, but upon release it swung down, releasing the bomb beyond the blades of the propeller. Second, the plane needed to adhere to certain dimensions. In order to fit inside the elevator used to transport planes from the hangar deck to the flight deck of an aircraft carrier, a plane's wingspan needed to be less than 42 feet in length.[49]

Heinemann had by now designed and built four planes; this was to be his fifth. Of course, like all such enterprises, the new aircraft was a collective venture. Jack Northrop, for example, played an important role, as did many others.[50] But the guiding spirit and genius throughout were those of Ed Heinemann. He quickly proposed an innovative design. Previous US dive bombers, such as the Curtiss SBC "Helldiver," were biplanes: they had a wing above and beneath the fuselage. This afforded a great amount of lift for a relatively small wingspan but created more drag because of the struts needed to fasten the wings together. Heinemann proposed a low-wing monoplane, whose wings would be short enough to fit onto a carrier elevator but wide enough to generate lift for flight. In fact, the surface area of Heinemann's new plane wings was greater than the surface area of its biplane predecessors: he did with one wing what other planes did with two.[51]

Heinemann could enlarge the wings because he designed them to be strong. Using techniques he'd learned from Northrop, Heinemann made his plane entirely of metal and reinforced it with an internal framework of metal cables coursing through its skin. This allowed the metal to endure much greater compression loads than was normal for planes of the time. The wings were also strong and lightweight because they were not solid but multicellular, composed of sections of ribs and lengthwise parts. As a result, his wings, unlike previous monoplane designs, did not bend to excess, but remained stiff and strong.

The performance characteristics of Heinemann's low-wing design were also particularly suited for naval aviation. Because the center of gravity was above rather than below the wing, the plane was easier to roll, a necessary maneuver in aerial combat. The plane could also land softer and take off from a shorter runway because of ground effect, that is, the deflection of air by the ground against the wing, which is stronger on low-wing planes. There were corresponding drawbacks, however. The ease of rolling Heinemann's plane meant that it required greater concentration to fly. Also, the early onset of ground effect, the same feature that softened the plane's landing and shortened its take-off distance, meant that the plane coasted when coming in to land and required a longer runway. The first problem was simply added to the job of a naval aviator. The second was rendered moot by the fact that naval planes came to a stop on deck by catching the arrestor wire.

Of course, Heinemann was not the first to design a monoplane. In the 1930s there were many technical advances, what one historian has referred to as a "design revolution" in aeronautical engineering, that made monoplanes a natural evolution. Streamlining, engine improvements, and structural advances meant that wings could be made that were stronger and larger than ever before. Working independently of each other, designers in Germany and the United States tested monoplanes.[52] But many companies still favored the biplane: it was compact and maneuverable, and they trusted it. Of the seven aircraft competing for the US Navy dive-bomber contract, four were biplanes. The only monoplanes were those proposed by Heinemann, Chance Vought, and Brewster.

Heinemann's design was further distinguished by its split flaps. All planes have flaps that extend beneath the trailing edge of the wings. These flaps increase lift at low speed and allow the plane to land in a shorter distance than they could without them. Heinemann added a second pair of flaps that extended above the wing. He also designed a hydraulic mechanism to extend either one or both sets of flaps symmetrically. In a dive, the extended split flaps acted as air brakes, slowing the plane and improving its maneuverability.[53] For obvious reasons, the development work was done in secrecy.[54] In November 1934, the US Navy awarded Douglas a contract to build the prototype, christened the XBT-1.

The prototype was tested at Mines Field, now Los Angeles International Airport, in July 1935. Heinemann went up with the test pilot, Vance Breese, and witnessed many of the dives from the back seat. This was partly for psychological reasons, to demonstrate "confidence in his product," and partly to observe the XBT-1's performance firsthand.[55] While Breese flew the plane, Heinemann operated a velocity-gravity recorder to gather data on the plane's airspeed and maximum acceleration. This information allowed him to calculate the speed and loading endured by the aircraft. He needed to make sure the plane could dive slower than the required 250 knots.[56] "I don't think there is anyone," Heinemann later said, "who has made more nine-G pullouts than Vance Breese and myself."[57] Many of these dives involved recoveries that brought on a force of nine times that of gravity. Heinemann must have experienced the same blackouts that sometimes overwhelmed naval pilots.

The risks of flight-testing an aircraft were considerable. One of Heinemann's greatest fears was that a set of flaps might fail to open or snap off. This would have caused "asymmetrical loading," a greater amount of drag on one side of the plane than the other, leading to "a wild rapid rotation of the aircraft about the longitudinal axis." The plane would twist out of control and quickly lose altitude.[58] But Heinemann climbed into the cockpit regardless in order to discover at first hand the many problems that would need to be solved before the prototype could be manufactured at scale.

The first discovery was that in a steep dive, when the split flaps were extended, the tail of the plane fluttered violently. Riding along in the plane, Heinemann saw the tail warp by as much as 2 feet. "This," as he later recalled, "scared the very hell out of me." The flaps created vortexes that disrupted the plane's lateral stability. Minor adjustments did not solve the problem. The National Advisory Committee for Aeronautics (NACA, now NASA) sent Charles Helm, a leading aerodynamic engineer, to El Segundo. After studying the problem, he suggested drilling a series of holes in the flaps to ease the flow of air over their surface.[59] As Heinemann complained, this made the aircraft, when its split flaps were opened, look like a "flying colander," but it did the trick. The plane was now capable of stable vertical dives without exceeding 250 knots.

Another problem was engine torching. The carburetor, which controlled the fuel-air mixture, was unable to accept the rapid change in pressure that took place during a dive. As a result, unnecessary fuel was injected into the engine and then sprayed out of the exhaust, where, as Heinemann remembered, "it ignited with alarming results." Skin panels were torched, the bomb displacement mechanism was rendered useless, and "flames would stream twenty or thirty feet along the bottom of the plane": each dive transformed the machine into an enormous plunging candle.[60]

There was no easy fix for this problem. It required lengthy experimentation, what Heinemann later called "the old fashioned trial-and-error method of engineering." He adjusted the carburetor on the ground and recorded the settings and then observed the plane in flight again and again until he was able to identify the mixture that worked. In all, it took "nearly 100 dive tests to eliminate the snags."[61]

Heinemann and Northrop were up against some stiff competition for the contract from some of the country's major aviation companies: Great Lakes, Chance Vought, Brewster, Grumman, and Curtiss.[62] In a reminder of the hazards involved, during a stall test the Vought prototype crashed over shallow water, killing both the pilot and Vought's representative. On paper, the Vought aircraft had the edge in performance, but compared to Heinemann's model it had "an excessive dive speed problem," which shows the importance of an effective dive brake.[63] The plane was also unable to handle a 1,000-pound payload effectively. Still, Vought received a contract, resulting in what later became a greatly inferior dive bomber, the Vought Vindicator.[64]

Heinemann's prototype was brought to Anacostia Naval Air Station for trials in December 1935. Cold weather revealed more problems, this time with the canopy and the landing gear. "Midnight rework corrected the problem," Heinemann remembered, "but hand filing the parts was tedious work."[65] The trials were satisfactorily completed, and the navy ordered fifty-two of the aircraft. Heinemann and his team delivered all but two—keeping those for continued improvements. The plane was difficult to handle at low speeds, so Heinemann made adjustments to the wing. He also upgraded the engine and the propeller and installed retractable landing gear in order to reduce drag. The plane then went to Langley Memorial Aeronautical Laboratory for tests in what was then the world's largest wind tunnel.[66] These resulted in further substantial improvements, which Heinemann oversaw. The navy project engineer, Edward Clexton, made a major contribution, as did another navy engineer, Walter Diehl.[67] The final plane can thus be described as a public-private partnership. The navy accepted the design in February 1939 and ordered a further fifty-seven of what Heinemann considered "a brand new airplane" compared to his initial proposal.[68] "The only thing remaining," said Heinemann, "was the split flaps used as dive brakes."[69] The plane went into production at the Douglas plant at El Segundo in June 1940, by which time war was already raging in China and Europe.

Six months later, Heinemann was called into Donald Douglas's office. The navy had wired with bad news: the first twenty planes that had been delivered were developing wrinkles on the wings. This indicated a structural weakness that could eventually disturb flight, or could even cause the wings to break off from the fuselage. Douglas asked Heinemann to personally investigate the problem. The planes were being used by a squadron of Marines under "austere conditions" at Guantanamo Bay, Cuba. Heinemann would need to travel there and, if possible, attempt to fix the problem in the field. His reputation, as well as the reputation of Douglas Aircraft, was at stake.

After two days of travel, Heinemann arrived in Cuba, landing in the midst of a jungle. Even in December, it was sweltering. A young lieutenant drove him out to the bay, where conditions were worse than Heinemann had imagined. The Marines were conducting flight operations on nothing more than "a coral airstrip with no facilities, just tents." Inspecting the wings, Heinemann found that there were indeed wrinkles, but he suspected the problem was not his design. The landing signal officer, who guided planes in for landing, was instructing the pilots to cut power very early in their approach. This was likely overstressing the wings at their roots.[70] "I need some more hard data," Heinemann told the pilots. "I'd like to take some pictures of a plane touching down." Referring to his personal camera, he said, "I brought a Leica with me." "You what!" said the senior Marine officer. It wasn't about personal safety but operational security. As Heinemann put it, "I'm sure there was a moment or two in which he questioned the intelligence level of a certain civilian engineer named Heinemann." It would be nearly another two years before the United

States entered the war in Europe, but there were already suspicions about German espionage.

After some discussion, the Marines relented. Heinemann lay beside the runway where the planes landed and took about sixty photographs. Once he developed the film, he determined that the problem was the excessive sink rate of the plane's approach. The airframe needed to be reinforced. He fashioned custom aluminum stiffeners to size and, with the help of twenty Marines sitting on top of the wing, was able to rivet the stiffeners into place. It took two weeks to retrofit all twenty planes.[71] Shortly afterward, the navy models began to enter service, tasked with both scouting and bombing roles.[72] The SBD (Scout Bomber Douglas), or Douglas Dauntless, was now ready for action.

As required, the Dauntless could perform a vertical dive with a payload of 1,000 pounds, accurately strike the target, and survive the enormous accelerational forces of recovery. Pilots loved the plane; it was stable in a dive yet lightly controlled in normal flight—benefits of Heinemann's low-wing monoplane design and split flaps.[73]

No plane is perfect, and the Dauntless was no exception. Compared to fighter aircraft it was slow, especially when climbing. The safety restraints for the pilot were also not sufficient—of this, more later. But these drawbacks were more than outweighed by its advantages. While the Dauntless had yet to see combat, it was already clear that Heinemann's plane was extremely rugged, capable of absorbing considerable punishment. One pilot, after surviving a crash of the prototype, remarked "that was quite a sturdy aircraft. As far as I am concerned it saved my life."[74]

Dive bombing was not a weapon unique to the United States. Germany had the Junkers JU 87A-1 "Stuka," and Japan had the Aichi D3A1 "Val." Britain and France had the Blackburn B-24 "Skua" and the Loire Nieuport LN-40, respectively, but these were never mass-produced. They numbered fewer than three hundred between them. The Dauntless, Stuka, and Val, however, were built in their thousands. The planes had many similarities. All were used to deliver a bomb of 500 pounds or more by means of a vertical dive; all were reliable and accurate weapons. The Stuka had the leading edge in development, demonstrating its effectiveness in the Spanish Civil War when the Val and the Dauntless were still prototypes.[75] But the Stuka, as Heinemann commented later, was not sufficiently armored, so it "was very vulnerable to attack by fighter planes." It could operate only in areas where the Germans already had air superiority. And it also had a remarkably low striking range: it was a land-based bomber and was not designed for the lengthy patrols or long-range attacks characteristic of naval aviation. The Val's range was greater than the Stuka but still lower than that of the Dauntless. To be specific, the Dauntless could fly 60 percent farther than the Val and 82 percent farther than the Stuka. In terms of speed, the Dauntless was slower than its rivals—but only in terms of its cruise speed, not its maximum speed. Fully loaded it was the heaviest by some 700 pounds. It had the smallest wingspan by several feet. Heinemann, one could say, had built the pocket battleship of airplanes.

There was considerable foreign interest in the Dauntless. A precursor to the SBD had been sold to Peru, Iraq, the Netherlands, China, Argentina, Norway, and Russia. The Dauntless itself was sold to New Zealand, France, Chile, and Mexico.[76] The British looked at the plane, but ultimately rejected it.[77] The prototype was sold to Japan with a export license, though it was not in the end put into production because the Imperial Navy chose the Val instead.[78]

The final obstacle to the Dauntless proved to be on Capitol Hill. During World War I, there had been huge waste in US military procurement. Senator Harry Truman, then still a simple congressman from Missouri, was anxious to avoid a repetition of this spending as the United States squared up against the Axis. He established a special congressional committee to audit expenditure.[79] Most of the time, the Truman Committee targeted local pork-barreling in the construction of barracks and other facilities. In 1941, however, shortly after the committee had been set up, it queried the number of dive bombers on order and recommended a reduction. Fortunately for the United States, the navy ignored this suggestion.[80]

At El Segundo, Heinemann was now chief engineer. The plant manager was Eric Springer, and the assistant manager was Heinemann's old collaborator Karl Peter Grube.[81] With war looming, these men, and many other German American engineers, threw themselves into the task of increasing production of the vital dive bombers. In late August 1941, the "El Segundo personnel in general and Ed Heinemann in particular" were commended by NACA, the Bureau of Supplies, and the Bureau of Aeronautics for the "dispatch and efficiency" of their work.[82] The Materiel Division of the Air Corps echoed these sentiments six weeks later.[83] A month after that, the inspector of naval aircraft praised the Dauntless drawings Heinemann had made for contractors as the "highest in their estimation . . . for completeness and accuracy and other necessary information."[84] Heinemann believed that he was building more than planes, describing his work as the "very important task of supplying our armed forces with equipment so vital to our freedom."[85] By the end of 1941, Douglas Aircraft was turning out twenty Dauntlesses a month.[86]

Heinemann, though, was determined to improve on this figure. In late March 1942, with war already well underway, he gave a rousing speech to the engineering personnel working under him. "We can't all be MacArthurs" or out there "with the men in the front," he said, "but one thing is certain, we can back them up by providing them with the best possible equipment in the shortest possible time." Heinemann urged his men to "cut out the horseplay," to avoid time-wasting, and to plan carefully. "Remember," he said, "there is still time to win the war, but none to spare."[87]

Heinemann and all those working in the US war industries did their job. By mid-1942 the plant at El Segundo manufactured some two hundred Dauntlesses, and there were enough on US carriers to take on the Japanese if conditions were favorable.[88] The question now was whether the US Navy had a commander capable of putting them in the right place at the right time.

2

THE STRATEGIST

IT WAS DARK ON CONNECTICUT AVENUE. ADMIRAL CHESTER Nimitz walked it alone, somewhat dazed. Nearly one week earlier, the Japanese had attacked Pearl Harbor, among other ports in the Pacific, catching the United States by surprise. President Franklin D. Roosevelt had fired the commander of the Pacific Fleet, and tonight he had just offered the job to Nimitz. For the hundredth time that day Nimitz thought of his son, Chester Junior, aboard a submarine operating out of Manila. Accepting Roosevelt's offer meant taking responsibility for his life as well as the lives of many others. It also meant returning to a place that Nimitz had been before. Thirty-five years ago, when he was a midshipman just out of Annapolis, he had visited Pearl Harbor. He wrote his father: "If once you were in this little Paradise spot here you would want to live here forever." But that was 1905, and now it was 1941. The midshipman had become an admiral, and paradise had become an underworld.[1]

✪

THE FUTURE ADMIRAL WAS born in the Texas Hill Country in 1885. His hometown of Fredericksburg was named after Prince Frederick of Prussia. It was a solidly German settlement in both language and culture. The people sang German hymns on Sundays and celebrated the *Christkindl* at Christmas. When a local boy wrote home from college asking advice on which foreign language he should study, his parents gave a telling response: "Take English, Son."[2] Much had changed since then: "Texas German" is hardly spoken nowadays in Fredericksburg, though the place is still referred to colloquially as "Fritztown."

It was the same region that produced the future US president Lyndon Baines Johnson, who was delivered by a German midwife, Mrs. Christian Lindig. Johnson's maternal grandmother was a Huffman (originally Hoffman). When his mother got angry, Lyndon's father would tease her by saying, "That's your German blood again."[3] There was a lot of it in the Hill Country.

All four of Nimitz's grandparents had been born in Germany. His paternal grandfather, Karl Heinrich Nimitz, came from Bremen. His maternal grandfather, Heinrich Karl Ludwig Henke, was from Westerbrak, Brunswick. It was natural, then, for the young Chester to have been brought up bilingually, speaking mainly German to his immediate family. There was also his physical appearance: the towheaded and blue-eyed young Nimitz was distinctly Germanic looking.[4]

We don't know what the young Nimitz made of the world around him. Reconstruction Texas had been a fraught place in the twilight of the Old West. Anxieties about Indian raids and civil war were gradually replaced by those of industrialization and racial segregation.[5] The international sky was darkening, too. In the nearby Caribbean and remote Pacific Ocean, the United States had gone to war with Spain in 1898. Afterward, it found itself in charge of a raft of new territories, including the Philippines, Cuba, Guam, and Puerto Rico. It also acquired Hawaii in 1898, and it had annexed the Midway Atoll in 1867. In 1899, US sailors and Marines saw combat during the Boxer Rebellion in China; starting in 1910, revolution in Mexico caused a break in US-Mexican relations. With all these developments, America emerged as a Pacific power.

The impact of these international events on the US Navy was immense. Nimitz's confidant and biographer described the turn of the century as a "glorious renaissance" for American naval power. The war with Spain meant naval battles in both oceans, moments when the United States earned important victories and inaugurated new heroes. Admiral George Dewey, for instance, became a household name after his fleet defeated the Spanish in Manila. The age also had its prophets, chief among them Alfred Thayer Mahan, whose book *The Influence of Sea Power upon History* argued that sea power was a combination of national character, colonial possession, and military capability. Published in 1890, it had been taken to heart by statesmen and sailors alike. The shipyards went to work to prove it. Until 1916 Congress authorized the construction of a new battleship nearly every year.[6]

It was during this time that Nimitz decided to join the military. His family had moved to nearby Kerrville, where his parents ran a hotel, by 1900. That summer, an army artillery unit was training in the foothills, and two officers stayed over for the night. Recent graduates of the US Military Academy at West Point, these men, for all their bearing and polish, were hardly older than Nimitz himself, who was then fifteen.[7] There wasn't much of a military tradition in the Nimitz family; indeed, many German Texans were refugees from militarism. His grandfather, a teller of tall tales, styled himself "captain," but while he had served in the German merchant marine, the title actually derived from his status in a Confederate militia. Yet Nimitz, partly fired by his determination and partly by wanderlust, knew what he wanted. He wrote to his grandfather, "I have made up my mind to try to get into either West Point or Annapolis."[8]

Enlisting was one thing; attending a service academy was something else entirely. Nimitz needed a nomination from a member of Congress or a senator, had to pass a physical examination, and had to outscore other applicants on an academic examination.[9] For the past two years, he had been at the head of his class in every subject, earning high marks in US history, Roman history, algebra, English grammar, and Latin.[10] But the examination covered other subjects, such as geometry, that Nimitz had not yet studied. His school superintendent volunteered to tutor him through the summer, however, and the hard work paid off.[11] The following year he sat his academic exam and received a high score. He then passed his physical, and a local congressman, James Slayden, awarded him an appointment to the United States Naval Academy in Annapolis. Nimitz boarded the train for the East Coast in 1901.[12] The rest of his life, in many ways, was lived at sea.

Like all new cadets, Nimitz entered the Naval Academy by swearing to "defend the Constitution of the United States against all enemies foreign and domestic," a significant oath for the grandson of a Confederate. Then came the descent into the hell of cadet life. Nimitz wrote home to say that during the first week, "the drilling was hard and long and caused several boys to faint."[13] This admission provoked his father to write with concerns about hazing, to which Nimitz replied, "There is never any bodily hurt done here. . . . [T]he kind of hazing here is more of a different kind." He went on to describe antics similar to what still goes on today: "I had to make love to my broom and dance with it while my roommate struck up the band."[14] His class numbered 150 cadets, at that point "the largest class in the history of the Academy."[15] Nimitz proved a decent rower and tennis player; he was an even stronger student, routinely placing high in his class for math and Spanish.[16] It was a time of discipline and examination as well as a time of camaraderie. He began lifelong friendships with other cadets, including William Halsey, R. Kelly Turner, Frank Jack Fletcher, and Raymond Spruance, who would also make important contributions to the US victory at Midway. When making funeral arrangements some sixty years later, Nimitz asked to be buried next to three officers, all academy graduates, Turner and Spruance among them.[17]

Nimitz took his German heritage with him when he joined the navy. Soon after his arrival at Annapolis, he wrote home to say that there were "a number of Germans in the Academy and all of them stand up well in their studies." These were fellow Americans that Nimitz referred to by their European origin. He also shared news that naval cadets from the German Empire were due for a visit.[18] His grandfather responded with a heartfelt letter that happened to coincide with Nimitz's birthday. "I know of nothing acceptable to send you for a birthday present," said the old sailor, "so I will . . . give you some family history." He then described the lineage of the Nimitz family as far back as the thirteenth century. It was a letter that Nimitz treasured, keeping it as long as he lived.[19] His classmates at the academy picked up on this part of his character, describing him in the yearbook as someone "who possesses that calm and easy-going Dutch [i.e., German] way that gets at the bottom of things."[20] And when aboard ship, if his men complained about the food, he would answer with a German proverb: "Hunger ist der beste Koch" (Hunger is the best cook).[21]

After graduating from the academy in the spring of 1905, Nimitz was posted to the battleship *Ohio*, the flagship of the Asiatic fleet. Sailing west meant sailing toward war; this was the year that Imperial Japan bested Tsarist Russia in the Battle of Tsushima. It was another streamer on the flag of Dewey and Mahan, a vindication of the battleship: a decisive confrontation in which speed, gunpower, and concentration of force were supreme. It also proved that Japan had joined the ranks of first-rate naval powers. Sailing into Manila Bay, Nimitz espied two Russian cruisers. "They were certainly battered up," he wrote to his grandfather, noticing that one displayed "eleven large holes in her starboard side—besides, all of these were marked all over with patches where shell had struck." Doctors aboard the *Ohio* were sent to treat the Russian wounded, some of whom were "cut up badly . . . with limbs shot away etc." Nimitz was phlegmatic even though he found it hard to believe: "It doesn't seem possible to think that here we are sitting on the quarter deck of a happy ship—and over there not more than three hundred yards away, are three ships all shot up—with so much suffering aboard. But all that goes to prove that they didn't toe the mark, or else they would have inflicted more damage and received less in return."[22] It was an early lesson in the human cost of failure at sea.

At the same time, US relations with Japan began to deteriorate. The forced commercial opening of that country by Commodore Perry fifty years earlier had created a double blowback for the United States. First, the growth of Japanese naval power posed a challenge to the American position in the Pacific. Second, the increasing integration of the Pacific Rim and the lack of opportunities in Japan, despite its remarkable economic growth, led to a substantial increase of Japanese immigration to the West Coast of the United States. This, in turn, provoked hostility among Americans worried about employment and societal cohesion. Like the Heinemanns and the Nimitzes, these new Americans were relatively recent arrivals, but they would have to struggle even harder to gain acceptance.

In March 1905, several months before the Russian defeat at Tsushima, the California State Senate unanimously passed a resolution requesting "the attention of President Roosevelt and the department of state to menaces of Japanese immigration."[23] There were economic concerns as well as the prejudices of class and race. As one newspaper explained, "Japanese contract laborers" and their "low rate of wages . . . [were] beginning to crowd out white labor."[24] The San Francisco School Board announced that Japanese students would be moved into "Oriental Schools" along with the Chinese in order to spare white children "association with pupils of the Mongolian race."[25]

The Japanese were doubly offended, considering it an insult to be both segregated from whites and forced to associate with the Chinese. California legislators refused to back down, traveling to Washington to meet with President Roosevelt and his cabinet. Some prominent figures rejected segregation on the grounds that "the so-called 'yellow peril'" was "'America's golden opportunity' . . . to preach the gospel . . . to the sons of the orient and gladly prepare them to return and help in the great awakening of China and Japan."[26] In other words, it was a chance to evangelize Asians in America so that Americans could evangelize Asia. Others contemplated war and the loss of US empire, asserting that "on the declaration of war Japan would seize the Philippines, take Hawaii and try to occupy Alaska."[27] By this point, Nimitz was in command of his own ship, a destroyer named the *Decatur*, and he was ready for a fight. He wrote to his father in December 1907, "If I knew for sure that we were going to have that war with Japan within the next twelve months I think I would try to hold on [to] my present job instead of taking leave when it comes due."[28]

Several months later, Nimitz was still in command of the *Decatur* when his ship ran aground. He stood on the deck that night wondering what to do. There were many reasons to be ashamed. The *Decatur* was a powerful four-stack, 420-ton coal-burning destroyer capable of 28 knots. It was named for Stephen Decatur, perhaps the greatest sailor in US naval history, responsible for victories in the Barbary Wars, the Quasi-War with France, and the War of 1812. Then there was Nimitz's failure to maintain attention as her commander. The ship had been entering Batangas Harbor south of Manila Bay. It was nighttime, and he should have continued to fix his position; instead he had estimated his position by dead reckoning. Yes, he'd been commissioned for only eighteen months; yes, he was only twenty-two years old. But neither youth nor inexperience were excuses. Nimitz remembered this as a "black night." During the subsequent court-martial, he was found guilty of "neglect of duty" and sentenced "to be publicly reprimanded by the Commander-in-Chief, U.S. Naval Forces in Philippine Waters."[29]

After a short break in Texas, Nimitz was assigned to submarines. It was meant to be a punishment, a demotion from the surface fleet, which was then considered the most prestigious arm of naval power, but it meant that Nimitz became an expert on the submarine's power plant: the diesel engine. In 1913, when the navy assembled a team to visit Germany, the international center of diesel engineering, Nimitz was the perfect candidate, conversant in both the technology and the German language. Shortly before departing he married Catherine, a ship broker's daughter who had never traveled outside of her home state of Massachusetts. The newlyweds enjoyed a weekend in New York before visiting the Nimitz family in Texas and then traveling to the shipyards of Hamburg. In Texas, the Nimitz family regarded Catherine with a little suspicion, considering her an Anglophone Yankee. In Germany, it was Chester's turn to be out of place. The German naval officers were frosty and aloof, although they improved a bit when they realized that Nimitz, who was dressed in civilian clothes, was a fellow sailor and officer. This was peacetime navy life: the sense of duty and estrangement, the momentary fanfare, the long sea voyages to and from the Old World. It was brought to an abrupt end by the outbreak of war.[30]

When the great conflagration came, it was both farther away and closer to home than Nimitz had expected. World War I broke out in distant Europe, not among the islands of the Pacific. But it directly affected Nimitz's family in Texas, because Germany encouraged Mexican claims to territory that had been ceded to the United States in the nineteenth century. The tension acquired a racial tinge in the notorious "Plan of San Diego, Texas" of 1915, a self-described "revolutionary plot" to "rise in arms against the government and the country of the United States of North America." The object was the reconquest of "Texas, New Mexico, Arizona, Colorado, and Upper California" by means of racial genocide: "Every North American over 16 years of age shall be put to death," read the movement's manifesto. "War without quarter" would be carried out by an army recruited solely from "the Latin, the Negro, or the Japanese race."[31] All this under a flag that read "Equality and Independence." Germany was suspected of promoting these schemes, though nothing was ever proved.[32] Then British intelligence intercepted and forwarded to Washington a telegram from the foreign minister in Berlin promising this same territory to Mexico in the event of war with the United States. This promise, along with the German resumption of unrestricted submarine warfare, forced President Woodrow Wilson to act. In April 1917, the United States entered World War I.

Nimitz had a relatively quiet war—but he was not resting. After returning from Germany he designed the engines for the first diesel-powered surface ship in the US fleet, the *Maumee*. The *Maumee* was a refueling ship, and Nimitz became its first executive officer and chief engineer. Once the United States declared war on Germany, it was vital to move destroyers into European waters to hunt U-boats. Destroyers could not make the Atlantic crossing without refueling, and the *Maumee* performed this task for nearly all the thirty-four destroyers sent during the first three months of the war. Along with the captain of the *Maumee*, Nimitz developed the first techniques for refueling and reprovisioning ships while underway. It was a feat of tactics and engineering that improved the navy's striking capability.[33]

With the outbreak of hostilities with the German Reich in April 1917, the German American community, including little Fredericksburg, was in the firing line. Anti-German feeling in Texas, as in other areas of the country, was rampant. The community reacted partly by drawing in on itself, and partly with compensatory patriotic ostentation. Honoring these efforts, Lyndon Johnson's father defended the Germans of the region in a speech in February 1918. The first American death in France, Johnson said, had been a German American, likely referring to Louis John Jordan of Fredericksburg. In fact, Johnson was only partly correct. Louis John Jordan was not the first American but the first Texan officer to be killed in the conflict.[34] What Nimitz himself made of it all is not known, but it is surely no coincidence that his homespun Germanicisms seem to have stopped around this time. All across the Union, in fact, German Americans were downplaying their German identity and unreservedly committing themselves to the cause of the United States.

While Europe recovered from war, the United States acquired a new enemy—or rather, rediscovered an old one. The Japanese, fearing subjection by neighboring powers and resenting their second-class status in the international system, stepped up their own imperial and colonial project. In 1931, they occupied Manchuria in northern China, the start of a long and exceptionally brutal campaign. The United States immediately objected because of its missionary and economic interests in the country.

Deep down, what drove the Japanese military buildup was a sense of inferiority. Their immediate rivals were Russia and China, but their proximate rivals were the United States and Britain. In many respects it was the latter powers that posed the greater threat. Unlike Russia and China, which were somewhat geographically discrete, the United States and Britain were distributed, spread out across islands and continents worldwide. Hong Kong, Singapore, Australia, and the Philippine Islands represented only a portion of the resources that either power could bring to bear in a conflict. There was also the fact that Japan had proved itself in battle against Russia and China but not against the United States or Britain. Finally, it was the United States and Britain that set the standard in terms of technology and industry.

The Japanese compensated in several ways. They pushed beyond the limitations set by the Washington Treaty in terms of naval tonnage, developed their regional influence, and trained hard. "The Japanese fleet lags a long way behind the West," Admiral Isoroku Yamamoto told a group of pilots in the 1930s. "That is why I regard death in training the same as a hero's death in action."[35]

✪

THE POST–WORLD WAR I US Navy was consumed by a furious debate about the naval battles of the future. One side favored gunpower, believing that the sturdy battleship and its big guns would remain the arbiter of victory. They believed that aircraft and the aircraft carrier were auxiliary weapons, a means of reconnaissance that would alert battleships to the presence of the enemy and, when it was time, improve the accuracy of a battleship's guns. The other side believed naval power had been transformed. It was now a question of airpower, they argued, and those who could marshal the greatest number of aircraft carriers in a battle would prevail. Battleships, from their perspective, were steel mastodons, destined for scrap at best, and the bottom of the sea at worst. In the 1920s and 1930s, all this was conjecture. Unlike the big guns of the battleships, the destructive power of aviation was untested in naval warfare.

Nimitz quickly grasped the capability of airpower. At the Naval War College in 1922, Nimitz wrote his thesis on the Battle of Jutland in 1916. Like the Tsushima conflict, this was a fight between battleships, a test of surface maneuverability and gunpower. British ships, sailing in a complex formation of paired columns, suffered twice as many casualties as their German opponents. Weather also played a role: fog and smoke obscured friend and foe alike. One solution to these problems was aircraft. Their altitude or position could provide the reconnaissance necessary for battleships to maneuver and fire more effectively. Nimitz also learned from his fellow student Roscoe MacFall. During war games, MacFall did not arrange his ships in columns, like the British at Jutland, but in concentric circles around battleships designated as capital ships. This strategy greatly improved fleet maneuverability, as ships were able to visually position themselves relative to one ship rather than several. Yet the age of the battleship, according to the president of the college, Admiral William Sims, was drawing to a close. Sims argued that the aircraft carrier would soon become the navy's capital ship. He understood that aircraft would eventually have a striking power far greater than battleships and would also be more flexible.[36]

At his next duty station, Nimitz combined both of these ideas. In 1923 he became the executive officer—that is, the second-in-command—of the US fleet stationed on the West Coast known as Battle Fleet. During exercises, Nimitz proposed the circular formation to his fellow officers. As MacFall had suggested, the ships would form in concentric circles around a capital ship, in this case the battleship *California*. "My greatest problem," Nimitz remembered, "was to convince the senior captains in the fleet that this was a proper cruising formation. I even had to persuade my own admiral to agree with me after he had had conferences with the captains, who did not like that cruising all alone out there by themselves on a point in the formation." They were right to feel vulnerable, because traveling at the edge of the formation meant they would be the first to make contact with the enemy. But this was the point. By drawing fire, these ships would give the central capital ship more time to respond and more security. The following year, Battle Fleet participated in exercises with the *Langley*, the first US aircraft carrier. Nimitz had his chance. As Sims had suggested, Nimitz placed the *Langley* at the center of his formation: the carrier, not the battleship, became his capital ship. From now on this formation would characterize US naval power. "I regard the tactical exercises that we had at that time," Nimitz later remembered, "as laying the groundwork for the cruising formations that we used in World War II in the carrier air groups."[37]

The development of new tactics was followed by an expansion of the US Navy more generally. This was necessary for several reasons. First, the navy was aging: US shipyards had lain silent since the end of World War I. Second, there was the US strategic position: a continental power with far-flung island possessions required a large, versatile navy. Third, European powers as well as Japan had been steadily launching new ships. US congressman Carl Vinson of Georgia thought the only solution to these problems was a determined plan of naval renovation. In 1934, Roosevelt signed the first Vinson-Trammel Act, providing funds for nearly one hundred ships and more than two hundred naval aircraft. Vinson lobbied for more, pushing through another round of expansion in 1938, calling it an "insurance policy for peace for the American people." "The last stand of the democracies," he said, "will be in this hemisphere, with the United States carrying the load." The Two-Ocean Navy Law followed in 1940, the authorization of hundreds of thousands of tons of ships in order for the United States to have, in Vinson's words, "complete freedom of action in either ocean while retaining forces in the other ocean for effective defense of our vital security."[38]

New ships meant new carriers. In 1931, the Naval Bureau of Aeronautics requested improvements in three areas: speed, armor, and operational facilities. With these concerns in mind, Newport News Shipbuilding, Virginia, which is now part of Huntington Ingalls Industries, designed the *Yorktown* class of aircraft carriers, the *Hornet*, *Enterprise*, and *Yorktown*. These ships, 809 feet in length and home to some two thousand souls each, were floating cities. Their most precious cargo was aircraft, 82 in total, which were brought up from the depths of the ship via one of three elevators. US carriers had two characteristic features that the *Yorktown* class continued. First, a prominent control tower stood several decks high above the flight deck. It was paired with the trunk of the boiler exhaust and eventually adorned with radio and radar antennae. From the bridge and flying control the captain and his staff observed flight operations. Second, there were enormous doors along the sides of the ship. These could be opened to provide the hangar decks with natural light or ventilation. For this reason, some called the *Yorktown*-class ships barn doors on bathtubs. Indeed, there was something ungainly about their flat decks and rugged towers. But one sailor turned historian found they were "graceful ships with clean, sharp lines."[39]

As the navy grew, so did the tension between gunpower and airpower. Because of their black leather footwear, traditionalists were known as "black shoes," while aviators, who wore brown leather boots, were dubbed "brown shoes." Added to this was resentment from the fact that pilots received danger pay, about 50 percent in excess of their surface navy counterparts. Wade McClusky was one of the brown-shoe aviators. He was a generation behind Nimitz, entering the United States Naval Academy in 1922. As a result, he was exposed to aviation early on. In 1925, the superintendent of the academy, Louis Nulton, decided that all new US midshipmen should receive basic flight training.[40] In time, this greatly increased the familiarity of the officer corps with airpower, putting it ahead of the Royal Navy and even the Imperial Japanese Navy in this respect.[41] Besides, not all US "battleship admirals" were opposed to carrier aviation; some adapted to it quickly.[42]

Similar debates and rivalries were raging in Japan.[43] There, too, advocates of gunpower contended with those who saw naval aviation as the weapon of the future. In 1934, the committed naval aviator Mitsuo Fuchida was horrified to hear Japanese officials propose "the total elimination of aircraft carriers." Fuchida was then part of a scouting squadron aboard the *Kaga*. In his opinion, the Japanese Navy remained hostile to airpower throughout the decade. By 1939 he was commander of the *Akagi's* Air Squadron, where he found that "it was accepted wisdom in the Navy that aircraft carriers were categorised as auxiliary forces." Aircraft could strike targets 300 nautical miles away, yet battleships, which had only a 24-nautical-mile firing range, remained the core of fleet strategy.[44]

Fuchida's frustration was shared by Minoru Genda, a farmer's son from Hiroshima Prefecture. Like Wade McClusky, Genda had been an acrobatic flyer in his youth, and he regarded aviation as a display of more than just technical prowess. It was Genda who first recognized the potential of massed air attacks launched from several carriers: the tactic immortalized at Pearl Harbor. By the 1930s, Genda penned an essay proposing that the navy scrap its battleships and rely entirely on the strike capability of airpower.[45] That same decade, Japanese naval aviators, Fuchida and Genda included, cut their teeth in the war in China, flying missions from carriers in support of ground operations.

Those in the upper echelons of the Japanese Navy, however, like many of their US counterparts, were wary of airpower. Admiral Yamamoto was the lone exception. Yamamoto commanded the carrier *Akagi* in the 1920s before rising to lead the First Carrier Division in the 1930s. Though not a pilot himself, he instinctively understood that the advent of airpower had fundamentally changed naval warfare. His lobbying was not entirely without success—as already mentioned, the Japanese naval air arm was immensely effective in terms of aircraft design and pilot training. But Japan's navy did not incorporate airpower into its tactics and strategy to the same degree that the US Navy did. Yamamoto, in other words, was no Nimitz. The proof of Japanese strategic obstinacy was the construction of the *Musashi* and the *Yamato*, a fearsome pair of super battleships that were already obsolete by the time their hulls were laid down in 1937 and 1938.[46]

✪

ALTHOUGH AIRCRAFT COULD PACK a powerful punch, the aircraft carrier was much more vulnerable than the capital ships it was trying to replace. Unlike battleships, the carrier was not built to take punishment; indeed, it could not be, given the need for a broad and flat deck to land and launch aircraft. This was true even for the early US carriers *Langley*, *Lexington*, and *Saratoga*, which were wooden, unarmored flight decks laid on top of collier or battle-cruiser hulls. The heavy armor of their hulls protected them from torpedoes and gunfire but not from the aerial attacks of dive bombers. This weakness was obvious during the "Fleet Problems" of the 1920s and 1930s, war games in which the navy experimented with airpower.

For instance, when the *Lexington* was surprised by enemy aircraft during an exercise held in 1929, umpires ruled it "heavily damaged" and temporarily reduced her speed.[47] The following year, another Fleet Problem was held in which the *Saratoga* and the *Langley* were similarly taken off guard—this time surprised by dive bombers and, after twenty minutes of attack, ruled destroyed. By 1937, the US Navy had estimated that each 1,000-pound bomb hit on a large carrier would result in 7 percent damage. They woefully underestimated: in World War II it ranged anywhere from 15 to 100 percent.[48]

Aside from their design, carriers were vulnerable because in the years prior to radar, enemy ships could conceal their approach by using weather or geography. Naval warfare, in other words, was often a surprise and a close-quarters fight. Even planned operations left carriers vulnerable. The short range of aircraft meant that carriers needed to venture close to their targets. And if one were detected, there was the likelihood of having to face massed aerial attack: flying in squadron formation, planes attacking not in ones or twos but in groups of nine to eighteen. This is precisely what happened in a Fleet Problem held in 1930, when the *Lexington* and *Saratoga* were attacked by forty-two dive bombers as well as other planes.[49]

How then should carriers be defended? In the US Navy, defense began with the circular formation pioneered and favored by Nimitz. Surrounding carriers with less important ships such as destroyers and cruisers meant that enemy planes had to travel over hostile airspace to approach their target. All these ships could contribute antiaircraft fire in attacking the enemy. The carriers would also then have more time to prepare their own countermeasures.

The main defense was mounted by the carriers themselves, by launching combat air patrols (CAPs). These were groups of fighter planes organized on the carrier by an officer in charge of what became known as the combat information center. With a radio and a grease pen, this officer would track the location of friendly and enemy aircraft and allocate duties and responsibilities accordingly.[50] Antiaircraft guns were the last measure of defense, but in the early stages of the war they were not considered particularly effective. In

Fleet Problems, antiaircraft fire was assigned a 5 percent effectiveness rate, not nearly enough to defend the carrier.[51]

Carrier crews also gave a lot of thought to damage control. Given the threat of burns, sailors were equipped with protective gear. "Everyone aboard ship," remembered one crew member aboard the *Hornet*, "wore special flashproof clothing, specially treated pants and a jumper worn over uniforms to protect against burns during explosions. A hood would protect your head and face . . . [and] gloves and a steel helmet gave additional protection."[52]

In the end, though, there was a limit to what such defenses could accomplish. It was widely recognized that some bombers would always get through. In many respects, the situation was epitomized by the Fleet Problem in 1929 in which opposing carriers hunted for one another by groping about with scouting planes and ships, attempting to coordinate between land and seaborne forces. In the end, the winner was the side whose planes discovered the opposing carrier first. It was a battle determined by offense, by tactical aggression.

✪

JAPANESE CARRIER DOCTRINE, LIKE American doctrine, emphasized the offense. But it differed in one obvious respect: instead of separating carriers into independent groups, each guarded by a ring of surface ships, Japanese carriers sailed close together. Minoru Genda remembered that each year the Japanese simulated "a decisive 'fleet versus fleet battle'" between "an inferior Japanese Fleet" and "a superior American Fleet." These war games determined that a Japanese victory was best achieved by "simultaneous attacks with 80 to 100 aircraft." Given the limitations of contemporary communications equipment, "it was difficult to rendezvous the various air groups in midocean."[53] The solution was obvious to many. Fuchida and others proposed "a concentrated deployment of . . . carriers" in order for aircraft to attack as "a single aviation fleet" under the command of one officer. Unlike the Americans, the Japanese would group their carriers together to synchronize operations.[54]

Part of the preference for a simultaneous attack was the Japanese strategic longing for a "decisive battle." In their view, a decisive battle—not attrition, or subterfuge, or alliances—would determine the outcome of a war. The Battle of Tsushima was an important milestone in this regard. Then, so the story went, Admiral Togo Heihachiro provoked the Russians to overcommit their naval resources, and they were lured into battle at a time and place of Japan's choosing. Togo's victory was so thorough, so striking, that Russia sued for peace. By the 1930s the moment defined Japanese naval strategy. According to Fuchida, Pearl Harbor and Midway were both imbued with the "dream of the Battle of Tsushima." The Pearl Harbor attack was named Operation Z in honor of Togo's use of a "Z" flag to signal the attack.[55] Six months later, the Japanese carriers departed to attack Midway on May 27: precisely thirty-seven years to the day after the battle that had commenced in the Tsushima Strait. Further invoking this history, Yamamoto's capital ship was not an aircraft carrier but a battleship.

Another important aspect of Japanese carrier doctrine was the Japanese military's attitude toward war. As early as 1936, a Japanese Naval Staff College study determined that a Japanese carrier on operations "must be prepared to be impaled as it impales the enemy."[56] This meant leading with a preemptive surprise attack. Americans largely had the same view of leading with a preemptive strike, but they would not have accepted a willingness "to be impaled." At its best, this was courage; at worst, an abnegation of life. The result was a costly naval strategy, but not because it was fatalistic or forlorn. To the contrary, sacrifice in Japanese naval doctrine was a means of victory. Loss of life was to be expected, even treasured, for it validated combat.

The Japanese determination to impale the enemy was reflected in the design of Japan's carriers. The *Kaga* and the *Akagi* were converted battle cruisers and similar in size and speed to the *Yorktown* class.[57] But later carriers, such as the *Soryu* and the *Hiryu*, laid down in 1934 and 1936, respectively, were sleeker, faster, and lighter. The *Hiryu* was nearly 100 feet shorter, 40 feet thinner, and 5,000 tons lighter than the *Yorktown* and cruised 2 miles per hour faster. But the *Hiryu* also carried about twenty fewer aircraft and one thousand fewer souls and had an operational range that was 2,000 nautical miles shorter. In other words, it was a component of a larger machine. It was designed to travel alongside other carriers, especially the older *Kaga* and *Akagi*, which retained some of their surface armament. As one Japanese mechanic on the *Akagi* recalled, the converted ship had "three big guns on both sides, which I thought were useless."[58] These 8-inch surface guns reflected a reluctance to rely on a circular formation of supporting ships as much as determination to press forward and attack. The *Yorktown*-class ships, by comparison, had no gun with a caliber greater than 5 inches—and all were antiaircraft guns.[59]

The difference in size had several consequences. American carriers, which were larger generally and hence had larger flight decks, had room to funnel their exhaust out of the top of their decks. This allowed for a taller island structure. The Japanese, by contrast, funneled exhaust out of the sides of their carriers and did not have island structures—only adding them later during refits.[60] In keeping with this style, the Japanese stowed their planes below in hangar decks. The *Akagi* and *Kaga* had three such decks, and the *Soryu* and *Hiryu* two, whereas US carriers, which stowed planes on the flight deck, had only one.

Japanese carriers were more vulnerable. Their ability to detect, defend against, and respond to threats was lower than that of their US rivals. Concerning detection, the Japanese were limited by two factors. The first was the lack of radar. Without it Japanese reconnaissance was somewhat haphazard. Bad weather could prevent scouting planes from being launched or severely impair their line of sight.[61] The problem was worsened by the fact that the Japanese did not routinely integrate scouting into their carrier air groups—it was a function provided by floatplanes launched from escort vessels. Institutionally, systematic reconnaissance was strictly a second order priority, and tactically it was performed by less capable planes that could not strike the enemy should he be found.[62]

In terms of defending from attack, the Japanese also had weaknesses relative to the Americans. First, their antiaircraft provision was inadequate.[63] The problem began with automated fire control. US ships were equipped with mechanical computers that predicted the future position and range of a target, allowing for greater accuracy of fire and sensitivity of ordnance fuse settings. The Japanese lacked this technology in every respect: their guns did not have sufficiently capable computers, nor did they have proximity fuses. Hence, it was much more difficult for them to hit fast-moving targets in the air. The guns themselves were also deficient. The light-caliber gun had a low rate of fire and an insufficient hitting power, was slow to train on the target, and had a slow elevating speed. Japanese sailors also complained that the gun suffered from excessive vibration when firing, as well as muzzle blast that obscured the target. Amid the smoke and clamor of battle, the gunners had little chance of hitting a dive bomber, especially if it was diving down from directly overhead.[64]

In these circumstances, the main defense against air attack was the combat air patrol. But the Japanese also had significant problems in this respect. Because of an emphasis on strike planes, a carrier would normally launch three fighters, with six held in reserve.[65] This was not an adequate number to provide circular coverage at the various attack altitudes: sea level, in the case of torpedo planes, and anywhere from 15,000 feet and higher for bombers. Moreover, if enemy planes were sighted, the Japanese also lacked an effective means of directing their fighters to respond. Japanese radios were so poor that some pilots removed them to save weight, relying entirely on hand signals to communicate with other planes. In short, Japanese carriers lacked an equivalent to the US combat information center.[66]

Another problem was that Japanese damage control procedures were fragile. In the first place, they were too decentralized. In the US Navy, a ship's damage control was the responsibility of one man: the assistant engineering officer. But the Japanese divided this responsibility in half. One officer was responsible for damage topside, another for damage in the engineering and auxiliary spaces below deck. Splitting the responsibility meant that resources could not be allocated effectively, and it was difficult to resolve hierarchical disputes if an officer of lower rank needed help from someone more senior. Moreover, the repair systems had no in-built redundancy. There was only one water pump for fighting fire—if it failed, then nothing more could be done.

The hangar decks were particularly vulnerable. There the main fire control system was a set of large curtains that could be drawn across the hangar to isolate and contain the fire. But this was only possible if the blaze was manageable.[67] It was also not possible to flush aviation gas lines with carbon dioxide. Crew readiness further added to the danger: Japanese sailors were in the habit of wearing "half-sleeved shirts and tropical shorts," which exposed them to burns.[68]

Like Japanese cities, which were lightly constructed because of the fear of earthquakes, and thus highly flammable, Japanese ships and planes were not built to last. The Zero, as one American pilot recalled, was built like a "paper kite" compared to Allied fighters.[69] In the same way, Japanese carriers were thinly protected, but crammed full of combustible material. The fire danger was therefore a serious issue: if set alight, Japan's airplanes and carriers, like Japan's cities, would burn.

✪

JAPANESE ARMS AND JAPANESE doctrine were tested by the war in China during the 1930s. The conflict commanded national attention. Taisuke Maruyama, who went on to become a naval aviator, remembered it as a time when "the school system gave full support to the military. For example, I wore military style shoes to school. The main reason for this was the war in China. I think everyone was influenced by this." The Imperial Japanese Navy's involvement began with the Second Shanghai Incident of 1937. Medium bombers and Zero fighters performed extremely well. It was obvious that aviation had become the most effective weapon in the naval arsenal. Senior military leaders, however, were still resistant to change for various reasons. The Washington Naval Treaty of 1922 and the London Naval Treaty of 1930 had just expired and so defenders of traditional naval power argued that battleship development, which had been delayed accordingly, would soon improve. There was also a cultural bias in favor of what was familiar: gunpower. The result was that Japanese doctrine remained unchanged. The distant history of Tsushima, combined with the recent history of the war in China, meant that a decisive battle fought by battleships remained the dream of the Imperial fleet.[70]

The United States reacted to Japanese imperialism by increasing its own naval power. Congressman Vinson, when introducing the Vinson-Trammel Act of 1938, warned that "peace on the terms of dictators is a Carthaginian peace." This was his conviction with regard to the Pacific as well as Europe. In May 1940, President Roosevelt moved the Pacific Fleet from California to Hawaii's Pearl Harbor.[71] His intent was not to provoke the Japanese but to deter them by means of a forward deployment. Looking for a steady hand, Roosevelt offered the Pacific Fleet to Nimitz. But Nimitz, considering himself relatively junior, turned it down. The job then went to Admiral Husband Kimmel instead.

Tokyo proclaimed the "Greater Asian Co-Prosperity Sphere," which would incorporate not only Manchuria, Korea, and China but also much of Southeast Asia, in August 1940. A month later, Japan occupied northern Indochina, the first tangible sign of an ambition to move south. Shortly thereafter, it aligned itself more closely with Hitler, through the Tripartite Pact between Berlin, Rome, and Tokyo of September 1940.[72] The three signatories agreed to support each other militarily in the event that they were attacked by a third party, by which they meant the United States.[73] The United States retaliated by imposing a scrap metal embargo, which hit Japan's armaments and shipbuilding industry. The tension mounted throughout late 1940 and early 1941, and war continued to rage in China.

Then, in the late summer of 1941, the Japanese occupied southern Indochina, which put them within striking distance of the British colony of Malaya and the oil fields of what were still the

Dutch East Indies. The United States responded by imposing an oil embargo. If nothing was done, the Japanese Empire would run out of fuel to power its commerce and warships. The British re-opened the Burma Road, through which the Chinese Nationalist forces of Chiang Kai-shek could be supplied. They also dispatched a battleship and a battle cruiser to Singapore in order to deter a Japanese attack on Malaya; the planned aircraft carrier to escort them never materialized. Admiral Tom Phillips, who commanded the force, was a believer in battleships and was well known in the Royal Navy for being dismissive of the impact of airpower at sea. One of his senior colleagues had reputedly predicted before the war that Phillips's last words, if his ship were struck by a dive bomber, would be "that was a fucking great mine."[74]

In late November 1941, US Secretary of State Cordell Hull issued a confidential proposal to Japan, an attempt at establishing a "mutual declaration of policy." The idea was to constrain Japa-nese imperial ambition. A drawdown was requested in the Pacific: "The Government of Japan," read the third point, "will withdraw all military, naval, air and police forces from China and from Indo-China." The proposal also attempted to alter Japan's relationship with the wider world. It went on to state that "the Government of the United States and the Government of Japan will endeavor to conclude a multilateral non-aggression pact among the British Empire, China, Japan, the Netherlands, the Soviet Union, Thai-land and the United States."[75] Agreeing to Hull's proposal therefore would have affected the Japanese at home and abroad. Regionally it meant a Japanese withdrawal from Asian continental resources, which meant starvation and humiliation: the end of imperial am-bitions. But it also meant changing one global alliance for another: Japan would leave the Axis powers and join the United States, Britain, the Netherlands, and the Soviet Union.

The Japanese government supposedly took Hull's proposal to be an "ultimatum," a view that remains contested by historians.[76] If the Japanese felt cornered by Hull and US aggression, then the surprise attack on Pearl Harbor appears reasonable, if not unavoid-able. The ultimatum theory also helps explain why the Japanese attacked the United States when most Japanese leaders knew they had little chance of defeating such an industrial heavyweight. "If I am told to fight regardless of consequence," Admiral Yamamoto famously remarked, "I shall run wild for the first six months or a year, but I have utterly no confidence for the second and third years." He also said that "a war with so little chance of success should not be fought." Yamamoto predicted that it would be a long conflict that would end in the exhaustion of Japan.[77] He believed that Japan's navy and naval aviators were the best in the world, but knew that ships and pilots could not be replaced quickly. Only Hull's "ultimatum," an affront to Japanese honor, could explain and justify the eventual attack.

Hull's proposal was not the only document directing future events. On November 15, 1941, nearly two weeks before Hull sent his proposal, the Japanese emperor had endorsed a strategic statement titled "Draft Proposal for Hastening the End of the War Against the United States, Great Britain, the Netherlands, and Chiang Kai-shek." Japan felt that war had already begun—not just with the United States but also with other powers in the Pacific and Europe. Along with these enemies the document specified that Japan had two particular allies: Germany and Italy. There were several reasons for the government of Japan to reject integration into the Anglo-American international order. First, the Japanese had yet to forget their rejection at Versailles in 1919.[78] Then there was their confidence in their military power, earned from nearly a decade of war in China and the previous victory against Russia.[79] Less reasonable was their own racial and religious prejudice, which made it unlikely they would agree to such a relationship with the West. Finally, it must be remembered that by 1941, the world situation, and especially the situation in Europe, had changed—Japan had entered into an alliance with Hitler that required its leaders to think globally.[80]

The resulting strategy was straightforward. According to the emperor's document, "a quick war" would be waged to "destroy American and British bases in eastern Asia and in the southwest Pacific region." This would allow Japan to secure "a strategically

powerful position . . . for a protracted period of self-sufficiency."
The coup de grace would soon follow: "At the appropriate time,
we will endeavor by various means to lure the main fleet of the
United States [near Japan] and destroy it." Regional dominance was
part of a global strategy. Japan would "work for the surrender of
Great Britain in cooperation with Germany and Italy, and to destroy the will of the United States to continue the war." It would
also monitor "the war situation in Europe" and "the policy vis-a-vis
India," all while increasing "diplomatic and propaganda activi-
ties directed against Latin America, Switzerland, Portugal, and the
Vatican."[81] What had begun with conquest in Manchuria would affect the entire international order.

✪

BY DECEMBER 1941 NIMITZ was stationed in Washington, DC, with
his family. He was then working as the chief of the Bureau of
Navigation, responsible for the "procurement, training, promotion,
assignment, and discipline of officers and enlisted personnel in the
Navy," a position to which he was appointed by President Roosevelt. Nimitz didn't much care for the job—he preferred a ship
to a desk—but it suited his rank and it involved important work:
the organization of the recently enlarged navy. There was also the
benefit of spending time with his family. His son, Chester Junior,
was on a submarine based in the Philippines, having graduated
from Annapolis in 1936. But his three daughters—Kate, Nancy, and
Mary—all lived at home and usually had dinner with their parents. Like any family, there were disagreements. Nancy, according
to Nimitz's confidant and biographer, "had acquired strong leftist,
even pro-Soviet, leanings," going so far as to apply for membership
in the Young Communist League at George Washington University,
though she was rejected because of her "bourgeois background."[82]

One Sunday after lunch, Nimitz and his wife were listening
to the New York Philharmonic on the radio. They enjoyed classical music, and there was a performance of Shostakovich's First
Symphony and Brahms's Second Concerto, featuring the pianist

Artur Rubinstein. Nimitz had just settled down to listen when the music unexpectedly stopped. "We interrupt this program," said the announcer, "to bring you a special news bulletin. The Japanese have attacked Pearl Harbor, Hawaii, by air, President Roosevelt has just announced." Nimitz leapt from his chair, going to change into his uniform. Among other things, he would've thought of his son, Chester Junior. If the Japanese attacked Pearl Harbor, wouldn't they also attack Manila? The phone rang. It was a staff officer: a car was on the way to pick him up; they would take him to Naval Headquarters. He wouldn't see another quiet Sunday for several years. Nimitz shouldered his coat and kissed Catherine. "I won't be back," he said, "till God knows when."[83]

Although it was afternoon in Washington, it was morning in Pearl Harbor. Six Japanese carriers had launched more than three hundred attack aircraft into the sky. Many were flown by seasoned pilots with an average of two thousand hours' flight time, including combat experience in China. The leader of the strike was Mitsuo Fuchida. He and the first wave of 183 aircraft had launched at sunrise. "It looked exactly as if our naval flag filled the entire sky," he remembered. "I took this to mean the dawn of Japan."[84] Once the attack began, however, "black smoke filled the entire airspace" over the harbor. Looking down with his binoculars, Fuchida saw the devastation on battleship row: the *Nevada* and the *Arizona* were smoking badly, and the *West Virginia* and the *Tennessee* were "enveloped by fierce flames." Aboard the USS *West Virginia*, the African American mess steward Doris Miller manned a machine gun against the attackers and helped to bring his wounded captain to safety.[85] Airfields and airplanes were also ablaze, having been hit by dive and level bombers.[86] Deterrence had failed.

Thankfully, the aircraft carriers, which were at sea ferrying planes to defend the Pacific garrisons, were not in Pearl Harbor when the Japanese struck. But the damage was bad enough as it was. Within twenty minutes, Japanese aircraft had destroyed three American airfields, including 231 planes parked on their runways or in their hangars. They had also hit all eight American battleships in the harbor—crippling five of them. By the end of the morning, the *Enterprise* Air Group had lost six men from its Dauntless aircrews, and many planes were damaged.

Those who believed that Japanese success at Pearl Harbor was solely the result of surprise had to think again three days later. Shortly after the attack, the British sortied to attack what they suspected were Japanese landings in Malaya. The battleship *Prince of Wales* and the battle cruiser *Repulse* had neither air cover nor adequate antiaircraft guns. They were caught out by seventy-three shore-based Japanese bombers on December 10, 1941, and the two ships were sent to the bottom as clinically as the US Pacific Fleet had been in Pearl Harbor. It was the torpedoes that did the decisive damage—each ship was struck by at least four of them and sank within two hours of the start of the assault.[87] There could now be no doubt about it: capital ships without air cover, no matter how big, were easy prey.

Senior figures in the Japanese Navy recognized the sinking of the *Prince of Wales* and the *Repulse* as significant. Fuchida thought it marked the end of an era. He wrote in his memoirs that "this should have convinced the leaders of the Japanese Navy of our argument of the non-utility of battleships." Genda supposedly disagreed, but he did not elaborate on his skepticism. Admiral Matome Ugaki also recorded the event—writing conflicting assessments in his memoirs in the days and weeks after the attack.[88] On the US side, Admiral William Leahy, then US ambassador to Vichy, France, wrote in his diary that it "pointed to a failure of the British Royal Air Force to be where it was needed when it was needed."[89] The obvious conclusion was that planes were more powerful than ships.

Japan was now dominant in East Asia. By December 14, the Japanese Empire had attacked Hawaii, Midway, and Wake Island, capturing Guam and making advances on the Philippines and Malaya. "The Pacific Ocean," read one newspaper in Washington, DC, was now "the biggest war front in the world conflict."[90]

On December 16, President Roosevelt summoned Nimitz to the White House for a brief interview. Once again he offered him command of the Pacific Fleet. Afterward, Nimitz walked home, about a mile and a half, somewhat dazed. Once home, he found Catherine resting in bed. She could tell something was on his mind. "What is it?" she asked. "What's happened?"

He said, "I'm to be the new Commander in Chief in the Pacific."

"You always wanted to command the Pacific Fleet," she said. "You always thought that would be the height of glory."

"Darling, the fleet's at the bottom of the sea. Nobody must know that here, but I've got to tell you." The news of his greatest promotion was more like the news of his greatest defeat. At dinner that night he tried to figure out how to tell his daughters. His daughter-in-law was also with them while her husband was at sea. Nimitz didn't want to leave, but he didn't want to stay either. Before he could say what he wanted, the girls guessed what had happened. Catherine laughed, and for a moment it was nothing more than dinner on a Tuesday night.

Eventually the conversation turned to the press. What should Admiral Nimitz say when the news was officially announced? He took out a notepad and pencil and wrote down a one-sentence response. He passed it around the table to see what the girls would say. Kate, the oldest daughter, read what her father had written: "It is a great responsibility, and I will do my utmost to meet it." She tore off the paper and folded it to keep in her pocket, saying, "I'm sure this is history."[91]

Nimitz took the train to California dressed in civilian clothes. He'd accepted Roosevelt's offer but was reluctant to be recognized. The commander in chief of the Pacific Fleet wanted to remain anonymous, especially now. He needed time to think. In his luggage was a stack of damage reports and a bottle of scotch. As the train sped across the continent, he set to work. He also began writing letters to Catherine, a habit that he continued throughout the war. "As I get more sleep and rest," he told her, "I find myself less depressed. . . . I am sure by the time I reach Pearl Harbor I will be able to meet the requirements of the situation. I only hope I can fulfill the expectations you and Mr. Roosevelt have in me. It is an awesome task and I need your prayers."[92] He arrived in Pearl Harbor on Christmas

Day, his plane touching down after sunrise. Perhaps it would've been better to land at night, to see the devastation in glimpses. But as it happened he saw it all from the plane's window: five mighty battleships burned out and submerged in the harbor, streaming black tails of oil. And then, when the door of the plane opened, he was accosted by the smell of charred wood and rotting bodies.

The first orders from Washington for the new commander of the Pacific Fleet were straightforward. First, he was to hold the line against the Japanese from Hawaii to Midway, maintaining communications with the West Coast. Second, he was to maintain communication with the west coast of Australia, chiefly by holding the line from Hawaii to Samoa, and, if possible, to Fiji.[93] Nimitz wrote to Catherine, "There will be more action in the Pacific than elsewhere for many a day to come."[94]

This prediction came true. The Japanese quickly occupied Hong Kong and Malaya. Singapore fell in February 1942. Not long after, they sent the Allied fleet defending Java to the bottom of the sea and captured the oil fields of the Dutch East Indies. The Japanese even raided Darwin on the northern coast of Australia. The Americans were putting up more of a fight in the Philippines, but the end there was just a matter of time. To many, the Japanese seemed invincible.

Nimitz needed to upset the Japanese advance, to break their momentum, and he needed a victory to lift morale, to prove that the US Navy could hold its own. But his options for attack were limited. His only offensive weapons, aside from his submarines, were his four carriers and their supporting forces. Luckily for him, American carrier aviation was probably the best prepared of all the US combat arms at the start of the war.[95] Some senior officers argued against sending these ships on the attack. Carriers were vulnerable, and there were also suspicions of an ambush. One admiral on Nimitz's staff believed that the Japanese, "by means of agents communicating via Mexico," knew of US plans to reinforce Samoa. When US ships departed, he warned, the Japanese would attack Pearl Harbor again. Nimitz, however, had confidence in his carrier task forces. Admiral William Halsey had been commanding carriers since 1935 and was restless to go on the offensive. Nimitz decided to send him out with the *Enterprise* and the *Yorktown*. After escorting the reinforcement of Marines to Samoa, the carriers would proceed to attack the Gilberts and Marshalls, Japanese-held islands in the Central Pacific. For the time being, Nimitz settled on a strategy of what he termed "raids of hit-and-run." Soon after the carriers returned from the Gilberts and Marshalls, he sent them on another mission, to strike Wake and Marcus, small islands that were a further 2,000 miles west of Hawaii, and therefore much closer to Japan than the continental United States was. There was also a mission to hit Rabaul, a vital port in Papua New Guinea, north of Australia. These were short missions that still caused him considerable anxiety. He wrote to Catherine, "I lie awake long hours."[96]

None of this activity inflicted much damage on the Japanese, but it did achieve several things. For one thing, the raids greatly lifted American morale at a time when good news was rarely heard. Second, they demonstrated the quality of US naval aviation. If the torpedo planes performed badly due to malfunctioning torpedoes, the dive-bomber pilots repeatedly demonstrated their skill in attacking heavily defended ground targets. The rugged Douglas Dauntless proved its effectiveness, and the pilots gained invaluable combat experience. Nevertheless, so far, most of the destroyed Japanese ships were small and had been bottled up in harbor. Whether US dive bombers would be able to deal with the Japanese First Air Fleet, the *Kido Butai*, on the wide ocean remained to be seen.

Above all, Nimitz rattled Yamamoto. The apparent speed of the American recovery highlighted Japan's strategic predicament. In order to achieve regional dominance in the Pacific, Japan needed to isolate the United States and destroy its naval capability. But US forces were dispersed in island bastions and mobile carriers. The Japanese preference for mass attack and decisive battles was of little use against an enemy that did not stand and fight. Then there was the problem of the clock. Japan could not stand still, given its comparative disadvantage with the United States in terms of economic and military resources. To do so invited an early American air attack on the homeland, something Yamamoto greatly feared.[97]

Yamamoto needed to strike again to destroy the will of the United States to fight before it could shift from hit-and-run raids to large-scale offensive operations. He had several options. He could strike west into the Indian Ocean, threatening the British hold on the Indian subcontinent. He could move south, neutralizing Australia, either by direct assault or by occupying the surrounding islands. He could fight east, invading Hawaii and pushing out the United States. Or he could take another approach altogether, attacking not land, but ships. He could lure the American carriers to their destruction somewhere on the high seas. This strategy would turn the dispersal of US forces into a Japanese advantage. Along this line of thinking, Yamamoto could attack a critical base like Midway in the Central Pacific, provoking Nimitz to respond. When the US carriers arrived, the Japanese would have the decisive battle they wanted.

Despite the run of Japanese successes in the early months of 1942, Yamamoto was still cautious. In May he wrote to a friend that "the 'First Operational Stage' of Operations has been a kind of children's hour and will soon be over, now comes the adult's hour."[98] He anticipated a change in tempo once the United States found its footing. He also knew that the Japanese Navy was tired after several months of sustained operations.

Many other officers in the Imperial Navy did not agree. They were bursting with confidence, not to say hubris, after their recent triumphs. The Japanese fleet had sailed 50,000 nautical miles, winning battles and seizing territory.[99] "Morale could not have been better," remembered Fuchida of that spring. "Skill levels had matured to the point of matching those of the gods."[100] This atmosphere, however, made for terrible planning. The attack on Midway, which Yamamoto had been organizing since February, was profoundly affected. "At that time everyone thought that the mission would be a simple task to accomplish," remembered one naval aviator. "That's why I feel we didn't do enough planning before the Midway operation." A former aircraft mechanic said something similar: "Because of the success that we had in Hawaii, Japan was not as careful as it should have been. We also were too confident."[101]

The Japanese believed that the United States was pliable and re-active, not plotting and offensive. Fuchida thought this kind of perspective was contagious and debilitating, that it was a "malady of over-confidence," a "Victory Disease."[102] Even Admiral Chuichi Nagumo had succumbed, telling his men prior to the battle that "although the enemy is lacking in fighting spirit, he will probably come out to attack as our invasion proceeds."[103]

Nimitz's carrier raids should have given the Japanese pause, but for months they had won victory after victory. In late March and early April, the *Kido Butai* conducted a brief raid into the Indian Ocean. It attacked the British bases in Colombo and Trin-comalee, damaging the port facilities and sinking two Royal Navy cruisers and an elderly aircraft carrier. Once again, the Japanese had triumphed. So far, so familiar, but there was a moment when they showed a surprising vulnerability. This was when nine British Blenheim bombers evaded the combat air patrol over the *Kido Butai* and were able to release their ordnance. All of them missed, though some came close. It was the first time Japanese carriers had come under serious attack, and they had not responded well.

✪

IN MARCH 1942 THE *Hornet* docked at Naval Air Station Alameda, in San Francisco Bay, where it received an unusual cargo: sixteen North American B-25 bombers. When the *Hornet* sailed out past the Golden Gate Bridge and along the Farallones, Captain Mark Andrew "Pete" Mitscher, the skipper, announced on the ship's in-tercom, "This ship is going to transport these Army bombers to the coast of Japan and we're going to bomb Tokyo." At this mo-ment, Richard Nowatzki, a deck gunner, remembered that a loud cheer erupted on the ship.[104] The men were thrilled to have their chance at war. Soon the *Hornet* and its task force arrived off the coast of Japan to launch the attack. Like Nimitz's earlier carrier raids, the Doolittle Raid—named for Lieutenant Colonel James Doolittle, who planned and led the attack—did hardly any physi-cal damage, but its psychological impact was immense, not on the Japanese public, which was largely unaffected by the incident and unaware of it, at least outside of the immediate area, but on the Japanese military, and especially on the high command.

Yamamoto was incensed. "About the raid," he wrote to a friend, "one has the embarrassing feeling of having been caught napping just when one was feeling confident and in charge of things. Even though there wasn't much damage, it's a disgrace that the skies over the imperial capital should have been defiled without a single enemy plane being shot down."[105] This defeat brought with it the realization of an enduring strategic problem. As one Japanese historian wrote, "Neither the person of the Emperor nor his sacred soil was safe while enemy carriers ranged the seas."[106]

When the torpedo-bomber pilot Juzo Mori returned in late April 1942 from successful operations against the British in the Indian Ocean, he saw the blown-out windows in houses near the harbor. He was forced to endure the reproaches of the local population. "We thought you navy guys could protect us," they charged. All Mori could do, he remembered, was to "hang his head in shame."[107] It was clear, therefore, that the Americans were still very much in the game.

The shock of Doolittle's raid thus added urgency to the Midway operation. Yamamoto's plan had two goals. The first was the seizure of territory in the central and northern Pacific before the United States could fully develop its naval power. The second was the luring out of the US fleet. Yamamoto believed this would occur once the Imperial Army attacked Midway. When US reinforcements arrived, six Japanese carriers would be waiting to strike. This would be the kind of decisive battle that the Imperial Navy longed for—ending US influence in the Pacific and perhaps bringing an end to the war itself.[108]

In early May, the Japanese war-gamed the Midway operation. As they were supposed to do, these exercises revealed all kinds of problems. Soon after the simulated attack began, US aircraft based on Midway discovered the Japanese fleet. The umpire, however, ruled that the damage sustained by Japanese carriers was negligible. The result of air combat was, as Fuchida remembered, "similarly juggled, always in favor of the Japanese forces." When the verdicts were challenged, the umpire stepped in again. Fuchida thought the entire exercise rushed. Plans were executed rather than tested. When problems were discovered—such as the need for better radio communications or the vulnerability of the aircraft carriers to aerial attack—there was no search for corresponding remedies. "Some officers," Fuchida remembered, "privately whispered that Combined Fleet Headquarters seemed seriously to underestimate enemy capabilities."[109] Later historians have agreed with Fuchida, finding the exercises hasty and poorly judged. It must be recognized, however, that the Midway war game was part of a four-day meeting during which the next three months of operations were discussed. The Midway occupation was but one part of this larger set of plans, which included seizing the western Aleutians, attacking Australia by air, and undertaking a full-scale assault on Hawaii. In other words, the war games did not reveal a Japanese problem with the Midway operation so much as a major flaw in their entire plan for the Pacific: it presumed that the US fleet was on the defensive.

Lastly, the perspective of the umpire himself should be considered. This was Utome Ugaki, a senior admiral in the Imperial Navy, who kept a detailed war diary. From his perspective, the war games were helpful for two reasons. First, they revealed the importance of the combat air patrol to protecting the strike force and compensating for the "vulnerability of the carrier." Second, they revealed that "the surface force must be prepared to sacrifice itself in its place when necessary."[110] Both remarks, which have so far gone unnoticed by historians, call to mind the Imperial Navy's strategic determination that the Japanese carrier force "be prepared to be impaled as it impales the enemy."[111] They also suggest that the war games were not so much ineffective as their lessons unheeded.

✪

AT PEARL HARBOR, ONLY two men were allowed an immediate audience with Admiral Nimitz regardless of his schedule. The first was his flag secretary, Lieutenant Paul Crosley; the second was Commander Edwin Layton. Layton had graduated from Annapolis in 1924 and, after duty in the surface fleet, completed language training in Japan, where he became acquainted with Japanese officers, including Yamamoto. In 1940 Layton became the senior intelligence officer in the Pacific. When Nimitz arrived at Pearl Harbor at the end of 1941, it was Layton who could provide the most accurate insights into Japanese operations. "I want you to be the Admiral Nagumo of my staff," Nimitz said to Layton. "I want your every thought, every instinct as you believe Admiral Nagumo might have them. . . . [I]f you can do this, you will give me the kind of information needed to win this war." The Japanese, by contrast, did not have a full-time intelligence specialist appointed to the Japanese Combined Fleet until much later.[112]

Layton's information came from Station Hypo. Owning territory throughout the North Pacific allowed the United States to build a network of listening posts for eavesdropping on Japanese radio communications. Seattle, Oahu, the Philippines, and the Marianas all had radio towers and staff performing this function. The US diplomatic presence in China also meant that a post could be set up in Shanghai. Station Hypo was the office on Oahu. It was run by Joe Rochefort, a quiet, mild-mannered linguist who, because of his basement office, sometimes worked in a red quilted smoking jacket. He and his team of cryptologists, nicknamed "crippies," continually pored over their fragments of radio transcriptions and attempted to determine the position of the Japanese fleet. Even though the United States had captured a Japanese codebook, the messages were not always easy to understand. Abbreviations were used instead of place names, a weak signal could garble the radio transmission, the cryptologist might incorrectly transcribe what he heard, or the Japanese might deliberately spread false information—there were many reasons to be skeptical of what Station Hypo produced. "Radio intelligence has never been an exact science," Layton said in his memoirs. A great amount of guesswork was involved to piece together the details. Layton had to do his best. Each morning at 0800, he briefed Nimitz and his staff on the suspected position and plans of the Japanese fleet.[113]

Fortunately, the more Rochefort and his crippies eavesdropped on the Japanese, the more they understood the Japanese code. The Doolittle Raid was particularly helpful in this regard. After the attack Station Hypo intercepted a flurry of Japanese radio communications. There were other events that tested Rochefort's predictions. In late April he determined that the Japanese were preparing to seize Port Moresby in the Coral Sea. Looking at the evidence, Layton reported to Nimitz that the operation would "start very soon," perhaps within the week.[114]

Meanwhile, the El Segundo plant was turning out Dauntlesses. By the start of 1942, carrier squadrons received Heinemann's latest model, which featured several important improvements. Originally the plane had two forward-firing .30-caliber guns operated by the pilot and one rear-firing flexible gun operated by the rear-seat gunner. The new model had more than doubled this firepower, sporting two forward-firing .50s and two rear-firing .30s. The fuel tank was also improved: it was enlarged, increasing the plane's bombing range from 860 to 1,225 miles, and it was now self-sealing, lined with a synthetic material that would reseal itself if punctured by enemy gunfire. Protective armor was also added to the fuselage to protect the crew.

Heinemann believed that manufacturing more Dauntlesses was an urgent matter. In March, in a letter he distributed to all engineering personnel, he opened with a quote from Donald Nelson, chairman of the War Production Board: "Every weapon we make today is worth *ten* that we might produce next year. This year—1942—is the critical year in the existence of the United States." The war for the Pacific, as much as it was a contest between opposing strategies, was also a competition to manufacture weapons and the engines that would deliver them. "This timely quotation," Heinemann told his engineers, "sums up in a few words the importance of all out action *now*."[115]

When the Japanese moved south in early May, Nimitz—forewarned by Layton and Rochefort—was ready for them.[116] A US carrier group surprised the enemy in the Coral Sea, an area of outstanding natural beauty between New Guinea and Australia. It was the first naval battle fought between two mutually invisible carrier forces. Over two days, May 7 and 8, both sides hurled aircraft at each other. The Japanese lost a small carrier, the *Shoho*, and a large carrier, the *Shokaku*, was seriously damaged. The Americans lost one large carrier, the *Lexington*, and another, the *Yorktown*, was badly damaged. Overall, the Japanese lost more aircraft and pilots than the Americans. Tactically, the battle was a narrow Japanese victory, but because the American interception turned back their invasion force, it was a strategic defeat for Tokyo.

Much more important were the lessons both sides learned, or failed to learn, from this engagement.[117] The sinking of the *Shoho* by dive bombers and torpedo bombers blinded the Americans both to the vulnerability of the torpedo planes and to the unreliability of their torpedoes. It also reinforced their doctrinal assumption that the combined dive- and torpedo-bombing attacks were the best way of sinking a carrier. The effectiveness of the dive bombers, by contrast, was underestimated. This was partly because the tropical air caused bombsights and canopies to mist up during dives, putting pilots off their aim, and partly because the Dauntlesses had suffered heavy losses at the hands of Japanese fighters. It was not a fault of design or training, but of tactics—the Dauntlesses were more vulnerable while circling over the target. They performed this maneuver in the belief that it was more effective to attack simultaneously with the slower torpedo bombers. It was not only more dangerous but it also forfeited the crucial element of surprise.[118] The false deduction that American analysts made after the battle was that fighter protection should be given to the dive bombers in the first instance, rather than the torpedo bombers, which needed it most. These misjudgments would cost the Americans dearly a month later.

The Japanese also drew some fatally wrong conclusions. They did not ask why the Americans had suddenly appeared, or why the *Shoho* had been surprised so completely. It was similar to the raid on Colombo, when the Japanese were caught out by British Blenheims: attacking aircraft were a mortal threat to ships, but the seriousness of the problem eluded the Japanese. At Coral Sea, the carrier *Zuikaku* was able to escape into a rain cloud before the US Dauntlesses could set to work. And the sister carrier, *Shokaku*, which had been hit, managed to survive. A maintenance officer aboard the ship during the attack remembered that the fire was small enough to be controlled by foam and a "water hose from the flight deck."[119] There was no reason to expect that other attacks would turn out differently. More generally, the Japanese had failed to grasp how formidable an enemy the American naval aviators were, a critical point of information if war games and strategy were to be of any use.

Nimitz, however, learned a vital lesson. The intelligence coming out of Station Hypo could be trusted.[120] Thanks to Layton and Rochefort, he had been able to put his carriers right on top of the Japanese. Having done it once, Nimitz knew he could do it again.

Confidence in his abilities did not lighten Nimitz's darkness at Pearl Harbor. It was a city under siege. During the day the sidewalks were thronged with US soldiers, sailors, marines, and steel-helmeted plant workers of various nationalities. Then came the eight o'clock curfew and the war showed a different face. One visitor during the summer of 1942 said that "the streets of Honolulu are as black and silent as a deserted mining town."[121] Nimitz felt a similar desolation. There was little to show for months of campaigning: his raids bothered the enemy, but they had delivered no prizes. He needed a victory.

Then Rochefort reported that another operation was in the works, this time in the Aleutian Islands and Midway. Layton and Nimitz were inclined to agree. Convincing Washington, however, was another matter. There the navy had another office of cryptoanalysts with ideas of their own: they believed the real target was Hawaii, Johnston Island, or Australia.[122] Nimitz tried to confirm Rochefort's intelligence. On May 2, he visited Midway itself, inspecting the fortifications and gun emplacements. He spoke with the commander of the Marine forces there, asking what was needed to defend the atoll. When the officer answered with a list of equipment, Nimitz replied with another question: "If I get you all these things you say you need, then can you hold Midway against a major amphibious assault?" The Marine answered, "Yes, sir."[123]

By mid-May Nimitz's suspicion was stronger. Intercepted radio transmissions from the Japanese contained repeated references to Midway. By May 15 he had managed to convince Washington, and then he planned accordingly. He dispatched Seventh Air Force bombers—as well as other planes, tanks, and antiaircraft guns—to the airstrip on Midway. He requested support from one of three British carriers in the Indian Ocean (a request that was refused). He ordered submarines to monitor possible avenues of approach to Midway. He also ordered planes to perform search missions, hoping to gain advance warning of the Japanese arrival.

The date of the planned Japanese attack was unknown, but Rochefort thought it was imminent. The *Enterprise* returned from the Coral Sea on May 25, and the *Yorktown*, still badly damaged, was expected soon after. The next day Rochefort and Layton determined that the Midway Operation would begin on June 3. Nimitz needed to take stock of his forces. He visited his ships, holding award ceremonies and inspecting their condition. The *Yorktown* arrived on the 27th, "trailing a ten-mile-long oil slick." It had taken a hit from a Japanese dive bomber that had penetrated its flight deck and opened seams in the hull. Pulling waders over his khaki uniform, Nimitz walked through the ship. The gash in the hull was the most worrying damage, but there were other problems too: the radar and refrigeration systems were shot to pieces, fuel tanks were leaking, and the boilers had been hit. It was estimated that the necessary repairs would take three months. Nimitz didn't have that long. More than a thousand welders and shipfitters were assembled to work on the ship round the clock. Nimitz gave them three days.[124]

Meanwhile, Nimitz was preparing not merely to defeat the Japanese but to memorialize his expected victory. In late May, he asked the navy's Field Photographic Unit for volunteers for a dangerous mission to an unnamed location. The celebrated movie director John Ford, then serving with the unit, immediately stepped forward. Soon he was on his way by speedboat, and then destroyer, to Midway. Ford, who still had no idea what lay ahead, naturally assumed that he had been sent to make a leisurely documentary about life at a remote outpost. On arrival, he threw himself into filming the garrison and the local wildlife. "Up here for a short visit," he wrote to his wife, Mary. "This is some place."[125]

On May 28, orders for the Midway operation were delivered to ship captains by hand. In essence, Nimitz was setting an ambush. The Japanese were expected to attack Midway from the northwest with four or five carriers and a host of supporting forces. Lying in wait would be two US carrier task forces, the same formations Nimitz used during the Fleet Problems of the 1930s. The first was Task Force 16, which included the *Enterprise* and the *Hornet* along with eighteen supporting ships. The second was Task Force 17, the *Yorktown* and eight supporting ships. Task Force 11, the *Saratoga* with eight ships, was departing from California and would arrive by June 5. If one included Midway, which had an airstrip of its own, now filled to a bursting point with aircraft, the balance of forces between the Japanese and the United States was more or less equal.

But the more important fact was not the number of ships but their orientation. Nimitz was not sending out his carriers to challenge the Japanese head-on. Instead, he wanted the Japanese to remain fixated on Midway, so that his carriers could attack at will. In this sense, the atoll was acting as a support-by-fire position— it would keep the Japanese occupied while the US carrier air squadrons approached from the flank. The open sea northwest of Midway was a perfect kill zone for the US Dauntlesses. Nimitz told his captains, "In carrying out the task assigned . . . you will be governed by the principle of calculated risk which you shall interpret to mean the avoidance of exposure of your force to attack by superior enemy forces without good prospect of inflicting, as a result of such exposure, greater damage to the enemy."

In late May, the main Japanese striking force assembled at the island anchorage of Hashirajima off the western Inland Sea of

Japan. A group of newsmen were embarked on the *Soryu* in order to record the expected victory. Security seems to have been lax. On the eve of their departure, some officers bragged about the Midway attack to girls in the local brothels. "Prior to our departure," remembered one Japanese naval aviator, "everyone was talking about our Midway plans, so it wasn't a secretive mission like the Pearl Harbor attack." He took it as a "bad omen." A maintenance officer had the same experience, finding that "even Japanese civilians knew that we were going to attack; but it was supposed to be a secret."[126]

There were other ominous portents. The *Kido Butai* deployed without the *Shokaku*, which was still being repaired from the damage sustained in the Battle of the Coral Sea. The *Zuikaku* was also staying behind. It was undamaged but had lost much of its dedicated air group. Mitsuo Fuchida was also removed from battle, though he was on the *Akagi*. Soon after departure, he was struck down with appendicitis. The final warning sign was a failed intelligence mission. The Japanese had planned to send a plane over Pearl Harbor to confirm the location of the American carriers. But Nimitz, anticipating this move, had placed an American destroyer where the Japanese plane would be refueled at sea. As a result, the plane was forced to turn away; it would not be able to inspect Pearl Harbor. Yamamoto and Nagumo thus sailed into battle without any idea where the American carriers were.[127] The Japanese were setting a trap, but they were about to fall into it themselves.

Juzo Mori, back on the carrier *Soryu* and steaming east, had no sense of foreboding. Morale remained good. The slogan for the operation was "In high spirits for certain victory!" Some of the pilots gathering on the fantail of the ship to smoke thought that casualties would be high, especially among the torpedo pilots, but Mori was unworried. The same had been said before Pearl Harbor. He spent every day with the maintenance crews working on the planes. Mori was soon covered in grease, but he felt the effort was worth it, as it made him more familiar with his aircraft.[128] Like the rest of the *Kido Butai*, he had no idea what was about to hit him.

✪

NIMITZ HAD PUT HIS carrier task forces in the right place to surprise Nagumo. He had also reinforced Midway, making it a robust support-by-fire position. Thanks to his judgment call, the US Navy would be able to snare the snarer. In the Douglas Dauntless, his carriers had a weapon capable of delivering devastating force against the enemy. The admiral had done his part. Now it remained to be seen whether the pilots who manned those planes could do theirs.

3

THE PILOT

LIEUTENANT DUSTY KLEISS WAS FAR FROM HOME. HE WAS stretched out on his bunk aboard the USS *Enterprise* with a pen in hand, writing to his girlfriend, Jean. "I'm living temporarily in another world—one I hope you never know," he told her. "It is a cold and ruthless world filled with hate and incalculable cold-bloodedness. But it is necessary for some of us to live there now and then to protect the other world, the one I'm in when I'm with you." The following day, if all went according to plan, he and his squadron would ambush the Japanese fleet. That was the reason for his tense tone. His work had suddenly seemed to become nothing more than a complicated kind of killing. But he didn't flinch from it. He was filled with a longing for courage, good fortune, and fortitude. He wanted to fight as he had trained. "Give me courage, Jean, and luck," he wrote to her. "Sometimes I need them badly and I know that you can supply them." He signed his letter, sealed it, and lay down in his bunk. The command for lights out came and then Kleiss lay still in the darkness.[1]

✪

NORMAN JACK KLEISS WAS born in Coffeyville, Kansas, in 1916, the descendant of Germans who had settled in the United States in 1859. He was just too young to experience the German America that had shaped Nimitz and left its mark on Heinemann. Kleiss was an all-American boy who had been raised in a Methodist Episcopalian household that took religion seriously. "I came to believe God routinely intervened in the affairs of humankind," he recalled when describing his youth. "All of the inexplicable occurrences—good or bad—were part of his plan." Kleiss's childhood was one of adventure; guns were close at hand. He received early instruction from a formidable aunt, Helen Ruthrauff, the women's shotgun champion of Kansas, and from a neighbor. The latter taught him how to shoot a jackrabbit on the move, which later helped him to perfect his aim while dive bombing. In both cases, he explained, the "shooter must aim for where the target is going to be, not where it is." Faith, family, and firearms: this was the world that Jack knew.[2]

He was also aware from a relatively young age that there was another world out there, one of loss and conflict, both at home and abroad. His beloved mother died when he was in his early teens, and Kleiss recalled that the "only solace" he found was in religion. Four years later, during his final year in high school, Kleiss opted to write an essay on the famous Kellogg-Briand Pact of 1928. This idealist measure, which, in Kleiss's words, "outlawed war," was hailed by many who remembered the horrors of the trenches. Kleiss, writing in 1933, two years after the Japanese had occupied Manchuria, and the year in which Hitler came to power, knew better. He queried the "idea that savvy diplomacy and moral progressivism would make war obsolete." "Nations would always go to war," Kleiss believed, and so "there would always be a need to fight."[3]

At the heart of Kleiss's view of the world was the belief in a supreme God who respected human action. This is why, in his thinking, there would always be a need to fight for one's country. It was also how he dealt with another contemporary event: the Scopes Trial of 1925, a reaction to the rise of the theory of evolution. When applying to the University of Kansas, Kleiss was closely questioned on the issue. He described his response as the product of two perspectives: "I felt no desire to compromise my belief in the biblical account of creation, but at the same time, I respected the natural sciences."[4] In other words, he believed that God's creative power did not cancel out or negate man's power to explore. For Kleiss, life was a gift as much as it was something he decided for himself.

One of his first great decisions was to fly. Having joined the Kansas National Guard as a cavalryman, he was "killed" by a swooping aircraft during joint exercises. From that point on, Kleiss was determined to leave horses behind and fly planes instead. Inspired by newspaper reports of the new aircraft carriers, he resolved to join the US Navy as an aviator.[5] Instead of enrolling at the University of Kansas, Kleiss accepted a place at the United States Naval Academy at Annapolis.

✪

KLEISS ENTERED THE NAVAL Academy in 1934, two years after Nimitz's son, Chester Junior. Much had remained the same in the thirty years since the elder Nimitz had graduated. It was still a place of intense discipline, physical hardship, and camaraderie. During the week, academic coursework had to be balanced with military exercises, and on Sundays the midshipmen attended chapel. Religion there, according to one professor, was "cheerful, manly, natural, and far-reaching . . . closely linked with a man's highest impulses and feeling for service."[6] It was also, like nearly everything else at the academy, mandatory. Trying to make friends with upperclassmen, and thus escape the hazing, Kleiss joined the wrestling team as a welterweight at 145 pounds.

His best friend was Tom Eversole from Pocatello, Idaho. The basis of their friendship was their mutual desire to pursue the newest area of naval operations, an area that represented one of the greatest changes to the navy since the elder Nimitz's days: aviation. Both Kleiss and Eversole wanted to fly. A near contemporary of the two men remembered that, during the 1930s, aviation "was receiving progressive attention" in the navy: "All members of our class were given indoctrination flights as well as lectures on fleet employment of aircraft of all types including from our three carriers."[7] There had been other changes as well. Because of developments in technology, midshipmen studied electricity, radios, and aeronautics. The history curriculum had also been updated. What had previously been "limited to the achievements of the American Navy" was now expanded to include a "substantial course in the political and social history of the United States," as well as modern European history from 1789 to the "conditions and problems following the World War."[8]

In 1935 and 1937, Kleiss went on two "summer cruises" on the battleship USS *Arkansas* that were designed to give midshipmen like himself some practical experience in seamanship, gunnery, engineering, and other skills required by the navy. These trips were largely uneventful; the only danger he remembered was an explosion set off in the battleship's forward turret. It was caused by bored sailors trying to make a "pink lady," an alcoholic cocktail made from medicine and torpedo propulsion fluid. The strict "no alcohol" policy on US navy ships did not mean that sailors drank nothing, but rather, that they'd drink anything. The cruises took Kleiss twice to the German port of Kiel, which gave him insight into the increasingly threatening atmosphere in Hitler's Third Reich. The "other world" was beginning to encroach on him.[9]

Kleiss graduated in 1938 roughly in the middle of his class, with a somewhat weak performance in the humanities and languages but a strong showing in mathematics and engineering–related subjects. The commencement address was delivered by none other than President Franklin D. Roosevelt. Roosevelt alluded to the growing "world problems" in his speech, and perhaps for this reason dropped a hint that the new "Bachelor of Science" graduates should not "place too much emphasis on the word 'Bachelor.'"[10] In other words, they should get married quickly, before hostilities began. That year, the academy yearbook, known as *The Lucky Bag*, contained photos from Kleiss's second cruise to Europe, one of them showing a busy street in Berlin lined with swastika flags.

The first posting for all academic graduates was in the surface fleet. Kleiss was sent to the cruiser USS *Vincennes*. His real element, however, was not the sea, but the air. Aboard the *Vincennes*, he served as the aircraft recovery operations officer for the ship's scout seaplane. It allowed him to work alongside aviators and also exposed him to the tension that existed between the traditional "black shoe" navy and the "brown shoe" pilots. He was definitely one of the latter, though he understood that "aviators would only earn their place through success in combat."[11]

Kleiss did not take the president's advice. While based in Long Beach, California, he met and fell in love with Eunice Mochon, a blue-eyed beauty of French Canadian parentage, whom he later called "Jean." Engagement soon became a topic of discussion. There was a problem, however. Eunice was Roman Catholic and Kleiss was Protestant at a time when such differences mattered intensely.[12] Kleiss's father wrote repeatedly to warn that marriage to a Catholic would be a violation of family tradition. Eunice was determined to retain her faith and send her children to Catholic schools. Kleiss insisted that she give up these aspirations and convert to Methodism. He felt a sense of family piety; he was also repelled by what he considered to be the Catholic church's "oath-taking."[13] When Kleiss left Long Beach on the *Vincennes*, bound for Norfolk, Virginia, the matter was still unresolved. With Eunice, he couldn't make up his mind. He was not in control; he was in love.

Aviation was different. "In an airplane," Kleiss said, "I could be my own commander, make my own decisions."[14] Aviation, more than any other area of the navy where he might have served, leveraged Kleiss's independent streak. Success or failure resulted from his actions rather than those of a large crew. When taking off or dive bombing or returning to land, he was alone, in charge of his destiny.

Aviation offered other incentives. There was extra pay, for example: pilots "received 50 percent additional hazard pay beyond the normal $125 per month base pay," he later wrote in his memoirs. There was also "the excitement" of flight. And finally, there was the fact that Kleiss believed that war had changed: "Planes, not surface ships," he wrote, "would win the navy's future battles."[15] The truth of that statement had yet to be proven, but it was the way Kleiss saw things. So, in early 1940, his time aboard the *Vincennes* coming to a close, Kleiss applied to flight school.

At the same time, he decided what to do about Jean. Calling her on the phone, he proposed marriage. Jean had proposals of her own, however. She would accept his Protestantism, but she intended to maintain her faith by having a Catholic wedding and raising their children in the Catholic tradition. Kleiss fired back heavily anti-Catholic broadsides. "The dispute," he recalled, "deadlocked any chance of marriage."[16]

Without Jean, his life was dominated by the navy. In the autumn, he reported to Naval Air Station Pensacola on the Florida Panhandle for flight training. He was a quick study. His closest friend in ground school was his Naval Academy classmate Tom Eversole. "We did everything together," Kleiss recalled. "Two closer chums could not be found."[17] Soon he went on to learn carrier flying at the navy fighter school in Opa-Locka, at the other end of Florida. The town was a northern suburb of Miami. Shortly before leaving Opa-Locka he was near the airstrip when a new pilot failed to recover from a spin. Kleiss watched appalled as the pilot bailed out and his parachute failed to open. He hit the ground, making a terrible noise and breaking nearly every bone in his body. Despite his injuries, the stricken aviator was able to get out some last words before he died. "Pray for me," he said, "and tell my family to pray for me." These words made a deep impression on Kleiss. Suddenly realizing that "we humans have only a short abode on earth," he resolved to waste no more time.[18]

The whole episode was another reminder of the relationship between science and religion, the subject Kleiss had considered back in Kansas. For him, the tension proved a creative one, because what sustained him in the ordeals ahead was not reason, but faith and love.

Kleiss dedicated himself to his trade: flying planes. Nearly all of what he knew so far related to biplanes, such as the N3N-1 "Yellow Peril" or the SU-2 "Corsair." Two wings made the biplane agile but restricted the pilot's view. They also added a large amount of drag, slowing the plane's speed. The one exception was the NJ-1 "Texan," manufactured by North American Aviation. Dutch Kindelberger, the man who had offered Heinemann his first job in aviation, designed the plane in 1935, the same year that Heinemann designed the Dauntless, and the planes shared a somewhat similar silhouette. But the Texan was a weaker plane by comparison: made partly of fabric, it was lighter and more fragile; its engine was also less powerful, it had a different wing structure, and it lacked Heinemann's dive brakes. Biplanes or not, these planes were largely characterized by the design principles of the World War I era. Engines had become more powerful, but the next generation of aircraft had yet to be introduced.

The instruction given at Opa-Locka was similarly out of date. Pilots were taught the basics reasonably well, but the initial training for carrier landings was rudimentary. The instructors simply painted the outline of a carrier on the field and told the students to land within it. The landing signal officer (LSO) would stand at the side of the simulated deck, guiding in approaching planes by means of colored paddles about the size of tennis rackets. With these paddles, the LSO would indicate changes in speed, altitude, or direction. Landing in such a confined space was hard enough, but it bore little resemblance to the challenge of bringing a plane down on a real carrier traveling at speed and in seas that might cause the flight deck to rise and fall by as much as 10 to 15 feet.[19]

Kleiss earned the treasured pilot's "wings" in April 1941. He was then ordered to San Diego to join Scouting Squadron Six, or VS-6, part of the Enterprise Air Group.[20] The Pensacola graduates appear to have been assigned at random—Kleiss did not ask to become a dive bomber. Tom Eversole, for his part, does not seem to have chosen the role he was given either, which was that of a torpedo bomber in Torpedo Squadron Six (VT-6), based on Kleiss's ship.[21] The luck of this particular draw would have profound consequences for both men.

Kleiss lucked out in another way as well: being stationed in San Diego meant he was closer to Jean. He still thought about her constantly, and his experience with death, the moment he had knelt beside the pilot who had fallen from the sky, had caused him to reconsider his qualms about her faith.[22] Soon after he arrived on the West Coast, he visited her in Long Beach. It was, as he remembered, "a momentous reunion." Afterward he wrote to her, promising marriage. But he waited to formally propose, thinking it would be better to finish settling into Scouting Six. It was a decision he would greatly regret in the months ahead.

One of those selected as a torpedo bomber at around the same time as Eversole was George Gay, who had been born in Waco, Texas, in 1917, a year later than Kleiss. His parents were of English, Irish, and German descent. Like Kleiss, he believed war was an inevitable part of the human condition, and he was convinced that the United States would eventually be drawn into the conflict brewing in Europe. Like Kleiss, too, he wanted to fly, and if he had to fight in any war, he wanted to do so in an airplane. Unlike Kleiss, whose path to his "wings" had been smooth, Gay had had to battle for a pilot training slot. The US Army Air Corps had turned him down in July 1939 on account of a weak heart. When the war in Europe broke out not long after, Gay thought of joining the Canadian Air Force or even the Royal Air Force instead. Then someone suggested he try the US Navy. So, in February 1941, Gay wound up at Opa-Locka for flight training.[23] On completion, he was assigned to Torpedo Squadron Eight (VT-8), aboard the aircraft carrier USS *Hornet*.

Meanwhile, the man with whom Gay's destiny would forever be associated, John Waldron, was completing a stint as the naval inspector of ordnance at the plant of Carl L. Norden, Inc., in New York City. Norden was the designer of the celebrated "Norden bombsight," which supporters of high-altitude bombing believed would deliver bombs on target. We do not know what Waldron made of those claims, or of the Norden sight itself. Ironically, he was soon posted to take command of Torpedo Eight, which operated a weapons system about as far removed from that of the Norden and high-level bombing as it is possible to imagine.

✪

THE *ENTERPRISE* AIR GROUP, like all US carrier air groups, was made up of four squadrons: a fighter squadron, a torpedo-bomber squadron, a dive-bomber squadron, and a scouting squadron; the latter—to which Kleiss belonged—also doubled as a dive-bomber squadron because both used the Dauntless. The difference was that the scouts were armed with 500-pound bombs, whereas the regular bombers had 1,000 pounders. This allowed the scouts to travel farther in order to perform reconnaissance, a task that sometimes required scouts to launch without ordnance. All told there were about 540 men in the entire air group, including mechanics and other flight deck crew.[24] Seventy-three of them (40 officers and 33 enlisted men) were in Scouting Six.[25] At this point, the navy's standard dive bomber was the Curtiss SBC "Helldiver." The Helldiver was a biplane with a strong engine so it could climb fast and carry a 1,000-pound bomb, a considerable upgrade in ordnance from the previous generation of dive bombers. It was constructed of fabric and metal, however, so pilots had to handle it with caution when dive bombing at a steep angle.

So far, the *Enterprise* had had an uneventful year, much of it spent shuttling equipment back and forth between Hawaii and the West Coast. The air group had conducted little aviation training.[26] When Kleiss caught up with the *Enterprise*, its crew had just finished stripping out all of its combustible material, such as "wooden furniture, canvas, excess rope, and inflammable paint."[27] This precaution was normal and had to be done because fires started by enemy action could turn the entire vessel into an inferno. Clearly, the captain of the *Enterprise* was preparing and clearing his ship for action.

In the summer of 1941, Scouting Six was equipped with a new airplane: Heinemann's SBD Dauntless. Immediately, Kleiss would have noticed its shape. Instead of two wings, the Dauntless sported one low mono-wing, trimmed with its characteristically perforated split flaps. The Dauntless also felt different in flight. It had nearly the same engine as the Helldiver but its climbing speed was more than one-third slower. In fact, the Dauntless barely climbed faster than the first plane Kleiss had ever soloed in, the N3N-1, which had been developed in 1917. This was because the Dauntless was heavy: 40 percent heavier than the Helldiver, to be exact.

Walking out to his Dauntless, Kleiss made his way to the rear of the wing and stepped onto where it met the fuselage. From here he could continue along the fuselage to the front cockpit, then slide back the canopy and climb into his seat. Sitting in his seat he fastened his lap belt. Before him were some fifteen dials and gauges used to monitor his engine, altitude, speed, direction, and attitude. A chart board was stowed inside the panel beneath these instruments; in flight it was often taken out and used as a workspace for his notes and map. A compass, a lever for propeller control, and a pull knob for letting engine heat into the cabin were located below that. Between his knees was his control stick, and at his feet, the rudder pedals. His relief tube, or "p-tube," was stowed by his left foot, and at his left elbow he would find the "T" handle for the fire extinguisher, his arresting hook lever, and a rudder tab wheel. Then, at his left hand, there were fuel gauges, a magneto switch, and controls for his throttle and fuel mixture. Beneath these, just far enough away that he had to lean down to reach it, was the release lever for his bomb. On his other side, at his right elbow, were the controls for his split flaps along with an oxygen supply indicator. At his right hand was the rear end of his .50-caliber machine gun; his electrical distribution panel, with fuse box and various switches; and an auxiliary panel with engine controls. Except for the split flaps, most of this was familiar to Kleiss, but because the navy had yet to standardize instrument panels, each model of aircraft was different.

Another unique aspect of the Dauntless was the mess. It was certainly not the first plane with a front-mounted air-cooled engine. These typically consumed a vast quantity of oil—as much as one gallon per hour—some of which sprayed back onto the plane, coating the wings. In those days, as one pilot said, "oil was cheap, and soap was cheap."[28] What was unique about the Dauntless was the complex system of hydraulics that Heinemann had designed to smoothly operate the split flaps while the plane was in flight. The tubing wound its way through the cockpit and, as Kleiss discovered, "if it sprang a leak, fluid sprayed out in a nasty stream."[29]

Over the next few months, Kleiss trained intensively. Even in peacetime, flying was an arduous business. For hours at a time, he had to navigate as well as control the plane. Food, if any was provided, came in the form of a box lunch.[30] If he was cold, he let in hot air from the engine. If he needed to relieve himself, he used the p-tube. The long flights required intense concentration to avoid drifting off course—on land there were terrain features to help him identify his location, but over the trackless sea there was only math: navigation required a precise calculation involving his heading, speed, and duration of flight. Equipment malfunction was an added danger that might cause him to be stranded at sea. Somehow he needed to overcome these physical and mental challenges to deliver his ordnance when and where it was required.

Dive bombing was the essential function of the Dauntless. It effectively meant, as one pilot put it, "firing the bomb like a bullet rather than dropping it."[31] The airplane had to be pointed more or less straight at the target, allowing for wind and the movement of the enemy ship. The commander of Scouting Six, Wilmer Earl Gallaher, took his men to practice on the kelp beds off the California coast. At other times, the pilots made diving runs on a sled towed by a destroyer. Usually in training, they dropped dummy bombs filled with water; on rare occasions, they used live ordnance. Pulling up from a dive, a pilot could look over his shoulder to observe the accuracy of his bomb. It was an irresistible urge: to see the effect of one's weapon. But Gallaher warned them never to do this in combat; it could distract a pilot when he was especially vulnerable to enemy fighters. Better to focus on climbing away to safety instead.[32]

Dive bombing required not only great courage and faith in the machinery but also skill and endurance. Usually, the attack would begin at about 20,000 feet. From that altitude, Kleiss recalled, the target "appeared to be about the size of a ladybug on the tip of a shoe."[33] If the target was moving, as ships usually were, Kleiss would note its direction and speed to gauge how steeply he needed to dive. He would also consider the heading he would take after his recovery. Then he would begin his attack routine, keeping one hand on his control stick at all times. He would stow his chart board, sliding it back into the instrument panel, and fold away his map. He would then glance about the cockpit, stowing any loose items to prevent them from flying about during the dive. Sliding his canopy open brought in a gust of cold air, but he did this to prevent it from fogging up during the rapid change in temperature. He would then smear ephedrine under his nose and inhale deeply. This cleared his sinuses, making his descent to sea level—and with it the tremendous change in pressure that would take place in less than two minutes—less painful. On his engine, he would switch to low blower, allowing it to operate better at sea level. Finally, he would extend the dive brakes, and, when that was finished, it was time. He would "push over," that is, push the stick forward, and thus the plane down into a dive. For a moment, the plane would accelerate, but because the dive brakes were open, it would steady at 275 miles per hour and remain responsive to minor adjustments in controls. As it plunged, buffeted by wind, the noise was deafening. Throughout the dive, Kleiss had to keep the target in the center of the telescopic bomb scope while glancing at his instruments. The key dial was the altimeter, which gradually jerked its way counterclockwise, registering the height of the plane to within 1,000 feet.[34]

Bomb-release altitude varied considerably. The lower you were, the more precise your aim. Pull up too early—you would miss. Pull up too late—you would hit the water or be hit by fragments from your own bomb. The recommended release height was 2,500 feet. While pulling up from steep dives, Kleiss would briefly lose his eyesight: the perceived force of gravity intensified some six to nine times because of the change in direction, pulling blood from his brain into his backside. In other words, the 150-pound Kleiss, while undergoing 6 Gs, would feel as though he were 900 pounds—resulting in a considerable increase in stress on both his body and the structure of his Dauntless.

In a way, dive bombing was like tennis. During the war, the navy produced an instructional film on dive bombing that began with two men on a tennis court, batting the ball back and forth. In the game, because points are counted in multiples of fifteen, the winning score inevitably suggests a large difference in skill between winner and loser. But in truth, as the narrator of the film pointed out, "the expert or the champ" is determined by who "will get the smallest average error." Winning the game was not so much about having more skill than one's opponent as it was about making fewer mistakes. Dive bombing was similar. Like hitting a ball over a net, it was a straightforward task. But in order to score, one had to concentrate, make fine adjustments, coordinate hand and eye—and make fewer mistakes than the competition: in this case, other pilots, who were also plunging down at a target, aiming for a bull's-eye.

The glamour and importance of dive bombing were reflected in the widely watched Hollywood movie *Dive Bomber* (1941), which was released not long before the United States joined the war. Set both on land and aboard an aircraft carrier, it emphasized the hazards of the job and the need to understand the stresses that pilots were under during the descent. Kleiss regarded the film with mixed feelings. "The . . . movie 'Dive Bombers' had lots of our old planes in it and lots of nice color shots," he wrote to Jean in mid-November 1941, "but as a movie there are few worse."[35]

Some pilots were better than others. As one pilot, Clarence Dickinson, from Jacksonville, Florida, said in 1943, "men don't fly with equal skill any more than they play tennis with equal skill."[36] Kleiss repeated this analogy verbatim some seventy years later.[37] Hollywood suggested that piloting skills were quasi-mystical. *Dive Bomber*, released the same year that Kleiss arrived at the *Enterprise*, portrayed pilots as continually at risk of the malicious spirits of blackouts and fatigue. Either would attack at inopportune times, and, should death occur, the pilot's memory would haunt his comrades. Survival was often the result of good intuition. Kleiss's experience, however, suggested a more mundane reality, where survival depended on discipline and repetition. This did nothing to undermine the brotherhood or rivalry within the squadron. To the contrary, it amplified it: pilots were notorious for overestimating their hits.[38]

While the dive bombers were an effective plane, it was already clear, long before a shot had been fired, that the Douglas TBD Devastator torpedo bombers and the torpedoes they carried were seriously deficient. Kleiss discussed these problems at length with his friend in Torpedo Six, Tom Eversole. The Devastator was too slow and ungainly, at least at the low altitudes where it mattered. In one exercise, 40 percent of the torpedoes they carried sank directly upon hitting the water, and another 50 percent went off in the wrong direction. Kleiss observed this himself in another exercise, when he saw the torpedoes "spinning in a circle like a dog chasing its tail." It was clear that there was something wrong with the guidance system or propeller, yet Kleiss was warned by a superior officer not to speak about what he had seen.[39] Whether the torpedoes would actually explode when they hit the target was unknown, because the Bureau of Ordnance forbade live-firing exercises on grounds of expense (each torpedo cost $10,000).[40]

Watching the problems with the Devastator caused Kleiss to concentrate even more on his responsibilities in the Dauntless. The key to success was teamwork: on the ship, within the squadron, and in the aircraft itself. In this context, the relationship between the two Dauntless crew members was important. Obviously, the gunner had to operate the twin .30-caliber guns that were used to defend the plane from attack. This required shooting skills not unlike those Kleiss used in dive bombing—that of leading the target. It also meant being able to service and repair the guns should there be any malfunction during operations. The gunner also had important duties with the radio: he was responsible for changing the coils, the means by which different frequencies were selected for communication. The role was dangerous because it was more difficult for gunners to bail out. "With twin guns that weren't designed for the plane, and armor plate in the seat that folds in front of your chest and stomach, you haven't got much chance to bail out at that altitude," said one gunner, when asked about escaping from the Dauntless if he got into difficulties soon after take-off.[41] Then there was the final consideration, as to whether the pilot could trust the gunner should the plane crash. Both men would need to rely on one another in extreme circumstances, perhaps even in captivity.

The selection of the gunner was thus one of the most important decisions a pilot would make. Kleiss used the training period to size up the gunners' abilities and dismissed many of them outright, noting their deficiencies in his notebook. Then his eye fell on John Snowden, who at the age of twenty was younger than many of the others but had extremely high gunnery scores. He swooped in before any of the more senior pilots noticed and carried Snowden off as his gunner in late July 1941. It was to prove a stable and warm relationship until the navy divorced them shortly after Midway. "I never quite got over breaking us up," Snowden later wrote. "I didn't care so much about where we went so long as we went together."[42]

✪

"A MELEE OF ORGANIZED confusion": that was what George Gay had heard about Torpedo Squadron Eight before he joined it in Norfolk, Virginia. So it was when he arrived in the fall of 1941. The skipper was Lieutenant Commander John Charles Waldron, a graduate of the United States Naval Academy, class of 1924. Originally from North Dakota, Waldron was part Sioux. "Whenever he solved a problem ahead of others," Gay remembered, "he always credited it to 'the Indian in me.'" He was a brash disciplinarian, especially hard on junior pilots, insisting that "the most dangerous time in the life of an aviator is when he starts flying." For their first one thousand hours, in his view, pilots were too cocksure to take instruction and woefully deficient in their knowledge of their aircraft and the nature of naval air warfare. On the wall over his desk was a big sheet of paper with the names of all the squadron members and a tally of their flight hours and experience. The goal was to bring all the pilots up to the same level. "Before we are done here," Waldron told his men, "you are going to wish every airplane was in hell, and that I was down there with 'em."[43]

In the air, the pilots practiced stalling the plane and returning to level flight in all possible conditions and altitudes. This training allowed them to understand the tendencies and character of their aircraft. They practiced landing on a short field runway, pretending it was a carrier, and bringing their planes to an abrupt halt. There was also "bombing practice with tin, water-filled bombs." On the ground with a blackboard and notebook, there were lectures on navigation, aircraft maintenance, and similar topics.[44] The attack on Pearl Harbor, when it came, validated Waldron's sense of urgency.

Most of the pilots, including Gay, were bachelors, and so lived in a house together in town. At night, if there were no squadron duties, they would drive out to the movies or the beach. Gay remembered it as a time of dancing, drinking, and adding to "Cupid's score" with the girls—a kind of merriment that played out against the "premonition of what fate held in store for us." They all knew that Norfolk would not last forever.[45]

If Gay was fiercely loyal to Waldron, all was not well within the Hornet Air Group. Its commander, Stanhope Cotton Ring, was deeply unpopular among the crew. Tall and handsome, with his perfectly tailored uniform, erect figure, and aristocratic swagger stick, Ring was the very model of a modern naval aviator. Unfortunately, he was an indifferent pilot and a woeful navigator: during one training flight over the Gulf of Mexico, he was unable to lead the air group back to the *Hornet*. With all the men looking to him for direction, he had become lost on a clear day.[46] Ring was also afflicted by an arrogant and aloof manner, which was said to have been influenced by snobbery picked up on a posting to a British carrier. Playing on his acronym—CHAG (Commander *Hornet* Air Group)—the men called him the "Sea-Hag" behind his back.

Traveling to Pearl, the *Hornet* was following the path of the *Yorktown*, which had charted the same course soon after the Japanese attack in December 1941. One of the senior pilots aboard the *Yorktown* was John "Jimmy" Thach. Born in Pine Bluff, Arkansas, Thach had graduated from the Naval Academy in 1927 and soon ended up in aviation. In 1940, while commanding Fighting Squadron Three, he had developed a maneuver that came to be known as the "Thach Weave." It was a defensive tactic by which an aircraft could escape enemy pursuit. A pilot would crisscross or weave his path with his wingman. As he passed in front of his wingman, so, too, would the enemy aircraft in pursuit. At that moment, the wingman would open fire, or so the theory went. Thach had tried out his maneuver in various exercises, but he had yet to employ it in combat.

Another fighter pilot eager to test himself in combat was Lieutenant James Gray, the commanding officer of Fighting Squadron Six aboard the *Enterprise*. He had learned to fly at Milwaukee County Airport in 1929, where his instructors had drilled home two principles: "Only a fool runs out of gas in an airplane," and "Don't lose flying speed." The first adage was obvious—pilots needed to know where they were and how long it would take them to return home. The second line of advice was a bit more obscure—it related to avoiding stalling speed, or the speed at which an aircraft's wings were no longer able to generate enough lift for flight. Gray went on to attend the Naval Academy, graduating in 1936, two years ahead of Kleiss. In Fighting Squadron Six, he flew the F4F-3A, a sturdy plane that was, however, less agile than the lightweight Zeros.[47]

The men on the *Enterprise*, the *Hornet*, and the *Yorktown* defended the same flag, but they were also divided in significant ways. Rank, obviously, was a major form of classification, distinguishing officers and enlisted men. Pilots were almost invariably officers and therefore addressed their gunners, who were usually enlisted men, by their surnames, while they were addressed in turn as "sir" or "mister." Moreover, gunners were not briefed in advance of a mission, and at this point in the war they were not admitted to the pilot ready rooms, which doubled as the officers' mess. Pilots and their gunners were not close off duty.[48] Kleiss and Snowden were an exception.

The pilot-gunner divide was often, though not always, a matter of socioeconomic class. Alvin Kernan, an ordnance man aboard the *Enterprise*, remembered that "in the early days of the war almost all enlisted men were from blue-collar, lower- or lower-middle-class homes." They didn't necessarily feel that they were inferior, preferring to believe that there was no such thing in America as an "underclass." Moreover, not *all* officers were upper class. On the contrary, most were from the middle class, similar to Kleiss and Nimitz and Heinemann. Their families had come to own property, but they knew what it meant to go without. Unsurprisingly, this social division was more pronounced when viewed from below than from above. Kernan recalled that "there was always a lot of tension between the enlisted men and the officers." It was reflected in the way the officers, especially early in the war, attained a "god-like status." Partly this was because of their dress: the enlisted ranks sported workshirts and dungarees that were often stained with sweat and Cosmoline, a waxlike petroleum used throughout the ship to prevent rust, whereas the officers wore open-necked khaki shirts and trousers, and were therefore much more presentable. But the tension in the ranks would also have resulted from the fact that the men were afraid. Each day they sailed closer to war. They looked to officers to lead them through to the other side.[49]

Underlying all this as well was a racial divide, which may not always have been obvious to white crew members. Black naval enlistees were routinely assigned the more menial jobs as mess attendants, cooks, and pantrymen; it was the same for Americans of Asian descent.[50] For this reason there were no Black Dauntless pilots. The question of whether Blacks should be allowed into more senior and fighting roles was much debated behind the scenes by the political and naval establishment, but had so far foundered on the objections from segregationists.[51] Unaware of these confidential discussions, Kernan remembered "a lily-white navy that never gave its racism a thought." Nor did it worry much about what Kernan described as its "covert" antisemitism.[52] In both respects, of course, the navy simply reflected some of the wider fissures in American society at the time.

There was also constant tension between the ship's crew and the air group, whose members, whether they flew or not, were known as "airdales." Bill Norberg, of Lemington, Wisconsin, who served as a yeoman aboard the USS *Enterprise*, recalled that "the Air Group was an entity unto itself," and that its members, with the exception of the plane handlers on the flight deck, had very little interchange with the rest of the ship's crew.[53] Ship's officers resented the better-paid aviators. The enlisted crew resented the privileging of the airdales in the chow line for food. Once the war began, the airdales were allowed to jump the queue, because they needed to be immediately available to launch or recover aircraft. Joseph Underwood, who served on the *Hornet* during this period, recalled that "we would walk to the front of the line past the throng of ship's crew waiting to eat." "The grousing and catcalls would follow us," he said, "but we felt great because even though I might be a seaman I would pass higher ranking Petty Officers to eat before them."[54]

At this time, maintenance crews were attached to the air group rather than the carrier. The aircraft required a whole army of mechanics, armorers, radiomen, parachute riggers, and other skilled personnel to remain operational. Their work was critical to every mission. The pilot about to launch needed to be confident that his engine had been properly checked, his plane fueled, and his parachute safely packed. Kleiss, for instance, became close with Chief Curtis Myers, one of the men responsible for his plane.[55] When the air group went ashore, the maintenance men went with it, and when it transferred to another carrier, or to a shore establishment, they moved, too. They and the ship's crew generally did not mix. "We were transient," one airdale recalled, "and they were not."[56]

Life on a carrier was inherently dangerous even in peacetime. The maintenance crew faced the possibility of work accidents daily. A moment's inattention risked death or mutilation. Tired men could walk into rotating propellers or be blown into them by a sudden gust of wind. Other injuries were more mundane but no less painful: fingers were smashed in hatches, skin was burned by hot steam from the boiler pipes, toes were stubbed, heads were banged on aircraft wings or gun barrels. In one particularly dramatic incident, an aircraft snapped an arresting wire, sending it snaking across the flight deck until it coiled around a nearby sailor's neck. Incredibly, he survived.[57]

It was worse for the aircrew. Some aircraft were lost at sea because the pilot failed to concentrate, ran out of fuel, or suffered a technical malfunction.[58] But the greatest hazards were experienced during launch, and especially recovery. When an aircraft was laden with a bomb or torpedo, there was often a tricky moment when the plane dipped below the bow and sometimes hit the water before gaining altitude. The risk was greater for the planes that were the earliest to depart: a full deck of planes meant that the first aircraft had little room in which to generate speed for flight. On landing, the pilot risked crashing into the deck, missing the arresting hooks and hitting the crash barrier, careering into the island structure, or simply plunging over the side into the sea. A particularly intense mishap for Kleiss occurred in the spring of 1942, when he prepared to land on the *Enterprise* only to realize that the ship's antiaircraft guns were firing at him: he had been mistaken for a Japanese plane.[59] Another pilot on the *Enterprise*, Perry Teaff, was taking off when exhaust fog from the ship's stack obscured his visibility. He veered off course and crashed into the water. Fortunately he was rescued by a nearby destroyer.[60]

Crash-landing in the sea was no less dangerous than doing so on land. The Dauntless generally sank within seconds of hitting the water, so the crew had only a very short time to disentangle themselves from the plane. Moreover, seatbelts in the Dauntless had no shoulder straps; there was a constant danger that, upon impact, the pilot would lurch forward and knock his head against the instrument panel.[61] One memory that particularly haunted Kleiss was watching a close friend and fellow pilot—Bill West of Minneapolis—crash in the ocean. At first, West was dazed, perhaps unconscious. As water poured into his cockpit, he came to his senses and climbed onto the spine of his plane. Suddenly the plane nosed over in the water and plunged downward, his boot catching the radio antenna. It dragged West under.[62] For others, even escape did not necessarily mean survival. Then they were at sea, floating in an inflatable raft, where they might capsize in a storm or, if not rescued quickly, perish from thirst, heat, exposure, or hunger. One way or the other, on ship or in the air, death and injury were routine on an aircraft carrier long before war broke out.

Danger and proximity made carrier life peculiarly performative, almost theatrical. You were constantly being watched and judged. It was most stressful for the pilots. They effectively had to earn their status every time they landed their aircraft, with the entire carrier as audience, or so it seemed. The gallery on the island at which spectators would congregate in the hope of watching a good crash was known as "Vultures Row."[63] Landings were routinely filmed for propaganda or training purposes. The pilot knew he was in trouble if he saw the photographers suddenly animated and straining to get a good angle of his imminent misfortune.[64]

Take-offs had a pageantry of their own. That was when, according to one crew member, "the flight deck looked like a big war dance of different colors." Cloth helmets and T-shirts were color coordinated to indicate different roles and responsibilities: red for ordnance men, who prepared and loaded bombs and torpedoes; brown for plane captains, who ensured the planes had what they needed prior to launch; green for the hydraulic men operating the arresting gear and catapults; yellow for the LSO, who would wave his paddles at planes in the queue; and purple for the oil and gas kings manning the fuel lines.[65]

Hidden beneath this fanfare were the men themselves. In their downtime they exercised by running laps around the deck of the carrier—a journey that was nearly a third of a mile one time around. They wrote letters home. They argued or teased each other. They smoked cigarettes. Crossing the equator was a momentous occasion and involved an elaborate ritual. Initiates of all ranks would strip to their underwear, have their heads shaved, and perform ignominious tasks—all at the behest of a sailor designated as "Neptunus Rex" and his minions, that is, the more experienced crew. Usually, however, leisure time was marked by far less grandiose events, such as games of checkers or cribbage—and there was plenty of gambling over hands of poker and bridge.

At port or during normal conditions at sea, life aboard ship followed a strict routine. Stanford Linzey of Houston, Texas, ended up on the *Yorktown* as a clarinetist in the band. He remembered reveille being broadcast every morning on the ship's loudspeakers at six o'clock followed by the raspy voice of the boatswain calling out, "Reveille! Heave out and trice up! Sweepers start your brooms! Clean sweep down fore and aft! Reveille!" After a shower and shave, Linzey would breakfast in the mess deck. Then the day's work would begin, pausing around noon for lunch. At four o'clock another bugle call would announce "liberty." In port, the men would go ashore or watch a film in the hangar deck; at sea, they would kill time some other way. The day would end at ten o'clock sharp; over the loudspeaker the chaplain would say a prayer, followed by the slow and mournful sound of taps.[66]

In the mess deck the menu rarely changed. For breakfast there were beans, sometimes Spam or dried eggs, dry cereal with powdered milk, and prunes or some other dried or canned fruit, all washed down with coffee.[67] Lunch and dinner would be a variation of the same ingredients, often beans and spaghetti.[68] Sometimes "potatoes" were served, but these were suspected to be no more than ground-up beans.[69] The longer the ship was at sea, the blander the food became as supplies dwindled.

Religion was not much of a draw, at least in a formalized setting. Bill Norberg, the yeoman from Wisconsin, recalled that only half a dozen sailors attended the Protestant services on the *Enterprise*.[70] Linzey, on the *Yorktown*, found the chapel services so wanting that he started his own Bible study group. He and several men would meet weekly in one of the flight ready rooms.[71] Bibles were everywhere, however, and the men often received them as presents, either before leaving home or in the mail while at sea.

The other major fact of life aboard ship, especially once the war began, was death. Funerals would be held on the hangar deck. Bodies, tied in canvas, would, after a two-minute time of prayer, be committed to the sea. Death was sobering; it reminded the men that their job was serious and awful. However, it also meant promotion for those left behind, as junior sailors or airmen filled the vacancies.[72]

In many ways, life aboard a Japanese carrier was very similar. There were similar routines arising out of the servicing of similar equipment. There were the same hazards and accidents. Like the Americans, the Japanese emphasized training and operational efficiency. There were the same divides between officers and enlisted men. The former, as one veteran of the *Akagi* recalled, were sometimes served "elegant" three-course meals, while the other men had to make do with "tasteless, but nourishing" dishes.[73] Teii-chi Makishima, a civilian cameraman assigned to the *Akagi*, spent much of his time with the officers. He remembered eating "soup, sashimi, grilled fish, boiled vegetables" and, at a special evening meal prepared each night at 2100, sweets such as "shiruko, mitsu-mame, shortcake, castella, and rice cake." Overall, the carrier was "another world," he said. Exploring the noisy workrooms and stuffy hangars felt "like entering a munitions factory somewhere." "The only thing that can't be produced," remarked Makishima to another sailor, "is a woman."[74]

There were some important differences between the American and Japanese routines, however. In operational terms, the Americans usually armed and fueled their aircraft on deck, while the Japanese preferred to do this below, in the hangars. Moreover, unlike the American hangars, which were open to the elements, Japanese hangars were enclosed. This provided a more comfortable workspace and improved light discipline during night operations, but it made the Japanese hangars stuffy with potentially combustible aviation fumes. Unlike the Americans, who wore long trousers, shirts, and flashproof clothing on operations, Japanese crews were permitted shorts when serving in the tropics. Shorts were more comfortable, but in combat they gave little or no fire protection.[75]

In cultural terms, the differences were also significant. Instead of Christianity, however nominal, the faith aboard the Japanese ships was Shintoism. It was customary for carriers in the Imperial Navy to display a portrait of the Emperor Hirohito, whom they held in reverence. On the *Akagi* this portrait was covered by a silk curtain, so that his image would not be sullied by the profane gaze except in homage.[76] On each carrier there was also a small replica of the Kompira Shrine, which was dedicated to seamen. It rested between two electric candles and was a place where members of the crew could come to ask for spiritual blessing.[77] Pilots would often stop to pray before embarking on their missions.[78]

Perhaps the most notable cultural difference was to be found in the relationship between the pilots and the maintenance men, which both groups, among the Japanese, remember to have been warm. Though the aviators were given better living quarters than the maintenance men, they often used them to socialize with the crew, or smoked with them on deck. Sometimes aircrew and maintenance men would drink together. The dive bomber Kiyoto Furuta, who flew from the *Akagi*, remembered getting "to know [his] mechanics very well."[79] On occasion, pilots would even help with the maintenance work. The camaraderie was probably due to the fact that, unlike the US pilots, many of the Japanese pilots were enlisted men rather than officers. Whatever the cause, it certainly boosted morale and cohesion. By contrast, as one maintenance crew member on the *Enterprise* recalled, "few enlisted men knew an officer as a person, which meant that the deaths of the pilots were not felt very personally." "We felt them," he continued, "as fans feel the loss of a game by their football team."[80]

✪

ON DECEMBER 7, 1941, Kleiss's training on the *Enterprise* was suddenly interrupted by news of Pearl Harbor. The attack caught Scouting Six unawares, with eighteen of its SBD Dauntlesses in the air bound for Hawaii. One of these pilots was Clarence Dickinson, who was over Oahu when his wingman suddenly erupted in flames. Suddenly, he saw four or five Zeros coming straight at him, firing their machine guns and automatic cannons. The muzzle flashes were mesmerizing: "They seem to be winking at you with jewelled eyes, and it's pretty to watch but you know each wink is an effort which may kill you very, very dead." Dickinson felt the bullets clatter into his plane, then his rear-seat gunner let out a scream, "a yell of agony."[81] He bailed out of his smoking plane, noticing his gunner slumped over in the rear seat, unresponsive. Under his parachute canopy, Dickinson drifted down to Oahu and was picked up by an elderly couple—a Mr. and Mrs. Otto F. Heine—on their way to a picnic. The woman refused to believe an attack was underway.

On the *Enterprise*, a senior officer in the squadron tried to grab everyone's attention: "Pearl Harbor is under attack by the

Japanese. This is no shit!"[82] The entire experience was surreal. Dusty Kleiss remembered scanning the radio, trying to find information. There was only a station playing "Sweet Leilani": "I dreamed of paradise for two, you are my paradise completed, you are my dream come true."[83] Then a Japanese plane roared overhead "using his guns as a shovel to scrape the road," killing two people in a nearby car.[84] The danger was apparent, but the situation was still hard to believe.

Kleiss launched twice that day, but he could find neither enemy ships nor enemy aircraft, though he heard a series of garbled reports on the radio. All told, Scouting Six lost six aircraft; six men were killed and three were wounded.[85] Shortly after, the *Enterprise* returned to Pearl. Kleiss was shocked by the sight of the "splintered and smoldering" fleet.[86] The "other world" had finally come to him; his universe would now be one of pain and violence.

"The sights and smells and all that of Pearl are still with me today," said Bill Norberg some eighty years after sailing into that devastation as a crew member aboard the *Enterprise*.[87] For many, the experience justified the war. John Crawford, a gunner aboard the *Yorktown*, was one of many sent out to collect the dead floating in the harbor. "We developed a great hate for our Japanese friends there," he said, remembering that duty.[88] Even Kleiss, no blowhard, vowed that he was "ready to speak the language those little men can understand."[89]

At the same time, Kleiss sought to shield Jean from the realities of the "other world" of fear and suffering into which he had been thrust. When Jean discussed "doing her part" in the war, Kleiss responded chivalrously. "I guess I'm sort of old fashioned," he replied. "War is a man's game and a woman's role is to give love, inspiration, a return to reality." He wanted her to be "an ideal he cherishes, wishes to protect, and whose dreams he wishes to fulfill." He was afraid that "wearing a uniform" would cause her to forget "the larger and more important side of life."[90]

In February 1942, the men of Scouting Six had their first chance to hit back. Nimitz sent them to attack Japanese air bases and shipping in the Marshall Islands. Kleiss saw his first action, encountering intense antiaircraft fire and Japanese fighters. The raids were characterized by confusion and poor intelligence on the American side; the torpedoes launched by Torpedo Six, in which his friend Tom Eversole flew, failed to sink a single one of the moored Japanese tankers in harbor. There was no sign of any Japanese carriers. Soon after, the *Enterprise* repeated this performance in Wake and Marcus Islands, again accomplishing little in strategic terms.

Throughout all of this, Kleiss yearned for Jean, but he admitted that he had barely time to open her letters. His two worlds were in collision. "I want to say beautiful things to you tonight," Kleiss wrote to her in mid-February 1942, "but I just can't." "My mind's so full of thinking how to bump off Japs," he confessed, "there isn't room for anything else."[91]

The shock of Pearl Harbor generated a wave of hysteria against Americans of "enemy" descent. Most of this ire was directed against Japanese Americans, who were soon interned in camps for the duration of the conflict. No such collective measure was inflicted on German Americans, who by and large escaped the obloquy they had experienced during World War I. That said, a presidential proclamation was issued to observe the conduct of "alien enemies," that is, "all natives, citizens, denizens or subjects of Germany being of the age fourteen years and upwards" within the territory or jurisdiction of the United States who were "not actually naturalized."[92] Citizens were also investigated. Kleiss himself was targeted on account of his German background and surname. Around this time, officers repeatedly interrogated him wanting to know whether he maintained contacts with "the Fatherland," and asking him multiple "leading questions" designed to flush out Nazi sympathies.[93] There were rumors that his squadron mate Lieutenant Ben Troemel had suffered similar treatment, though his pacifism might well have helped to incite the investigation.[94] It is also likely that the intelligence services took a good look at Severin Rombach of Torpedo Six, who had been head of the German club at the University of Ohio before the war.

These months were a time of intense training and activity on the American carriers. The crews familiarized themselves with their equipment and practiced their attack routines. Kleiss learned to fly his Dauntless blindfolded, a precaution taken in case his visibility was impaired from injury, smoke, or weather.[95] With more hours in the cockpit, the men became better pilots. They improved on the basic skills of flight, such as take-offs and landings. Navigational skills and formation flying were also tested during training hops throughout the Hawaiian Islands. The men of Scouting Squadron Six and Bombing Squadron Six honed their dive-bombing skills by practicing on land targets near Ewa Field on Oahu. For a moving target, the carrier towed a wooden raft, and the Dauntlesses would attack with smoke bombs. Repetition was essential, so that the men could deliver their ordnance during the stress of combat. Forgetting one step in the bombing procedure could have disastrous consequences. One pilot in Bombing Six, Lew Hopkins, for example, forgot to open his dive brakes on one dive. The plane hurtled toward the ground at 400 miles per hour, 40 percent faster than the prescribed speed. Yanking back on the stick, he just managed to restore the plane to level flight.

One year earlier, in 1941, US Navy doctrine for carrier aircraft had been revised. Admiral Bill Halsey oversaw the writing and publication of this document, *Current Tactical Orders and Doctrine, U.S. Fleet Aircraft* (USF-74). By the winter, Halsey was based on the *Enterprise*, so it is certain that Kleiss and the other members of the air group took the revised doctrine seriously. "Carrier based aircraft are essentially offensive weapons," read the document. "Their major offensive power is the heavy bomb. All other missions of aircraft are therefore secondary to the delivery of heavy bombing attacks." The reason that bombing was so essential was that "the surest and quickest means of gaining control of the air is the destruction of enemy carriers, tenders and bases by bombing attacks." Offense, in other words, was key.[96]

But the torpedo bomber, not the Dauntless, was considered the most effective kind of bomb. It was, according to doctrine, "the heaviest striking arm with which a carrier is equipped." This was a serious error in judgment for two reasons. First, the method of delivering the torpedoes—that of the Devastators flying level, directly at their target, some 100 feet above the ocean—was incredibly dangerous. It was obvious that many would be shot down during the attack, yet according to doctrine, antiaircraft fire was treated as though it were an equal threat to both dive and torpedo bombers.[97] Second, the torpedoes, as demonstrated in live-fire exercises, rarely detonated against their targets even when they hit them. They were an almost useless weapon.

Another issue that USF-74 dealt with was command and control. But it did not clearly explain how a leader would assign targets to his pilots. In one section of the document, it said that when a formation of planes approached multiple targets, the planes in the lead of the formation should attack the far target, leaving those in the rear to attack the near target. But in a later section, it said that target distribution was the sole responsibility of the group commander and should be done "prior to ordering the attack."[98] There was the further problem that multiple targets might present themselves such that all appeared to be the same distance away.

However, the first few months of the Pacific campaign validated the main thrust of the doctrine: "carrier based aircraft" were indeed a preeminent "offensive weapon" in naval warfare. And Halsey recognized this in advance of the attack on Pearl Harbor, the point at which this doctrine became popularly acknowledged. Another important point about USF-74 relates to the purpose of doctrine. Doctrine is a teaching: it is not an iron rule that must be followed at all times. In 1942, naval aviation, especially because of recently developed technology such as Heinemann's Dauntless, was changing rapidly. Kleiss began his pilot training in August 1940. From that time until his first combat mission in December 1941, he flew some seven different kinds of aircraft, which, on the whole, represented a dramatic improvement in technology. All the more reason, therefore, to regard doctrine like that of USF-74 as a standard from which leaders could deviate or improvise, especially in combat.

Meanwhile, to fill gaps in the *Enterprise* Air Group, replacement pilots arrived. As rookies, these new men were in dire need of training, especially on basic skills such as carrier take-offs and landings. Kleiss, who by now had become a section leader, gave instruction while Scouting Six was based on Ford Island, Pearl Harbor, for about six weeks, from March to May 1942. It was the new pilots' first chance to train on land targets that were easier to observe than those at sea. Richard "Dick" Best, of Bayonne, New Jersey, was the commander of Bombing Six. He thought his skills improved immensely during this time. He was also able to see his wife and daughter, who were then living on Oahu.[99]

Dauntless pilots came in many shapes and sizes. Some were men of action who did not think much about their task or who masked their insecurity with bravado. Others were very moral creatures, pondering the war and the ethics of killing. "War is a serious business," Lieutenant Commander Waldron of Torpedo Squadron Eight admonished his nephew, "and it is not a sport."[100] Ben Troemel was a devout Lutheran and had severe doubts about his right to take lives. "It isn't right," he said to his fellow pilots, a confession that possibly had him removed from service.[101] Kleiss, who was very introspective, nevertheless arrived at a somewhat brusque conclusion: "I did my job and that's it."[102] Once Pearl Harbor occurred it provided a logic of its own. Most men were in little doubt why they were at war—and why they should kill and, if necessary, be killed. The United States had been attacked, and they were defending their country, their families, and themselves.

Morale was generally high aboard the *Enterprise*, but there were tensions within the air group. In March 1942, Wade McClusky was appointed its commander. Contrary to a tenacious myth, McClusky had plenty of dive-bombing experience, but he'd had little time in the Dauntless, which he flew first on March 20. His most recent roles had involved flying fighter aircraft. Over the next ten weeks McClusky did his best to familiarize himself with the plane, but he never actually used one to drop a bomb.[103]

Relations between McClusky and Best were tense. This seems to have been primarily a generational issue. At nearly forty, McClusky was somewhere between the worlds of the new "brown-shoe" aviators and the old "black-shoe" surface navy. At just thirty, by contrast, Best was a born and dedicated "brown shoe" who did not hide his skepticism toward the traditional navy. "Admirals," he later remarked, "didn't have much to do with what we did."[104]

Pride also played a major role. Japanese pilots such as Mitsuo Fuchida and Minoru Genda dreamed about mass aerial attack and the coordination of aircraft from multiple carriers. US pilots, such as Best and, later in the war, George Walsh, had a more independent streak. Their frustration with the "black shoes" or with other pilots resulted from a desire to get on with what they perceived to be the most important fighting technique in the naval repertoire: dive bombing. While there was an attempt to coordinate within the air group for fighter cover, the launching and recovery of aircraft was largely done independently of other carriers. There were serious rivalries among the pilots. Partly this was the nature of the work, as George Gay mentioned: the first thing he saw when walking into his squadron was a board of names where everyone was racked and stacked. When aboard their carriers, pilots were constantly judged and evaluated, vying for promotion and bragging rights. That was what naval aviation meant in many ways—it was a rivalry among friends rather than with the enemy. Dickinson, remembering the period after Pearl Harbor, wrote, "I saw men greet each other who were so glad to see one another alive that it was deeply touching. It was not until afterward that I began to realize that . . . in some cases they had not even liked each other."[105] Some two months later, things had returned to normal. "There has been some happenings of late," said Cleo Dobson, another pilot in Scouting Six, "that has made me hate this outfit worse than I ever hated anything in my life."[106]

Kleiss took part in this rivalry with gusto. Like all pilots, he kept a logbook, which he later self-published (*The Log of the War*), followed by a more detailed memoir in which he wrote that his "biggest competitor was . . . Clarence Earle Dickinson." He then proceeded to catalog slights going back as far as the United States Naval Academy, a period of some eighty years.[107] Perhaps the rivalry had been intensified by Dickinson's own memoir, which had been first off the press, published in 1943. In it, Dickinson recounted the story of how Kleiss earned his nickname, "Dusty," by landing on an unpaved airfield on Honolulu. His propeller had kicked up an enormous cloud of dust, provoking radio traffic from the control tower as well as other pilots. In a later scene in the book, Dickinson portrays Kleiss as a needless grumbler.[108] The supposed gist is that Kleiss is a fool, Dickinson a quiet professional. Kleiss's subsequent publications appear to be part of this back-and-forth, an attempt to name names and set the record straight. The commander of Kleiss's first ship, John Greeley Winn, was a man of "peculiarities" and "incompetence," Kleiss wrote. He had kind words, however, for Wilmer Earl Gallaher, a fellow Dauntless pilot and eventual commander of Scouting Six. "I liked him instantly," Kleiss remembered. "He was easily the true genius of our squadron."[109]

All this rivalry and introspection meant that Kleiss needed an outlet, some way of expressing himself. For him that was Jean, and he wrote to her constantly. "My heart poured out in these letters," he said, a correspondence that they kept up throughout his time in the navy and that culminated in his return to California and his proposal of marriage.[110] Jean kept and answered each letter. Her French Canadian parents likely supported his role in the Allied war effort. And it seems that she, too, despite their religious differences and despite the war, was in love.

Whatever pilots made of each other, they developed a close relationship with their Dauntlesses. It was not unlike that of cavalrymen with their horses. Aircraft, of course, do not have such strong personalities, and the pilots flew whatever machine was available. But the Dauntless in general commanded a strong sense of respect and affection. It was, as Dick Best recalled, "rock steady in a vertical dive, completely responsive to the controls, and ready to absorb punishment and still get you home." Norman Vandivier, a member of Best's squadron on the *Enterprise*, wrote home after watching a fellow pilot survive a crash, saying, "It's really wonderful what those planes will take and still protect the occupants."[111] After several months at sea, he said, "Our planes are holding up very well in the carrier operation."[112] Max Leslie, commander of Bombing Squadron Three (VB-3), then on the USS *Saratoga*, spoke of the "most perfect combination of ruggedness, stability, ease of maintenance,

[and] combination of performance, speed and endurance."[113] "I loved my SBD," Kleiss recalled. "In 1942, the SBD replaced the battleship. In my opinion, we owe everything to Edward H. Heinemann's plane." After surviving a dive in which the plane coped with incredible pressure without the wings coming off, Kleiss recalled thinking, "All honor to the folks at Douglas, they constructed their SBDs superbly."[114]

Moreover, it had become clear during the first six months of the Pacific War that the Dauntless was able to hold its own against Japanese fighters unescorted. There were three reasons for this capability. First, the Dauntless was built to take a lot of punishment, as Best said. Second, it brought considerable firepower to bear, particularly with its twin rearward-facing guns. In the hands of a skilled gunner like Snowden, these were often sufficient to send prowling Zeros off in search of easier prey. Third, the Dauntless was almost invulnerable during its dive. The angle was near impossible for antiaircraft fire. Zeros also had trouble: without dive brakes, they would overshoot the Dauntless if they followed it into a dive. Zooming past, they could do no more than exchange glances with their opposition.[115]

By contrast, it was obvious that the lumbering Devastator torpedo planes were not only vulnerable but ineffective. They had to approach their targets beam-on, ideally at a 90-degree angle, flying low. This requirement deprived them of almost any chance of surprise. It also exposed the Devastators to sustained, withering fire from all Japanese antiaircraft calibers, as well as to attacks from their combat air patrols, which would swoop down among them, scissoring back and forth. Even when the Americans were able to launch their "fish," the insistence on performing this maneuver low and slow caused the ordnance to enter the water horizontally instead of vertically. The impact "was the surest way to mess up a torpedo's directional and depth controls, causing the fish to run erratically."[116]

In April 1942, the torpedo crews were given a startling confidential briefing: navy intelligence estimated that during an attack only a fifth of a fifteen-plane squadron would be able to penetrate

Japanese defenses to launch their torpedoes. As Lloyd Childers, a radioman and gunner in the back seat of a Devastator, recalled, the news caused deep anxiety among crews, though they did their best to make light of it.[117] One pilot, "Abbie" Abercrombie, dubbed his squadron, Torpedo Eight, "the coffin squadron."[118] The navy tried to keep all this quiet, but among naval aviators such as Kleiss, Eversole, and Childers, it was an open secret.

By April 1942, the conflict was beginning to take its toll on Kleiss. He had not seen Jean for a year. He told her he could not "last six or seven years doing the things I am doing."[119] He had been at war for nearly six months, and what did he have to show for it? He had beaten up some island outposts. He had sunk a few smaller ships. He had seen good friends die in combat and accidents. So far this was not what he had been trained to do and not what needed to be done. He—along with the rest of the *Enterprise* Air Group—had missed the recent clash in the Coral Sea. He had therefore never laid a glove on a Japanese carrier or even seen one. The war would not be won this way.

In late May, Kleiss's spirits were suddenly lifted. The day after the *Enterprise* returned to Pearl Harbor, he was among a number of men decorated for valor personally by Nimitz. Among them was the Black messman Doris Miller, who had heroically engaged Japanese fighters from the deck of the stricken battleship USS *West Virginia* at Pearl Harbor and was honored alongside his white comrades. Kleiss himself stood next to Roger Mehle of Fighting Six. He overheard the admiral remark, as he pinned the decoration on his neighbor's chest, "I think you'll have a chance to earn another medal in a couple of days." When it was his turn, Kleiss received "the most careful look I ever experienced in my whole life." It went through him "like a shot of whiskey." Kleiss's nerves were steadied in that moment. "A leader," he recalled, "had put the fight back into me."[120]

✪

TO ATTACK MIDWAY, THE Japanese divided their forces into four groups. The first was a pair of light carriers along with supporting ships that would attack Dutch Harbor and the Aleutian Island chain. The second was the main body of the mobile force *Kido Butai*, commanded by Admiral Chuichi Nagumo. It included the aircraft carriers *Kaga*, *Akagi*, *Soryu*, and *Hiryu*. The third group included the transports carrying the troops who would storm the beaches at Midway. The fourth, which was well behind the *Kido Butai*, was centered on the superbattleship *Yamato*, from which Admiral Yamamoto oversaw the operation.

Each of these groups departed from a different place and at a different time. The first group left on May 26, 1942, from Ominato Harbor, near the northern end of Japan. The second, a day later, sailed from the Inland Sea into the Pacific, near the lower part of Japan. The third departed on the next day from Saipan, much farther to the south. And the fourth, on the following day, May 29, also sailed from the Inland Sea. This complex arrangement of forces was difficult to control, a task made even more daunting by the fact that they were trying to maintain radio silence. It was also telling that Yamamoto, the commander of the entire operation, was aboard the *Yamato* instead of one of the carriers. Practically speaking, it hampered his ability to direct and coordinate his main attack force, the aircraft. It also exposed his carriers to enemy attack, because they traveled in advance of his surface ships and their considerable firepower. From a symbolic point of view, however, Nagumo's forward placement conveyed a strong message: "The Midway plan," as Fuchida understood it, "rested on the obsolete concept . . . that battleships rather than carriers constituted the main battle strength of the Fleet."[121]

Nagumo had his reasons, however. The first was that he regarded American aviation with contempt. In one respect, this opinion derived from reports about the Battle of the Coral Sea, which stated that two US carriers had been sunk. If true, this meant that the United States had lost nearly half its carriers in the Pacific, a further stunning victory for Japan so soon after Pearl Harbor. But it was false, at least in part: the *Lexington* sank but the *Yorktown* survived. Added to this was what Fuchida considered to be Nagumo's "conservatism and passiveness."[122] Nagumo talked aggressively, but his plans seemed needlessly complex, ineffective, and outmoded. The Midway and Dutch Harbor attacks and the Pearl Harbor attack had quite different objectives. Pearl Harbor was an attack on US Navy ships, while this subsequent action was an attempt to capture territory. This kind of mission came with responsibilities: success would be determined not by offense, or even daring, but by logistics. It was not the kind of fight that suited naval airpower.

Nagumo also took a flattering view of the Japanese position. Until 1942 he had not lost a single ship to the Americans and only sixty of his aircraft had been shot down. He overlooked Coral Sea, since he had not been in command. "We have established an invincible strategic position," Nagumo said to his officers in early May, after studying the plans for the Midway attack. "In order to secure it tenaciously, we must keep on striking offensively at the enemy's weak points."[123] But from Fuchida's point of view, this was "arrogant over-confidence engendered by our early victories."[124]

The upshot of Nagumo's personality and assessment of the war meant that he did not place enough value on reconnaissance. The attack on Midway, for instance, was meant to be carried out after the establishment of a Japanese submarine cordon—that is, the deployment of submarines along the various lines of approach to Midway. If US ships arrived either in advance of the Japanese attack or after it had begun, these submarines would be able to strike. But the submarines were delayed; most did not arrive at their stations until June 4, when the US ships had already moved into forward position.[125] The only other kind of reconnaissance available to Nagumo came via scout planes, but these were another compromised resource. The Japanese conducted scouting operations with floatplanes lowered into the water from cruisers, which was cumbersome, rather than with carrier-based aircraft. There was also the problem of the weather. On June 2, as the Japanese crept toward Midway, they found themselves shrouded in fog. The fog would shield their forces from US planes or ships, but it meant that Nagumo could not launch planes of his own. Given that his submarines were not in place, he was in the position of preparing to attack Midway without knowledge of what was taking place around it or along its most likely avenues of approach.

✪

THE AMERICAN PILOTS HAD a sense that something was being planned, but what? And where? They had very little information about what was happening in the war. After returning from the Coral Sea, there was barely forty-eight hours before they were off again. Supposedly, "the Enterprise pilots . . . went ashore as soon as the ship moored and binged at the Waikiki hotels."[126] They had certainly done this in February, after returning from their raid on the Gilberts and Marshalls. But Dickinson didn't remember any partying in May: "We got new planes, a couple of new pilots and worked frantically to make them a part of the squadron."[127] Kleiss remembered only the sense of expectation: "We anticipated a big fight."[128]

Cleo Dobson, perhaps because he was writing in his diary rather than in retrospect, said that soon after arriving, the squadron went to visit Nancy West, Bill West's widow. "We told her all about how it happened," Dobson wrote, "and she asked us a lot of questions about Bill. For about two hours we sat around and tried to comfort her." Nothing seemed to help. Wanting to do something, the men took her out and bought her a sandwich and a milkshake. Dobson went to see her the next day and was angry that the squadron didn't join him. One of the other pilots "had to go whore around," and the others had excuses of their own.[129] Vandivier wrote home, trying to reassure his family. In April, a hometown friend of his, Wilbur "Tommy" Thompson, who also ended up in Bombing Six, had died when his Dauntless collided with another plane in formation. Thompson was the rear-seat gunner and failed to bail out before his plane hit the water. His mother wrote Vandivier two letters. "She wanted to know the name of Tommy's pilot, and I don't know what to do," he told his parents. "Everything was done that could possibly have been done."[130]

The air group from the *Hornet* flew to Ewa Field. Commander Stanhope Ring ordered them confined to base there.[131] George

Gay and Torpedo Eight celebrated in the best way they could: by dumping out gallon pickle jars, then filling them with ice, whiskey, and Coca Cola. They passed them around the room, each man taking a sip, until finally the jars were empty. Eventually a drunken fracas broke out. There were black eyes and cut faces, but no one was seriously hurt.[132]

Very likely theirs was a better night than the one Nimitz had. The senior officer in charge of Task Force 16 and Task Force 17 was Admiral Bill Halsey, commander of Task Force 16. Upon his return to Pearl, however, it was clear that Halsey was ill. He had lost some 20 pounds and had a psoriasis rash all over his body. Combat at sea for the past few months had taken its toll. Nimitz had to appoint a replacement on the eve of departure. He ended up choosing Admiral Raymond Spruance, a calm, professorial officer from Baltimore, Maryland. Spruance had the advantage of being suggested to Nimitz by Halsey; he had also performed well in the past few months in combat as the commander of Halsey's cruiser escorts. But Spruance was a "black shoe." The commander of Task Force 17, Admiral Frank Jack Fletcher, of Marshalltown, Iowa, who would be the tactical commander of both task forces, was also a "black shoe." The result was that neither of the men in charge of America's most powerful naval air force were pilots.[133]

On May 28, Lieutenant Commander Waldron took out his service .45 automatic. Around him were the pilots and crew of Torpedo Eight, sleeping soundly in a hangar at Ewa Field. Stretching out his arm, Waldron emptied his pistol, firing out of an open door into a nearby field of sugarcane. "I nearly came out of my skin," remembered George Gay. When the gun emptied, he heard the clattering of the brass on the concrete floor of the hangar. "Rise and shine," shouted Waldron. "We have work to do!"[134]

That day, Task Force 16, including the *Enterprise* and the *Hornet*, departed Pearl Harbor. The next morning, May 29, Spruance held a meeting with his senior pilots, including Dick Best, the air group commander. "The Japanese are planning an attack on Midway," Spruance told them. He then went on to describe the operation: on June 3 the Japanese would attack the Aleutians, but this would be a "diversionary feint." The main effort would take place on June 4, when the four carriers—the *Akagi*, *Kaga*, *Soryu*, and *Hiryu*—attacked Midway. "The detail was mind boggling," remembered Best. He thought it sounded too good to be true. "Suppose they don't attack Midway?" he asked. "Suppose they keep going east and hit Pearl again and maybe Honolulu?" One of Spruance's staff officers cut in to answer: "Well, we just hope they don't." To say more might risk giving away the source of the navy's intelligence. All that could be said was that on June 4 the pilots would fly west, hunting for four Japanese carriers.[135]

On May 30, Task Force 17, which included the *Yorktown*, put to sea, receiving repairs up to the last minute.[136] The band played "California, Here I Come," suspected by some to have been an attempt to deceive any Japanese agents at the port. But as Stanford Linzey said of the crew, "we all knew better." They, too, had a sense that something more important than a West Coast cruise was about to take place. The *Yorktown* Air Group flew out to join the carrier the next day, including squadrons from the *Saratoga* to supplement recent losses. Many of the pilots were rookies and this was to be their first carrier landing. One from this group, a fighter pilot, came in too fast and bounced on the deck, crashing into the plane ahead of him, a Grumman F4F, killing the pilot inside.[137] Once the *Yorktown* had left Oahu, passed Kauai, and made it to the open sea, word spread throughout the crew: "We were going to join the fleet at Midway to surprise the next plans of the Japanese," Linzey later wrote. In exchange for the remarkable turnaround and for sending the men out to sea so quickly, Nimitz promised a year's overhaul once it was over. Hearing this over the loudspeaker, Linzey remembered a cheer going up throughout the ship.[138]

At sea, the carriers settled into their usual routine. Each day one carrier from the group took responsibility for sending up Dauntlesses on four-hour scouting patrols. The planes would fly set patterns around the combined task forces in order to look for the Japanese. Regardless of what they found, the missions were harrowing for the pilots, especially the rookies. On the *Yorktown*, Paul "Lefty"

Holmberg, of Brunswick, Missouri, could hardly stand it. He had joined the squadron barely two months earlier and was apprehensive about taking off from a carrier, much less landing on one after a four-hour flight, to say nothing of combat. There were rookies aboard the *Enterprise* as well. In Scouting Six alone, which had seventeen pilots, only seven had dropped live ordnance before.[139]

If they were not in the air, the pilots waited in their ready rooms. On the *Enterprise*, Gallaher gave special instructions to his men. He told them to practice adjusting their homing devices so they could quickly pick up the signal of the *Enterprise*. Then he discussed how the squadrons would approach the Japanese fleet: by flying southwest toward Midway and then turning northwest, to hide the true location of the US carriers from the Japanese. Gallaher also said that no scouting planes would be launched on the appointed day. This mission would be different from most. As soon as the enemy fleet was sighted, the entire strike force would launch. To while away the time, the men in Scouting Six gathered scale models of a number of Japanese ships, including the carriers. Placing these models on the floor, the pilots would stand on a chair, imitating the perspective of looking down on a target ship from 20,000 feet and identifying them from attack height.[140] It was our "voodoo," said Dickinson. A way of conjuring their dream into real life.

If that was how the pilots expected things would go, they also had several important tactical issues to resolve. According to Kleiss, before departing for sick leave, Admiral Halsey had spoken personally with Gallaher. He had wanted to use the Wildcats to defend the carriers and then send Dauntlesses to attack alone, keeping the Devastators below decks. The reason for this was that Halsey knew the torpedoes were useless. Gallaher passed along this message. "The torpedo bombers—if deployed at all," he said, "would only be used for short-range scouting hops."[141] The battle would be won by finding the enemy quickly and then by striking first. Both of these tasks would be carried out by the Dauntlesses. Nimitz expected that action was imminent and he was sure the navy was ready for it. "Another busy day," he wrote on the night of June 2.

"One of anxious waiting for something to develop and for which we are better prepared than ever before."[142]

✪

FOR MORE THAN A week, the planes at Midway had been flying daily reconnaissance patrols of more than twelve hours each. These flights were done by PBY Catalinas, massive planes with an aircrew of seven, that were designed to perform a range of tasks, including attack and rescue operations. Ensign Jack Reid of Paducah, Kentucky, the pilot in charge on the morning of June 3, had just reached the halfway mark of his search. After six hours of flight, he was nearly 700 miles west of Midway and due to turn back when his crew asked for more time, hoping to come across Japanese aircraft based at Wake Island. Reid was willing to loiter for half an hour to see what turned up. Then he sighted specks on the horizon. It had been a long flight already—was his windshield dirty? He scrubbed at it with a rag. "My God," he said to his co-pilot. "Aren't those ships on the horizon? I believe we have hit the jackpot." At 9:25 a.m., he radioed, "Sighted main body." It was "a report that electrified everybody on our carrier," remembered Dickinson. "Our feeling was: At last! The long-sought contact."[143]

Nimitz knew better. He received the report at his headquarters in Hawaii and then radioed Admiral Fletcher aboard the *Yorktown*. "Main Body," Nimitz said, "that is not, repeat not, the enemy striking force." He rightly identified it as the invasion force—in other words, not the *Kido Butai* with its deadly carriers. Nimitz then sent a message to all his forces on or near Midway: "The situation is developing as expected. Carriers, our most important objective, should soon be located. Tomorrow may be the day you can give them the works."[144]

✪

THROUGHOUT JUNE 3, 1942, tension built on the American carriers. George Gay was waiting in the ready room of Torpedo Eight on the *Hornet*. The previous day, Stanhope Ring had convened his squadron leaders to tell them what to expect: a morning launch once the Japanese were discovered, and then repeated attacks in the afternoon. The Dauntlesses, with fighter escorts, would take the lead at altitude, and the Devastators in Torpedo Eight would fly much lower, bringing up the rear.[145] But at nightfall, Waldron came in and wordlessly handed out a printed message. Its tone alternated between encouraging and resigned. "I feel we are all ready," he had written. "We have done the best humanly possible" under "the most severe difficulties." Moreover, he hoped for "a favorable tactical situation." But "if the worst comes to the worst," Waldron went on, "if there is only one plane left to make a final run-in, I want that man to go in and get a hit." While his pilots were still reading the message, Waldron announced that "the approaching battle will be the biggest of the war, and may well be the turning point." "It is to be known," he said, "as the battle of Midway."[146]

There had also been a meeting aboard the *Enterprise*. Admiral Spruance summoned Lieutenant Commander Wade McClusky and the ship's captain, George Murray, to his quarters. It was the first that McClusky had heard of Halsey's illness and replacement. There, in the room, McClusky was allowed to read Nimitz's orders, which contained detailed information on the expected size and disposition of the Japanese fleet.[147] Midway, it was believed, would be attacked imminently by four to five Japanese carriers approaching from the northwest.[148]

In the ready room of Scouting Six, the pilots waited anxiously for information. A few men slept while the majority stayed up, "visiting back and forth, discussing possibilities." There was tension, but there was also a kind of satisfaction. "It was a pleasure," said Dickinson, "to exchange wicked grins with all your fellow officers, grins which said more plainly than words how we liked the idea of catching the Japanese at sea near our bases."[149] There was vindictiveness, a desire to inflict pain on the Japanese in retribution for Pearl Harbor. There was also something mischievous. Dickinson smiled at Gallaher because they were conspirators, proud to share a common fate.

Everyone took part in the preparations. Alvin Kernan remembered belting machine-gun ammunition for hours. These same belts were later loaded into the Dauntlesses to be used in their .50-caliber guns during the battle. The ammunition came in cardboard containers that were a fire hazard should they be kept aboard ship. Kernan and another sailor were ordered to haul the cardboard down to the incinerator on the night of the 3rd, in preparation for the battle the next day. The incinerator was a small room that was so hot the men had to strip down to their underwear, one man opening the door to the furnace, another shoveling in the cardboard. Every now and then a round that had been overlooked would cook off in the fire. All night they worked, Kernan remembered, "in the boiling heat that was filled with the stale smell of trash, flames weirdly lighting the small space."[150]

Meanwhile, on the *Yorktown*, the three squadron leaders slated to attack the Japanese carriers—Max Leslie of Bombing Three, Lawrence "Lem" Massey of Torpedo Three, and Jimmy Thach of Fighting Three—met to discuss tactics. The problem was what to do with the fighters. There were not enough to cover both the Dauntlesses and the Devastators. All the men were the same rank, that of lieutenant commander, and none of them possessed a personality like Waldron aboard the *Hornet*, who was willing to insist on a certain plan. Because of chivalry or bravado, all refused fighter cover: Leslie and Massey both insisted that the fighters should accompany the other. In view of the Coral Sea experience, in which the torpedo planes had done most of the damage, Thach decided he would escort Massey. He expected, though, that he would have at least eight fighters at his disposal the next day.[151] That same evening, Lieutenant Dick Cromwell of Fighting Three rammed home the importance of the battle ahead. "The fate of the United States," he told the assembled pilots, radiomen, and gunners, "now rests in the hands of two hundred and forty pilots," referring to the combined air groups of the three carriers.[152]

The men—and not just the aircrews—were in sore need of such encouragement. Unlike the crew on the other two ships, the *Yorktown* crew was tired. For the past 101 days they had been either in or preparing for action. In the ready room of Torpedo Three, pilot Wilhelm "Bill" Esders remembered targets being assigned.[153] Linzey felt that "a spirit of fear hovered over the *Yorktown* . . . a sense of foreboding." This despite having withstood the worst at the Coral Sea. "Some of the pilots," it seemed to him, "had a sense of nervous hilarity due to anxiety." They looked at their situation and laughed. But Linzey didn't see it that way. He lay on his bunk in the dark, unable to sleep. "I was afraid," he later wrote. "A terrific paralyzing fear gripped me—animal fear, wild-eyed fear. . . . It was smothering me. . . . I lay there alone in the darkness, consumed by my own fear of impending death."[154]

Across the three American carriers, men were making their peace with their families and their maker. James Gray, the commander of Fighting Six, recalled that "it was doubtful that there were any atheists on *Enterprise* on the night of 3 June."[155] On the *Hornet*, Waldron wrote to his wife, Adelaide, "We are up to the eve of a very serious business." Despite the positive message he had printed out and distributed to his crew, he knew the risks all too well. "If I do not come back," Waldron told Adelaide, "you and the little girls can know that this squadron struck for the highest objective in naval warfare—to sink the enemy." While he loved his family and "longed" to be with them, he said, his "place was here with the fight." Then he turned to "this business of the torpedo attack." "I acknowledge," he wrote, "that we must have a break."[156]

On June 3, Kleiss was more alone with his thoughts than at any other time since the attack on Pearl. Sitting in his squadron ready room, he looked at the other pilots and the map on the board and found that the sense of history made his mouth dry. He wrote in his logbook: "Tomorrow is likely to be a big day." That night he took out a sheet of paper to write to Jean. He found himself trying to put his "life and naval career in perspective." The first thing he noticed was that, for all his sense of foreboding, the feeling was familiar. After all, he had already survived three battles in the past five months. Whatever would happen at Midway was repetition. There was also a sense of regret. "I worried about this upcoming engagement. Would I die tomorrow? I fretted I might not make it home to marry Jean. My earlier reluctance gnawed away at me guiltily." There was nothing for it now but to perform well tomorrow. He wrote his letter to Jean and then went to sleep.

Among the men of the *Kido Butai* similar scenes were taking place. The Japanese did not expect to encounter the American carriers for a few days, but they knew that action loomed over Midway on the morrow. The pilot Juzo Mori, one of those who was slated to crater the runway there with his 1,700-pound bomb, tried to get some rest. But, as he recalled, "the combination of damp, stale air and the excitement of the coming mission made sleep impossible," at least at first. Lying in his bunk, Mori heard the banter of his fellow aviators as they prepared their equipment for what lay ahead. "Hey," said one, holding up a piece of clothing, "if I get killed tomorrow put this in my funerary urn." Slowly, the conversation ebbed, the last men turned in, and Mori eventually nodded off amid his snoring comrades.[157]

✪

HERE WAS THE COLD and ruthless world, the "other world," that Kleiss feared. It was the world through which he and his squadron members were flying. Somehow they had taken off from the world of their youth and were now hurtling toward violence, toward mayhem and fury. It would be violence committed by them and done to them. It was a violence they had been trained to perform and to endure. "Strange as it is to say," Kleiss admitted, "the fortunes of the Pacific War appeared to rest on our shoulders."

PART II

DURING

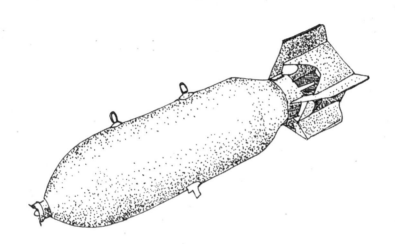

4

THE APPROACH

ON JUNE 4, IT WAS STILL DARK WHEN REVEILLE SOUNDED aboard the ships of the *Kido Butai*. Admiral Chuichi Nagumo and his staff gathered on the bridge of the *Akagi*. It was a small compartment, barely 15 by 12 feet in size, several decks above the flight deck, containing a map table, a chart locker, and several pedestal-mounted binoculars. With five officers it was crowded; Nagumo stood shoulder to shoulder with his men.

During the night there had been no surprises. The submarine cordon near Hawaii had nothing to report—which Nagumo took to mean that the US fleet was in still in harbor. And the *Kido Butai*, steadily plowing through rough seas, was now some 220 miles northwest of Midway. Peering into the dark, he could see that the fog had lifted but that low mountains of clouds blotted the stars. Soon Midway would be within striking distance. So far, all was going according to Admiral Isoroku Yamamoto's plan.

✪

BELOW DECKS THE MEN had been at work since 0130. Inside the enclosed hangars the crew armed the planes with contact bombs to attack Midway. These would explode on impact when they struck the ground installations. Each carrier would make a contribution, and the total strike force would number 108 planes, plus fighter cover.

One of the pilots was Juzo Mori, aboard the *Soryu*. He remembered waking up from a good night's sleep and feeling rested. "I felt confident," he said, "that I could properly carry out my duty." Breakfast was *sekihan*, a rice dish boiled with red beans that was eaten on special occasions. Then Mori changed into his flight gear and paid his respects at the ship's shrine, praying for "good fortune in the coming battle." Aside from his notepad and map, his hands were empty; the attack squadrons did not bring parachutes, believing captivity to be a disgrace.[1]

On the hangar deck, Mori helped load planes onto the elevators and then joined them topside. There was a bracing wind, and as the *Soryu* smashed through the waves, spray raked across the deck. Mori breathed deeply in the dark and found the salt air and the spray invigorating. He could see only several feet in front of him. Men shouted to one another, emerging from the dark, heaving aircraft into position as the ship slanted underfoot. Mori found his plane, and, with a dolly placed underneath his bomb, he tested the release mechanism. A simple lever yet such a complex operation: he was overwhelmed there in the darkness beside his weapon. To calm his nerves, he smoked a cigarette, and then it was time for the final briefing. The pilots and the aircrews gathered to synchronize their watches and note the *Soryu*'s exact position. Midway was by now only 180 miles away. The fight would come in less than one hour.

Loudspeakers announced a command: "All hands to launching stations." Then, when the pilots were seated in their cockpits: "Start engines." The planes roared to life, and the four carriers, already in their box formation, turned into the wind, a heading that made it easier for take-off. Mori checked his gauges and listened to his engine during the ten-minute warm-up. He placed his mouth in the speaking tube and called to his navigator and gunner. They were ready. Then he flicked on his wing lights, signaling "Prepared for take-off." The bridge ordered, "Commence launching," and the air officer swung his green signal lamp in a

wide circle. Men on deck for the launch and those in the gun tur-
rets alongside the ship all let up a cheer, waving their caps as the
Zeros and then the bombers sped down the deck and lifted into
darkness.[2]

Within fifteen minutes, 122 planes were airborne. Twelve of
these were Zeros to provide combat air patrol cover for the *Kido
Butai*. Two were torpedo planes to support reconnaissance patrols.
The rest, a total of 108 bombers, would attack Midway and were
led by Mitsuo Fuchida's replacement, Joichi Tomonaga. Tomonaga
was an able pilot and a veteran of the war in China. This would be
his first mission in the Pacific. Under his command, the Japanese
strike group assumed formation and headed south.

Tomonaga, however, was not leading the "first-string team"
of pilots, as Fuchida later delicately put it. Following Yamamoto's
plan, Nagumo held back his best pilots in case the American carriers appeared earlier than expected. Unlike the Midway strike
force, these planes waited below deck, armed with torpedoes and
time-fuse bombs to attack ships.[3] In the meantime, Nagumo sent
up a standard combat air patrol: each carrier contributed a *shotai*,
or group of planes, that was responsible for a different quadrant of
the sky above the *Kido Butai*. Half patrolled at 4,000 feet and the
other half at 2,000 feet. Altogether there were only twelve Zeros,
a small number for such a large sky. The carriers were sailing in a
box formation across 25 square miles of sea, with supporting ships
even farther out.[4]

Kaname Harada piloted one of the Zeros launched from the
Soryu as part of the standard combat air patrol. At Pearl Harbor
he had been stuck flying CAP as well. He hated this mission and
wished he could be on the attack instead.[5] Japanese aviators loathed
combat air patrol. Compared to offensive strikes it was uneventful
work, especially on a day like today, when the enemy was not expected for hours, if not longer. Harada expected a quiet day when
he took off.[6]

On the *Akagi*, Fuchida was not so confident. Still nursing the
wound from an appendicitis operation, he had managed to make
his way up to the flight control platform underneath the *Akagi's*

bridge, and there, amid the noise and pageantry of the launch, he found his pride overtaken by a growing unease. The low clouds offered concealment for the *Kido Butai*, but then again, they obscured any American planes that might be overhead as well. If the CAP was needed, Fuchida wondered, would twelve planes be enough? He was also concerned to hear that search planes had only just launched. Hours would pass before they could provide meaningful reconnaissance. In the meantime, under this cloud cover, the carriers seemed vulnerable. To what, he couldn't say. This anxiety, combined with his illness, suddenly made him dizzy. He retired below deck to rest.[7]

★

THE AMERICAN CARRIERS WERE 200 miles east of the *Kido Butai*. One hour before Tomonaga and his men launched, "general quarters" sounded aboard the *Hornet*, but many pilots were already in their squadron ready rooms, waiting on the word. At first, it was a repeat of the previous day. Like most of the ship, the Torpedo Eight ready room was a cramped space with a low overhead and bulkheads of whitewashed steel. It was dominated by a 3-foot-square reflector screen on which messages from the teleprinter machine were projected. The pilots lounged in leather reclinable chairs, some sleeping, some talking among themselves. All had pencil and paper near at hand. At any moment, the teletype machine might come to life, rattling off the position, course, and speed of the Japanese fleet. For now, though, the machine was quiet, and there was a restless atmosphere in the room.[8]

It was much the same aboard the other American carriers. On the *Enterprise*, reveille sounded and the crew and the air group began to congregate for breakfast. Each man was taking it in his own way. For some it was an unusually somber affair. The Dauntless pilot Lew Hopkins remembered the tension. "I don't think anyone was very hungry," he recalled, "and they kind of pushed their eggs around."[9] But there were others who, as Clarence Dickinson put it, "behaved, and with no pretence, as if this were just another day at sea."[10] The pilots then went to their squadron ready room, where they studied their maps, played cards, or dozed. Some, such as Earl Gallaher, experienced "butterflies" in their stomachs, less from fear than uncertainty.[11] Flight and general quarters were sounded at a number of occasions during the morning, but as the sun rose on the American carriers, there was still no order to launch.[12]

Dusty Kleiss was fully prepared. After breakfast, he changed into his flight gear: a long-sleeved khaki shirt and khaki trousers. Underneath his shirt he wore a sweater of Jean's that she had sent him. Then he checked and rechecked all his personal equipment. In his upper left arm pocket: the pencils he needed to plot his course. In his chest pockets: a flashlight and two lipstick-sized containers, one of Vaseline, the other ephedrine. In his trouser pocket: his spare flashlight, new batteries, and two woolen rags—one to wipe his chart board and the other to clear the plane's windshield. Around his neck was his life jacket, and slung on his back, his parachute. In one hand he carried his helmet and goggles.[13]

When he went down to the hangar deck, Kleiss was shocked to see that the Devastators were being armed.[14] His old friend Tom Eversole was nearby. With a worried look on his face, he told Kleiss that his squadron was being sent out with the strike. The two men shook hands and wished each other luck. It was a short exchange; there was no time for more. Kleiss, who knew that Eversole was unlikely to survive the attack, was suddenly overcome by emotion. As tears welled in his eyes, the face of his friend began to blur.[15]

✪

SINCE 0400, AMERICAN CATALINA reconnaissance aircraft had been searching the ocean. They fanned out from Midway looking for the *Kido Butai*. At 0520 one of them noticed a Japanese plane, then a Japanese carrier. And then, through a break in the clouds, a staggering sight came into view. Howard Ady radioed that he had seen "two carriers and main body ships" and "many planes." These reports came in quick succession. Spruance intercepted them and ordered his chief of staff to "launch everything you have at the earliest possible moment and strike the enemy carriers."[16]

This was a serious blow to Nagumo. The Japanese knew that the element of surprise had been lost because the Catalina escaped. It was also heard sending a long radio report. Any hope of striking Midway while the American aircraft were on the ground was now given up.[17]

While the planes made their way toward Midway, the contest at sea had already begun. The USS *Nautilus*, a submarine commanded by William Brockman, received the report of "many planes" at 0530 and went to investigate the suspected origin of these aircraft. Soon he sighted a formation of planes in the sky. One, a Zero, swooped down, firing its machine gun. Brockman submerged to 100 feet. Within minutes he was back at periscope depth, where he discovered "a formation of four ships," the advance screen of the *Kido Butai*. Drawing ahead to attack, Brockman was again strafed by a Zero overhead. Then came a pattern of depth charges. He dropped to 90 feet, hoping the Japanese would pass.

At 0555, radar on Midway detected a "large number of unidentified aircraft."[18] Eight minutes later, Task Force 16 received more details from the Catalina: "Two carriers and battleships bearing 320, distance 180, course 135, speed 25."[19] There was now a mad scramble to get the aircraft on Midway aloft before the Japanese struck.

"About 6 o'clock it began to get light," remembered Allen Rothenberg of Washington, DC, who was piloting one of the Catalinas out of Midway.[20] And with the day came the popping of engine starters as aircraft at the airfield came alive. The first to take off was a squadron of twenty-seven Brewster Buffalos that were meant to protect Midway itself. Then came the strike group, a somewhat ragtag group of different planes that included torpedo bombers, high-altitude heavy bombers, and dive bombers, many of them Dauntlesses. Including the CAP, this amounted to 84 planes, two-thirds the size of the Japanese force.

At 0615 Tomonaga signaled, "Target in sight."[21] Two minutes later, his pilots began to form up for the attack. Among them was Juzo Mori, "all tensed up and ready for battle." The island waited below, seemingly defenseless. Suddenly, the dive bomber in front of Mori burst into flames and dropped out of formation. Major Floyd

"Red" Parks and his fighters had arrived. "Shit," Mori thought. "They were up there waiting for us." It was pell-mell. Nearly 100 aircraft were careening about, angling for a position on each other. It was difficult to distinguish friend from foe. Parks himself was shot down, and though he managed to bail out, he was machine-gunned in his parachute by a Zero. Tomonaga and his planes kept on and within minutes had reformed as if nothing had happened.

The attack on Midway started at 0630.[22] To the men on the ground, already shaken by the summary dispatch of their fighters, the Japanese strike force bore a terrifying aspect, part of which was captured on film by John Ford. His camera recorded the wail of the air-raid siren, the clatter of machine guns, and the intermittent crashes of aerial bombardment. High above, Juzo Mori ignored the unexpectedly heavy antiaircraft fire. "You are never going to hit us with that lousy shooting," Mori thought.[23] Men ran in every direction, seeking cover.

By the end, the Marines counted "fourteen bombs dropped on Eastern Island." Fighters had also strafed gun positions repeat-edly. The powerhouse was demolished. Gas lines were broken. The sick bay and engineering tents were also damaged. Worse, the command post, mess hall, and post exchange were all destroyed.[24] Lieutenant Commander Yahachi Tanabe, skipper of the Japanese submarine I-168, watched from his periscope as "the island turned into a mass of flames" and was then covered with "a thick, black smoke."[25] The American pilots suffered greatly: fourteen fighters had been shot down, nearly half the CAP. Thirteen pilots were missing in action, one was confirmed killed, and four had been wounded. The island was now practically defenseless after an at-tack in which the Japanese lost only six planes.

Tactically, though, the attack was a failure. Only a few minor holes had been made in the runway: Midway was still an operational airbase that could mount attacks on the Kido Butai. Nimitz had re-tained use of what was effectively a fourth carrier. Even before he rallied his planes in the assembly area to head for home, Tomonaga therefore radioed Nagumo: "There is need for a second strike."[26]

✪

AT THAT VERY SAME moment, the *Enterprise* finally received the order to launch. Over the loudspeaker came the voice: "Pilots, man your planes." Immediately, Earl Gallaher's "butterflies" disappeared. He now had "a job to do."[27] Oddly, Wade McClusky did not convene a preflight conference to coordinate the operation with his squadron commanders. There had been last-minute changes to personnel. McClusky's regular gunner had smashed his glasses in an accident, so he was replaced by another man, Walter Chocha-lousek.[28] Severin Rombach in Torpedo Six also received a different gunner. Most, though, would take off with men they knew well. And they would perform a mission that was also familiar because of their training.

It was already warm on deck, and when the aircrews emerged into the open, they were momentarily blinded by the sun. The first thing they did was to check their planes, superstitiously kicking the tires.[29] Despite the heat, some were trembling. The gunner Don Hoff, an eighteen-year-old from Stockton, California, felt his legs shake as he scrambled up the wing of his Dauntless. When he gripped the fuselage to lower himself into his seat, he noticed that his hands were shaking, too. It was his first time in combat.[30] Others found it thrilling. Dick Best climbed onto his Dauntless and looked at his gunner, James Murray of Los Angeles, California, already in the back seat. "Murray, this is it," Best said. "Just like the movies."[31]

Alvin Kernan, by this point, had finished his trash-burning detail. He was exhausted but determined to help arm the planes that would participate in the battle. Changing into a clean uniform, he donned his red vest and red cloth helmet and climbed the network of ladders that took him to the flight deck. With another ordnance man he waited at the bomb elevator, a narrow shaft, 3 by 4 feet, that ran from the flight deck down to the bomb farm, a room near the keel where ordnance was assembled. As he looked down that shaft into the guts of the ship, a distance of several hundred feet, a bright yellow bomb was wheeled onto the elevator. It began to rise, steadily growing larger, until at last it appeared ripe in the sunlight, ready to be loaded onto the crutch of a Dauntless.[32]

The aircraft were spotted—that is, arranged and prepared on deck—by the maintenance crews. It was a kind of puzzle-fitting—some sixty planes were arranged at the tail end of the deck, wingtip to wingtip, so that the rest of the deck could be used for take-off. Once the planes were parked, the maintenance men weaved around them, ensuring they were fully fueled and armed with the required ordnance. Kernan and his red-helmeted ordnance men would visit each plane in pairs. With a special wagon, they moved the correct ordnance under each plane and then lifted it into place. Once it was fixed, they would insert the fuse into the nose of the bomb, then thread a long copper arming wire through the holes in the fuse vanes.[33] The bomb load and fuse settings were determined partly by the mission, partly by the ordnance available, and partly by the position of the plane on the deck; the shorter the run for take-off, the lighter the bomb load. Dauntlesses from scouting squadrons were equipped with a 500-pound bomb under the fuselage and two underwing 100-pound bombs; the rest were armed with a single 1,000-pound bomb. The larger bombs had delayed fuses and would detonate after penetrating their target; the smaller ones had contact fuses that would explode on impact. The torpedoes slung under the Devastators were also set to detonate on impact.[34]

Now that the planes were arranged on deck and armed and loaded, it was time for launch. The plane captain cranked up the inertia starter, which turned the engine and propeller enough to start the engine.[35] Kleiss fixed his goggles over his eyes. He glanced back at John Snowden, his gunner, and then settled into his seat. The engine found its rhythm. The noise—Kleiss remembered "a chorus of thirty-three angry buzz-saws"—was deafening.[36]

One by one, the Dauntlesses hurtled down the flight deck. McClusky launched first. Dick Best's plane, which carried a 1,000-pound bomb, plunged downward after zooming off the deck. His gunner, James Murray, noticed sailors running to the bow to see what had happened to them, but Best cleared the water, then stayed low and gradually gained altitude.[37] One of those coming behind him, Lew Hopkins, was apprehensive. It was his first time taking off with a live bomb.[38] His nervousness must have been apparent to his gunner, who held on to the sides of the aircraft for dear life, prepared to bail out if it came to the worst. In fact, both men were soon safely airborne. Their anxiety must have been widely shared among the many rookie pilots, including both of McClusky's wingmen. In Scouting Six, more than half of the sixteen pilots were new, and many of them had not seen action with live bombs.[39] Despite this, none came to grief during take-off. Soon Kleiss was in the air, too. Almost immediately, though, one of his wingmen, Eldor "Rodey" Rodenburg, noticed that his engine was malfunctioning, so he was forced to return to the *Enterprise*.[40]

Once they passed 14,000 feet, the pilots switched on their oxygen supply.[41] Immediately, the commander of Bombing Six, Best, noticed a problem. There was a burning sensation in his throat and lungs. It was caused by the oxygen from his mask, but he couldn't remove it; because of the altitude, there was nothing else to breathe. Later Best learned that one of his oxygen canisters was faulty. Caustic soda dust, used to drain moisture from the air, was filtering into the breathing tube. Best breathed in the dusty air for the next five minutes, causing fearsome damage to his lungs.[42] For a moment he considered returning for medical care, but he decided to remain with his squadron—a decision that would have important consequences for the battle that morning.

Some forty minutes later, Best and his fellow pilots were still orbiting above the *Enterprise*. They had been waiting for the rest of the air group to join them in order to launch a coordinated attack. "We stayed there and stayed there," recalled Tony Schneider, one of the Dauntless pilots, "until it seemed like an eternity."[43] The escort fighters and especially the torpedo bombers were taking forever to launch. Finally, Spruance received notice of a possible Japanese sighting and became insistent. Abandoning doctrine, which called for a coordinated attack, he decided to go ahead with the planes that were already in the air before any more fuel was wasted. He flashed McClusky the message that everyone was waiting for: "Proceed on mission assigned."[44]

Scouting Six and Bombing Six now assumed a "stepped-down" formation. Scouting Six took the lead, its planes arranged in groups of six, each set slightly below and to the side. In this way, the gunners had unobstructed vision and gun movement in case they were surprised by Japanese fighters. Behind them was Bombing Six, with the heavier bomb load and hence higher fuel consumption. Traveling in the rear would allow them to fly in the slipstream of Scouting Six. Once they reached the target, this formation would also enable each aircraft to peel off easily for its dive.[45]

Torpedo Six launched last because its Devastators needed the full deck run to get into the air. They were further delayed by the fact that their commander, Gene Lindsey, who had severe injuries from a landing accident several days prior, had to be assisted into his cockpit by a mechanic.[46] He ignored all entreaties to stay behind. Lindsey had helped to wind the clock; now he wanted to see it strike.

The launch from the *Hornet* was similarly disorganized. John Waldron, commander of Torpedo Squadron Eight, was acutely conscious of the vulnerability of his Devastator torpedo bombers and pleaded to be assigned fighter cover. The *Hornet* Air Group commander, Stanhope Ring, and Captain Pete Mitscher disagreed, claiming that the dive bombers, who had suffered so badly at the Battle of the Coral Sea, were more vulnerable. Waldron was still arguing on the bridge when the order to man planes came through. Pilot George Gay met him on the way down from the bridge and there was a tense exchange. Waldron swore that Ring had the location of the Japanese carriers wrong and that he, Waldron, would lead the torpedo bombers there alone.[47]

Unlike on the *Enterprise*, there was no set launch sequence aboard the *Hornet* that morning; planes departed in the order they were spotted by the deck crews. By chance, Gay was the first to take off. Astonishingly, it was his debut with a torpedo. "We had never even seen it done," Gay admitted in his memoirs. The additional 1,000 pounds of weight underneath his plane made it harder to launch, but he managed it. When the rest of the air group was aloft, they headed west in the direction of where Ring expected to find the Japanese carriers.[48] Counting both air groups, ninety-three planes were on their way to attack the *Kido Butai*.

✪

MEANWHILE, THE FIRST AIRCRAFT launched from Midway had already appeared over the *Kido Butai*. Hiroshi Suzuki, a maintenance man aboard the *Akagi*, was eating rice balls for breakfast when he heard the announcement that the enemy was approaching; this was followed by a bugle call to warn that the planes were close.[49] At 0710, six Avenger torpedo bombers from Midway, commanded by Langdon "Fieb" Fieberling, attacked the Japanese force, followed immediately by four army medium bombers.[50] They were engaged by about thirty fighters from the combat air patrol and promptly slaughtered. The American planes dropped their torpedoes too early and did no damage. One of the army planes nearly crashed into the command structure of the *Akagi*, which would have surely killed Nagumo. In this context, though, a miss was as good as a mile, and the *Kido Butai* steamed on unharmed.

Fieberling's martyrdom, however, exposed a deficiency in the Japanese fighter defense system. In the absence of radar, it depended entirely on visual sighting. As a result, American attacks could not be intercepted at a distance, but had to be engaged close to or directly above the *Kido Butai*. Nagumo's combat air patrol swelled in size as extra Zeros launched to assist, but they had very little time to accomplish their mission. They also had to dodge their own antiaircraft fire as the Japanese fleet engaged the Americans.[51]

Perhaps it was because of this vulnerability that Nagumo sided with Tomonaga: air operations on Midway were still a threat. A second strike was necessary. At 0715, therefore, he ordered that the aircraft that had been standing by, to deal with any American carriers that might appear, be rearmed with contact bombs. About this time, Juzo Mori landed on the *Soryu*, finding it "an absolute madhouse of frenetic activity." The flight deck crew hastily pushed his plane onto the elevator to arm it below. In the hangar, a torpedo was fixed in place, but then came Nagumo's order for a second strike on Midway, initiating a lengthy process of rearmament. Because the torpedoes and bombs were different shapes, each came with a different mount. The crew had to gently lower the torpedo and wheel it away, then replace the torpedo mount with that of a contact bomb, and finally hoist the contact bomb into place. All ordnance traveled from the magazine up to the hangar deck via an elevator. Because of the rush, the torpedoes were not returned to the magazine once they were removed from the planes. Instead, these 17-foot weapons were piled up inside the hangar.[52]

Meanwhile, the planes assigned to cover the *Kido Butai* were being constantly rotated. At 0730, the Zero pilot Kaname Harada and his two wingmen returned to the *Soryu*. They had managed several runs on Fieberling's hapless torpedo attack, but the lion's share of that kill went to others. After a relatively uneventful three-hour patrol, they had nothing to look forward to but breakfast.[53]

Nagumo, however, was beginning to sense a chance for sea battle. Half an hour after the first American attack, he received a report from one of his reconnaissance aircraft. There were ten enemy surface units 240 miles out from Midway, making 20 knots.[54] Maddeningly, the report made no reference to ship types. If these were cruisers and destroyers, they were of no interest. But if the American force contained carriers, then Nagumo would have the fight he wanted.

The admiral's ruminations were interrupted eight minutes later when the battleship *Kirishima* suddenly started to belch smoke. This was the signal given when enemy aircraft were sighted. It was another group of attackers from Midway, this time Dauntlesses commanded by Lofton Henderson.[55] The Japanese were puzzled by Henderson's approach at an intermediate altitude, rather than the high levels normally used by dive bombers or the sea-level attack position that torpedo bombers employed. Henderson, fearing that his pilots were too inexperienced to dive straight down, was leading his squadron in a glide-bombing run. The maneuver was both less accurate and more dangerous than a dive bomb: the pilots had to account for the horizontal movement of the bomb when aiming, and they had to withstand antiaircraft fire and enemy CAP during their gradual descent. Most of Henderson's planes were shot down, though some managed to attack the *Hiryu* with several spectacular near misses. Of the sixteen Dauntlesses, only eight returned home, all heavily damaged.[56] One plane, piloted by

Daniel Iverson, had taken no fewer than 219 hits but still made it back, a testament Heinemann's sturdy design.[57]

Very shortly after, the *Kido Butai* was surprised again. Fuchida had climbed above deck when several "dark geysers of water" rose up around the *Akagi*. Looking over at the *Soryu*, he saw the same thing taking place. He braced for impact but it never came. All the bombs had missed. High above he could see the silhouettes of planes he didn't recognize. Puzzled, he consulted his aircraft recognition chart and identified them as B-17s, the most modern US army bomber.[58] They had flown from Midway. Luckily for the Japanese, the Americans were at 20,000 feet: too high to accurately aim their bombs. Hiroshi Suzuki, the *Akagi* maintenance man, thought that the *Soryu*, which was completely obscured by the spray, must have been badly hit—but when the water settled, the ship steamed on, undamaged.[59] All that the pride of US Army high-level bombing had achieved was an iconic high-level photograph of the frantically maneuvering ships below.

By now the sea around the *Kido Butai* was full of Japanese and American pilots who had been shot down in the fighting. It was calm and warm, giving the pilots a good chance of survival, although for the Americans, rescue by the Japanese was a dismal prospect. At least two men would be executed that day. For the others, a Japanese prison often amounted to a death sentence. On the *Akagi*, Suzuki noticed that he could tell the two sides apart from their swimming strokes.[60]

At this point, Nagumo and his staff received two important reports from his scouting plane near the American fleet. The first, at 0811, said, "The enemy is composed of 5 cruisers and 5 destroyers." Then, not even ten minutes later, the scout plane sent a contradictory message: "The enemy is accompanied by what appears to be a carrier."[61]

What should Nagumo do now? If he attacked immediately, he would do so without a balanced force, because he did not have enough fighters to provide an adequate escort. In any case, Nagumo had no aircraft ready to go immediately. The original strike force set aside to deal with the American carriers was being rearmed with contact bombs to finish off Midway. Then there was Tomonaga, whose planes would soon return from the atoll short of fuel, some of them damaged or with injured crew members. They would need to land immediately and could not do so while other planes were being launched. Finally, Nagumo could not launch planes while his carriers were dodging enemy attacks; the high-speed maneuvering made air operations too hazardous.[62]

Brockman came closer to the surface in the USS *Nautilus*. What he saw imprinted itself on his mind: "Ships were on all sides moving across the field at high speed and circling away to avoid the submarine position."[63] The vigilant Japanese sighted his periscope, but he managed to get a torpedo off. It did not find its mark. The Japanese fleet scattered in all directions while the escorts engaged Brockman. Despite repeated depth-charge attacks, the *Nautilus* clung on below the waves, refusing to be driven off.[64]

No sooner had the *Kido Butai* dodged the enemy torpedo when it was once again under attack, this time by twelve planes from Midway, a squadron of Vought Vindicators led by Major Benjamin Norris. The Vindicator was an obsolete plane—slow and fabric covered—and Norris was leading them in a glide-bombing attack from 4,500 feet. They were such an easy target that even the gunners managed to hit some of them. Norris survived, but his squadron was destroyed.[65]

Aboard the *Akagi*, Nagumo and his officers debated what to do. It was 0830 and Tomonaga's planes were now overhead, ready to land, but some officers lobbied to attack. Admiral Tamon Yamaguchi, aboard the *Hiryu*, signaled to Nagumo: "Consider it advisable to launch attack force immediately." Fuchida agreed, though he kept his opinion to himself for the moment. He was laid out on the floor of the flight command post, a room immediately underneath the bridge of the *Akagi*, taking advantage of the lull in the fighting. Historians have since referred to this moment as "Nagumo's dilemma" or "Nagumo's ordeal."[66]

"Our feeling at that time," remembered Minoru Genda, one of the staff officers alongside Nagumo that morning, "was that we had been ambushed by the enemy force, which made us make up our minds to have a decisive engagement with the enemy force by all means." Ryunosuke Kusaka, another staff officer on the bridge, watched Nagumo closely when the scouting report announced the presence of an American carrier. "He might have been shocked for a moment," Kusaka said of Nagumo, "but I think anyone facing such an unexpected eventuality would have been shocked for a moment."[67] Within minutes, Nagumo made up his mind. The best means of effecting a decisive engagement would be a mass attack that required fighters to protect his bombers. He gave the order for Tomonaga to land his planes.[68]

✪

AT THIS MOMENT, THE opposite decision was made aboard the *Yorktown*. There the men had been awake since 0300 but Admiral Frank Jack Fletcher was holding them back. Unlike Nagumo, who preferred mass attack, Fletcher was willing for the arrival of his air groups to be staggered. Now he ordered them to launch.[69]

The delay, however, had made the men nervous. Lefty Holmberg, one of the Dauntless pilots in Bombing Three, sat in the ready room listening to his fellow pilots discuss their situation. By now the *Enterprise* and *Hornet* planes should've reached the *Kido Butai*— why hadn't they reported contact? Many assumed the worst: the men were lost or they had all been killed by the Japanese.

Jimmy Thach, commander of Fighting Three, was responsible for defending both the torpedo bombers and the dive bombers during the attack. It was a difficult task, considering that these planes made their approach at a difference of 15,000 feet in altitude. But that morning, Thach learned that instead of the usual eight fighters, he would have only six. Two of his planes would be held back to defend the *Yorktown* in case the Japanese launched a counterstrike. Thach spent so much time arguing fruitlessly for the decision to be reversed that he had only a few minutes before take-off to explain his strategy to the men. He told them to "stick together no matter what happened" and to defend the torpedo planes.[70]

When the order to launch came at 0840, the pilots climbed above deck in the glare of the summer sun. Immediately, Holmberg noticed something was different about his Dauntless: underneath the fuselage was a 1,000-pound bomb. If he managed it, this would be his first take-off with ordnance of that size. The skipper, Max Leslie, went first, and then it was Holmberg's turn. Despite his anxiety, his Dauntless steadied and then rose into the sky.

At the last minute, Admiral Fletcher decided to hold back the seventeen remaining Dauntlesses. He wanted them in reserve to carry out a follow-up strike, in order to defend the task force should the Japanese discover their location. All the airborne planes were now in formation and ready to head west for the enemy fleet. As they departed, the cruiser *Astoria* signaled to them: "Good hunting and a safe return."[71]

By 0905 all American carrier planes scheduled for launch were in the air. The strike had no overall commander. Going by experience, Stanhope Ring was the senior aviator of the three air groups, but he did not exercise any control over the day's operations. It was probably just as well, as it turned out. The carriers launched their planes much as they had fought against the Japanese during the past few months: independently.[72] There were now 151 American carrier aircraft on their way to the Japanese; of these, 84 were Heinemann's Dauntlesses.[73]

THE ACRIMONY AND CONFUSION of the launch continued as the American planes approached the *Kido Butai*. Among the Enterprise Air Group there were several problems. The Dauntlesses were disadvantaged from having spent nearly an hour's worth of fuel just waiting for the order to depart. When the order came, the torpedo bombers and fighters had yet to take flight. This meant that the air group was fragmented: the Dauntlesses and the torpedo bombers would not be able to attack in concert. Now on his way, McClusky gunned his engine up to 218 miles per hour, well above the normal cruising speed of 185. Kleiss winced, knowing that the faster speed would burn fuel that was already in short supply.[74] To complete the confusion, the *Enterprise* fighters and torpedo bombers were separated. James Gray's Fighting Six attached themselves to Waldron's Torpedo Eight, believing them to be Eversole's Torpedo Six.

The *Hornet's* air group set off together but soon became fragmented. They, too, had wasted precious fuel while waiting for all planes to launch, and some pilots already feared they would not make it back. Then, about half an hour after departure, an argument erupted between Waldron and Ring. Waldron wanted to change course but Ring ignored him. There followed an exchange heard over the radio by the entire squadron.

"I know where the damn fleet is," Waldron said.

"You fly on us," Ring replied. "I'm leading this formation. You fly on us."

Waldron pondered this for a few minutes. Then he announced, "The hell with you." And with that Torpedo Eight peeled off to the southwest. It was a stunning act of insubordination.

Soon Waldron had his planes fan out to form a "scouting line," in which they flew line abreast. This way they were able to scan a wider area of ocean. But there was a danger that planes on the end of the line might drift away and become lost, especially when passing through clouds. It was not worth the risk, so Waldron ordered the men into a closer formation. No sooner had he done so than Torpedo Eight spotted columns of smoke on the horizon.[75] It was the Japanese fleet. Waldron had been right. Now it was a question of whether he would enjoy the lucky break he had hoped for in his final letter to his wife.

The rest of the *Hornet's* air group stuck to their assigned course. Thirty minutes or so later, by which time they had been in the air for more than an hour, Ring's depleted command had seen no sign of the *Kido Butai.* The fighters were now seriously low on fuel. Two of the younger pilots turned back without permission, perhaps because they lost their nerve. Seeing this, the commander of the escort squadron, Lieutenant Commander Samuel G. "Pat" Mitchell of Fighting Eight, followed suit. Morale among the bomber crews, who were now on their own, plummeted. Even with his command disintegrating around him, Ring plowed on, maintaining his course. But he and his men were on what would later be dubbed "a flight to nowhere."[76]

Only the *Yorktown* flyers managed to maintain cohesion. Admittedly, their performance was not perfect. Max Leslie did not learn that half his Dauntlesses had been kept back until after he was in the air.[77] Still, the air group now had a substantial force of torpedo bombers, dive bombers, and fighters together and on their way. The bombers flew high at 15,000 feet, the torpedo planes low at 1,500 feet.[78] Thach positioned his fighter escort between them, doing S-turns to prevent his superior speed from taking him away from his lumbering charges.[79] Alone among the American forces searching for the *Kido Butai*, they would be able to deliver a coordinated strike. Moreover, unlike the other two air groups, the planes from the *Yorktown* were flying more or less directly to their target.

The threat to the *Yorktown* Air Group was not unit cohesion or bad navigation, but faulty technology. Two hours into their flight, the rear gunner, Lloyd Childers, was desperate to urinate. When he reached for his relief tube, he was alarmed by a large splash in the ocean to his right. Soon there was another. Not seeing any enemy aircraft, Childers guessed they were under attack from Japanese long-range guns. Then he saw another splash.[80] Holmberg was the first to know what had happened: "Capt. Leslie, the skipper, gave the signal to arm bombs," he recalled. "I watched him lean over in the cockpit and throw his electrical arming switch. Then, to my surprise I saw his bomb release from its rack and drop away cleanly from the wing." The planes had been outfitted with a new electrical arming system and some were wired incorrectly. The arming switch was activating the bomb release. Holmberg's switch worked fine but he could see Leslie, flying alongside him, furious about the situation.[81] Max Lane, another pilot who lost his bomb, said, "I was stunned . . . felt cheated and was frustrated at suddenly becoming powerless just as the moment of opportunity to hit the Japs a real blow approached." Now the seventeen *Yorktown* Dauntlesses only had thirteen bombs between them.[82]

★

AT THIS POINT, THE USS *Nautilus* came close to the surface again amid the Japanese fleet. Looking through the periscope, Captain Brockman could see a Japanese aircraft carrier about 10 miles away. It was changing course continuously, and, though the carrier did not appear damaged, the sky was filled with the black plumes of antiaircraft fire. Closer was a Japanese destroyer, the *Arashi*. Brockman fired a torpedo at the *Arashi* and then dived to 200 feet, hoping to close on the distant carrier.[83]

By 0910, the last of Tomonaga's planes had landed. On the *Soryu*, the pilots gathered beneath the bridge to be debriefed. Juzo Mori remembered the ship as an "absolute madhouse of frenetic activity." The flight deck crews were "swarming" over the planes, striking them down to the hangars for rearming and refueling. It was all punctuated by the clanging of the elevator bells as they went up and down. But for all the haste, it was a slow business. Mori was slated to carry a torpedo on his next attack, and each of these could only be loaded individually.[84]

Shortly after, Nagumo altered course to close the gap with the enemy. He could now think about launching his own strike. To do so, he would need clear decks on his carriers and time to get the strike force in the air. He got neither. A minute after the change of course, a fresh set of assailants appeared. The escorting cruisers began to pump smoke, partly to warn the rest of the *Kido Butai* and partly to confuse the enemy. More Zeros were scrambled to intercept, cluttering the decks.[85]

It was Torpedo Eight.[86] Waldron had found his quarry exactly where he expected it to be. He signaled for his men to spread out, bracketing the nearest carrier. They were several hundred feet above the water, traveling at just over 200 miles per hour, but vulnerable to the combat air patrol. Zeros swooped in, firing cannon and machine guns. The American fighters were nowhere to be seen. Waldron had lost visual contact with them a few minutes earlier, at exactly the moment they were needed most. He radioed for help but there was no response. His plane soon burst into flames. Waldron stood up in the cockpit to leap away but it was too late; his plane crashed into the ocean.

"Let's go back and help them, sir," said Bob Huntington, the gunner aboard George Gay's Devastator.

"To hell with that," Gay said. "We have a job to do." In a sense, Gay was responding without thinking. The event was too much for him to comprehend. "I cannot tell you the sequence in which the planes went down," he said years later. "Everything was happening at once, but I was consciously seeing it all." Machine-gun fire came over his shoulder, pouring into his control panel and windshield. He crouched low in his seat but continued to fly the plane.

"They got me!" Huntington said over the intercom.

"Are you hurt bad?" Gay asked. He looked over his shoulder but Huntington was slumped over, unresponsive. Gay began to swerve his plane, still making his way toward his target, the carrier *Kaga*. The Zeros came around for another pass and he felt the rounds clank into his plane. There was a knock against his left arm and he looked down, noticing a hole in his sleeve and blood on his hand. Feeling closer, there was a lump under his skin. He squeezed it as if it were a pimple: out popped a bullet. Gay looked at it, unsure what to do. It was a treasure, a memento of life nearly lost, but where could he put it? Because of his parachute harness, his pockets were no use. Intending to keep it safe, he put it in his mouth.

Looking around him, Gay noticed that his plane was the only one left. The carrier ahead was turning hard, trying to make itself a difficult target. Gay brought his plane down to 80 feet above the water and throttled back. He needed to slow down to launch his torpedo. He yanked the torpedo release lever, but, because his plane was so damaged, he couldn't tell if it worked. Soon he zoomed over the *Kaga*, seeing its flight deck loaded with "planes and men . . . bombs, torpedoes, gas hoses, and all kinds of gear." Then, as he sped away, the Zeros reappeared and finally managed to shoot out his engine. He crashed into the water, the impact so intense it knocked the bullet from his mouth.[87]

✪

MEANWHILE, BOMBING SIX AND Scouting Six from the *Enterprise* had followed the recommended course. When McClusky reached the expected point of interception at 0920, he "found the sea empty." There were sparse clouds and a visibility of 50 miles in all directions. No enemy was in sight. McClusky was certain he had not missed the Japanese on the way, and he was equally sure they were not lurking between him and Midway. The *Kido Butai* had to be in the semicircle to his right.[88]

McClusky now made a critical decision. Instead of turning back, as his dwindling fuel gauges suggested he should, he decided to fly west and then northwest. This was not, as was often claimed, guesswork or a mere hunch on his part.[89] McClusky *knew* where the Japanese were. He was conscious of the risks, though, because his fuel was running very low, and the planes behind him—which consumed more because of their need to constantly adjust their engines to maintain their place in the formation—were running even lower. If McClusky did not find the *Kido Butai* soon, the two Dauntless squadrons—the *Enterprise's* entire dive-bomber force—would not be able to return to their carrier.

This was an anxious time for the *Enterprise* dive bombers. Not only was their fuel running low, but they had been in the air for more than two hours, and the crews were struggling to concentrate. Kleiss sought to keep Snowden, his gunner, alert.[90] Pilots gave vent to their frustration. "Goddammit," one of them exploded. "Where are those fuckers?"[91] Matters were not helped by the fact that while it was warm below, it was very cold at 20,000 feet. Don Hoff's legs were shaking again, this time from cold rather than fear. To warm his hands, he drummed them on the side of the fuselage, but the noise distracted his pilot, so he had to stop.[92] His fellow gunner Ed Anderson of Bombing Six was also freezing. He had forgotten his winter flying boots. Then he felt an uncontrollable need to urinate. Getting unzipped in these temperatures—when the squadron could be attacked at any minute by Japanese fighters—was tricky, but Anderson did what needed to be done and then manned his machine guns again.[93]

Some of the aircraft were beginning to malfunction. Because they had to observe strict radio silence, the only way to communicate with another pilot/gunner team was to fly up alongside them and issue hand signals. One of the planes, piloted by Tony Schneider, drew up next to Best and warned him that they had engine problems and excessive fuel consumption. Shortly afterward, another plane, piloted by Edwin Kroeger, came abreast. His gunner, Gail Halterman, sent a manual Morse code signal to say he had problems with his oxygen. High-altitude flight was dangerous without oxygen, as it made the men drowsy. To reassure him, Best took off his own oxygen mask and descended to 15,000 feet to enable his men to breathe more freely.[94] The two bombing squadrons flew on, anxiously scanning the horizon for signs of the *Kido Butai*.

✪

NO SOONER HAD NAGUMO seen off Waldron than he was under attack again. Fuchida was alerted by a lookout on the bridge of the *Akagi*. "Enemy torpedo bombers," he called out, "30 degrees to starboard, coming in low." Despite his broken back, Gene Lindsey had taken Torpedo Six from the *Enterprise* to within 30 miles of the target. Spotting smoke on the horizon, he began his slow approach to the *Kido Butai*. It took an excruciatingly long stern chase, during which time the squadron was mangled by Zeros. Nine of fourteen planes were shot down. Lindsey himself was killed. So, too, was Tom Eversole, Kleiss's best friend. And so was Severin Rombach. None of their torpedoes made a difference.

From the perspective of those aboard the Japanese carriers, all this made excellent theater. They watched Lindsey's evisceration with "wild cheering and whistling," continuing as one American plane after another was destroyed.[95] But the end of Torpedo Six masked Japanese weaknesses, which were not only endemic but cumulative. Once again, as the surviving senior commander, Robert Laub, noted in his after-action report, Japanese antiaircraft fire had been totally ineffective.[96] Once again, the Americans had penetrated very close before they were spotted, and closer still before they were actually engaged by the combat air patrol. Once again, the presence of a major enemy formation—James Gray's fighters circling in the clouds above—was not even registered. Moreover, many of the Zeros had expended their cannon ammunition on Waldron and were left with only their smaller-caliber machine guns against Lindsey. This explains the length of time it took to deal with Torpedo Six.[97] It also explains why, as Laub also noted, many Japanese pilots were surprisingly reluctant to press their attacks home.

Yet the Japanese CAP, flawed as it was, worked. Or rather, it had worked against the valiant though haphazard American attacks thus far. In the past two hours, the *Kido Butai* had weathered attacks from more than one hundred American planes of all varieties and destroyed them in scores. All this while launching an attack on Midway and discovering the presence of the US fleet. Now Nagumo was preparing an enormous force, perhaps the most capable in the Pacific, to strike an American carrier, the quarry that had eluded him at Pearl Harbor.

✪

NAGUMO ATTACKED MIDWAY HOPING to provoke an American response, which he would then crush. So far, Yamamoto's plan had appeared to work too well. The Americans had appeared, albeit much more quickly than he had expected. Moreover, he had sought a decisive battle similar to what had happened in the Battle of Tsushima. This sort of confrontation with "the main fleet of the United States" had been Japanese strategy since as early as November 1941. All of which is to say that the surprise appearance of an American fleet was a welcome one. Nagumo was prepared to be impaled even as the *Kido Butai* impaled its enemy.

5

THE ATTACK

"HELLDIVERS!" SOMEONE SCREAMED. MITSUO FUCHIDA, FROM HIS place above the flight deck, looked into the sky. He saw "three black enemy planes" growing larger and larger in size. Unlike the previous attacks of the morning, which had come from sea level, these planes were plunging straight down on the *Akagi*. As Fuchida watched, "a number of black objects suddenly floated eerily from their wings." He knew what this meant. Immediately he fell to the deck and crawled behind a protective metal shield.

✪

JUNE 4, 1942, MARKED the high point of Japan's World War II expansion. Over the previous six months, Imperial forces had destroyed the American battlefleet at Pearl Harbor and captured Hong Kong, Malaya, the Philippines, and the Dutch East Indies. And for several hours, the empire seemed to be winning the Battle of Midway. The *Kido Butai* swatted away attack after attack by American bombers of various descriptions. They could have continued doing so for another three hours, and indeed longer. But at 1022 local time, their momentum was stopped. What then happened was neither a simple case of quantity turning into quality nor a curse of bad fortune or fatigue, but something altogether different.

At 0955, Wade McClusky's perseverance had paid off. Below, on the otherwise trackless sea, was the white scar of a Japanese ship traveling at speed. McClusky believed the vessel to be a cruiser, but it was in fact the destroyer *Arashi* returning from its latest tussle with the *Nautilus*. Convinced that this ship would lead him to the main force, McClusky gave chase. There was good visibility at his cruising altitude of 20,000 feet, although a torn veil of clouds lay across the sea at 3,000 feet. McClusky peered into the veil, following the *Arashi*, and three minutes later he saw the outline of the *Kido Butai*. "This is McClusky," he radioed to his two squadrons and the task force. "Have sighted the enemy."[1]

In the distance, the Dauntless squadrons could see two battleships, two heavy cruisers, a light cruiser, eleven destroyers, several oilers, and, for now, three carriers—the fourth was hidden by clouds. James Murray, one of the Dauntless gunners, could see the Japanese carriers "maneuvering hectically" to evade attacks from Torpedo Six. The carriers were nervous even though the Devastators were "really taking a beating" from the Zeros. One by one, as the torpedo planes were attacked, they caught fire and "cartwheeled" into the ocean. Over the radio, Murray could hear their frantic cries for fighter protection. Decades after the battle, Murray remembered that "it was a sickening sight."[2]

Elsewhere in the formation was Tony Schneider, who had worries of his own. The engine of his Dauntless sputtered to a halt: he was out of fuel. He quickly turned away from the Japanese fleet and headed toward Midway, switching through his tanks, hoping to find some fumes. McClusky and the other *Enterprise* Dauntless pilots watched him break formation and drift toward the sea.[3]

As Schneider went down, Dusty Kleiss glanced at his watch. He'd been in the air for more than three hours, and his own fuel tank, if the gauge was correct, was more than half empty. The mission was increasingly looking like a one-way attack, and ditching in the ocean so close to the Japanese would likely mean capture and execution. But he was determined to continue. Over the past five months, Kleiss had performed eight dive-bombing runs, three of which were in combat.[4] As he put it, "we had trained too hard and long to back out now."[5]

Instinctively, Kleiss began preparing to attack. Reaching down, he manually armed the bomb. On the intercom, he ordered his gunner, John Snowden, to turn on the Zed Baker. This was the homing device that would allow them to receive the location of the *Enterprise*. Several minutes later, Snowden called back with coordinates. Kleiss plotted these coordinates on his map, working out the heading he would take after his attack run. To obscure the position of the American carriers, he would dogleg there—first heading south before breaking northeast to his target.

McClusky then assigned targets to his two squadrons. Following tactical procedures, which urged commanders to avoid "dispersal of attack," he decided to concentrate on the two carriers ahead, the *Kaga* and the *Akagi*.[6] The carriers were equidistant. One was to the left of the planes, the other to the right. From McClusky's point of view, his order was clear. "Earl Gallaher," he said on the radio, "you take the carrier on the left and Best, you take the carrier on the right. Earl, you follow me down." In other words, Dick Best and Bombing Six would attack the *Akagi*, while McClusky, Earl Gallaher, and Scouting Six would attack the *Kaga*.[7] Best, however, missed the transmission—either because he was busy, his radio malfunctioned, or he was attempting to send his own message. The battlefield looked different to him. Trailing at a lower altitude because of his oxygen problems, Best judged that the *Kaga* was closer and it would be his target. He therefore radioed McClusky, "I am attacking according to doctrine." But McClusky never heard this rather stilted message, and it appears that most of the other pilots didn't either.[8] As a result, thirty Dauntlesses were preparing to attack only one carrier: the *Kaga*.[9]

At the same moment, Max Leslie and the air group from the *Yorktown* were sizing up the Japanese fleet from another direction. Whereas the *Enterprise* planes had flown south before turning toward the Japanese carriers, the *Yorktown* planes had managed to fly more or less straight to the target, approaching from the northeast. They also enjoyed two advantages. Their planes had more fuel than McClusky's and Ring's, and their air group was still together.

Leslie faced difficulties of his own, however. First of all, the faulty electronic arming switches had wasted several bombs. But Leslie's group was also smaller than he realized. He radioed to Walter Short of Scouting Five, "How about you taking the one to the left, and I'll take the one to the right?" But there was no answer. Leslie also tried raising his Devastator squadrons down below, but again, no answer.[10] He wouldn't learn until after the battle that Scouting Five had been kept aboard the *Yorktown* in reserve. And the Devastators, if they even received his message, were already engaged with the Japanese. Leslie decided to make do with what he had. He nodded to his left, signaling to his men that they would attack the nearest carrier on that side.[11] Seventeen Dauntlesses now prepared to dive on the *Soryu*.

One of the pilots watching Leslie's signal was Lefty Holmberg. For him, the morning had seemed routine. Years later, he said that "flying *en route* to the target, I can recall no 'jitters' or 'butterflies.' The attack was just like we had practiced in our training."[12] Like Kleiss, he was ready to perform his task. It also helped that the Japanese fighters had yet to appear. For the past few hours, the sky, like the ocean, had been empty. It was an emptiness that affected the pilots in different ways. Kleiss "breathed a sigh of relief." He was able to concentrate on his map and his aircraft.[13] Clarence Dickinson found it unnerving: "I could not understand why we had come so far without having fighters swarming over and around us like hornets."[14] After so much risk and uncertainty, the moment seemed too quiet, too easy.

As they got closer, the Dauntlesses got a better look at the enemy fleet. The *Kido Butai* provided a striking, almost beautiful vista. "The ocean was covered with ships," Earl Gallaher recalled exactly fifty years later. "It was a tremendous sight."[15] Dickinson found the view "intoxicating." Against the profound blue of the Pacific were the yellow rectangles of the Japanese flattops. There was a surge of emotion for Dickinson as he thought of what was about to come. "This was the culmination," he said, "of our hopes and dreams."[16] It was a chance to pay the Japanese back for Pearl Harbor and to avenge the deaths of the men who had been killed in the past few months.[17] It was also a test of ability, a chance to see who would perform while under fire, who would score and who would miss, who would survive and who would not. Aside from revenge or rivalry, there was the thrill of destruction: soon they would leave their mark on this vista. They would destroy or attempt to destroy the pride of the Imperial Japanese Navy, some of the largest aircraft carriers in the world. "We were captivated," Kleiss wrote, "by the sight of the pristine carriers beneath us."[18]

✪

ON BOARD THE JAPANESE carriers, the mood was relaxed, almost festive. The Zeros came and went, not for fuel but to replenish their ammunition, especially cannon shells, which were being expended on the Americans at a rapid rate. Nagatomo Yasukuni, who commanded an antiaircraft battery on the *Hiryu*, remembered how "we at guns and [those] at flight deck made praise and congratulated one another." "Our fighter attack was magnificent," they said.[19] Fuchida recalled that on the *Akagi* the maintenance crews "cheered the returning pilots, patted them on the shoulder, and shouted words of encouragement." As soon as his aircraft had been serviced, a pilot would nod, push back the throttle, and roar off into the sky. It was, as Fuchida recalled, a "scene repeated time and again."[20] The flight decks of the *Kido Butai* were thus in constant use.

One of those coming down to land was Ensign Haruo Yoshino from Chiba Prefecture. He had spent an uneventful morning flying a reconnaissance mission and returned to the *Kaga* around 1005.[21] On his approach he realized that the fleet was under attack. Flying close to the water, he watched as the Zeros of the combat air patrol dispatched the Devastators of Torpedo Six. At this point there were thirty-nine Zeros in the air, which, in theory, should have been arranged into two groups: one at 2,000 feet, responsible for the lower altitudes, and another at 4,000 feet, responsible for the higher altitudes. At the moment, however, the Zeros surged from one target to the next, striking out wherever their comrades were firing, moving together. This made short work of the Devastators, but it caused the Japanese to concentrate on the lower level of battle. They had no true command and control, and thus no real discipline.[22] They were also limited by technology. The Zeros either lacked radios or sported sets that were poor in quality. Instead, the pilots relied on hand signals or on their own situational awareness to maneuver and find targets. Given that the *Kido Butai* lacked radar, and so relied entirely on visual sighting, the distraction of the Zeros was particularly dangerous. To Yoshino, however, all seemed in hand. He "felt relieved that our fleet was safe, without any damage," and he watched as the surviving Devastators fled east. He brought his plane down on the *Kaga* and immediately went to find the air commander, Takahisa Amagai, in order to give his report.[23]

Admiral Chuichi Nagumo also took advantage of the lull in the fighting. He needed time to finish rearming his planes for an attack on the American carriers. Contrary to myth, however, the *Kido Butai* was nowhere near ready to launch this strike.[24] The dive bombers and torpedo bombers were still in the hangars below, waiting to be lifted topside, because the decks had been busy handling the combat air patrols. At least forty-five minutes were needed to lift the aircraft from the hangar and then maneuver them into position for launch.

What had been achieved, though unintentionally, was the accumulation of a terrifyingly large amount of combustible material in the bowels of the *Kaga* and the *Akagi*. Both of these ships held torpedo bombers, which the Japanese armed inside their hangars, unlike their dive bombers, which were loaded on deck. When preparing to attack Midway, they had loaded the torpedo bombers with contact bombs. Once the American fleet was discovered, these bombs were exchanged for torpedoes. It was a laborious process and many men were involved in the work. On the *Akagi*, for example, Lieutenant Kiyoto Furuta ordered the younger airmen down into the hangars to help. The heat was unbearable. Small windows were opened for ventilation, but they offered little relief. Seventeen planes were reloaded, and, in the hustle, there was no time to send the contact bombs deeper down in the ship for safe-keeping. By ten o'clock that morning, the hangar was filled with thirty-eight fully fueled aircraft, seventeen of which were loaded with torpedoes—a total of 8,800 pounds of explosives. Then there were the bombs, recently unloaded—another 3,500 pounds of explosives. On the *Kaga*, which had more aircraft, it was worse: nearly 19,000 pounds of explosives were piled up unsecured in the hangar.

✪

AT THIS MOMENT, A lookout on the *Akagi* spotted a new threat. Another squadron of American torpedo bombers was approaching from the northeast. Nagatomo Yasukuni saw them at 1009. One minute after that, the cruiser *Chikuma* opened fire to mark the intruders. At 1011, the *Akagi* took evasive action, turning its stern to the American squadron.[25] Soon, all four carriers had turned their backs on their new assailants, and another chase began. On the *Kaga*, Ensign Yoshino was told he would be unable to speak to his air officer right away because "enemy planes were approaching."[26] He went down to his squadron ready room to wait for a better moment. It would be the last time Yoshino would see that familiar flight deck intact.

The new arrivals were Lem Massey's Torpedo Three from the *Yorktown*. Once again, the Americans came in obligingly low and steady. This time, though, they were escorted by Jimmy Thach's fighters. He assigned two of his planes as close cover for the Devastators and took the rest to engage the Zeros. The appearance of these new squadrons was a welcome relief for the remnants of Torpedo Six, who, having finished their attack, were attempting to retreat.[27] The Zeros let them run and turned back to defend their carriers.

Many of the men of the *Kido Butai* had spent the past hour with their eyes at sea level as the drama of Torpedo Eight, Torpedo Six, and now Torpedo Three played out. The American planes would appear as specks above the horizon, gradually increasing in size. Ten miles or so from the target, the planes would either break into two groups, to execute an anvil attack, or attack in successive waves by division. From aboard ship, it was a mesmerizing sight and hard to ignore, not least because the intended target was never clear until the planes had finally committed. So it was with Torpedo Three, which was now crawling along the surface of the ocean toward the Japanese fleet, commanding everyone's attention.

This was Massey's vital contribution to the course of the battle.[28] It was his long attack run that provided the crucial distraction that the dive bombers needed. Torpedo Eight's sacrifice an hour earlier was already history, and despite legend, it is highly unlikely that George Gay could have seen much of what was about to unfold, because the Japanese fleet had shifted position since his crash. Likewise, Torpedo Six's more recent attack had just been thwarted, and while some of the Japanese fighters would no doubt have continued to pursue the survivors, the bulk of the combat air patrol pilots would probably have resumed their station above the *Kido Butai*.

Massey ensured that this did not happen. Instead of patrolling the higher altitudes, the Zeros descended to deal with Torpedo Three. They were joined by virtually all the other airborne Zeros and together spent the next twenty minutes focused on the fourteen Devastators and their escort of six Wildcats.[29] Thach counted about twenty enemy fighters, and to his surprise, many of them attacked him and his Wildcats rather than heading straight for the torpedo bombers. Then came another large group of Zeros "streaming" past him to engage Massey.[30] Once again the Japanese fighters had left the crown of the *Kido Butai* exposed.

One Devastator in this battle was flown by Harry Corl of Saginaw, Michigan. His gunner, Lloyd Childers, was in the back seat. As the Zeros charged them head-on, Childers mashed his butterfly trigger, but nothing happened. He had left on the safety catch, a common error in the heat of battle. He prepared to fire again when "all hell broke loose." Japanese antiaircraft fire was erupting all around them even as Zeros strafed the formation. Corl dived to 100 feet, hoping to make their plane a harder target, but it didn't work. Soon his elevator controls were shot away and his engine was malfunctioning. He didn't turn back, however. All of Torpedo Three, as Childers remembered, "chugged more or less straight ahead."[31]

The Americans would have suffered more but for Thach and his Wildcats. Thach had developed his weaving maneuver in the months leading up to the battle. In the Thach Weave, two Wildcats flying abreast of one another would cross paths and then veer away. The motion was repeated so that the planes wove together and each could cover the tail of the other. Thach had yet to test the maneuver in combat, but this was the perfect time. "The air was just like a beehive," he recalled, as Zeros swooped down on Corl and the rest of Torpedo Three. Thach signaled to his wingman, Robert A. M. "Ram" Dibb, and they began to weave—crossing paths and then veering away. A Zero soon appeared behind Dibb, and when Dibb came in front of Thach, Thach opened up with his twin .50-caliber guns. The Zero burst into flame. There was no time to watch him splash because another Zero soon fell in behind Dibb. The weave worked again. Thach began marking each kill on his kneepad.[32]

By 1020, the Wildcats and Devastators from the *Yorktown* were about 10 miles out from the Japanese carriers. Childers looked down from his wounded plane and saw the deck of an enemy cruiser. "The sight," he recalled, was "frightening." The enemy was suddenly much closer than he had realized. Up front, it seemed that Corl was talking to himself. "We are not going to make it," Corl said, to which Childers responded, "Let's get the hell out of here!"[33]

Aboard the *Kido Butai*, many watched intently as Torpedo Three continued its achingly slow approach. Then something alarming was spotted directly overhead. At 1019, a sailor aboard the *Hiryu* noticed planes at a high altitude approaching the *Kaga*. He reported to the bridge and a message was flashed: "Enemy dive-bombers over your ship!"[34]

By now, an ensign, Takeshi Maeda, had also seen the Dauntlesses. Maeda was standing on the flight deck of the *Kaga* when he noticed a "twinkling reflecting the sun." "I knew they were dive bombers," Maeda recalled; he also knew that there was no fighter cover.[35] He ran to report to the bridge. Then one of the ship's lookouts spotted them as well. The reports from the two men and from the *Hiryu* must have reached the bridge at almost exactly the same time. With what must have seemed like excruciating slowness, the *Kaga*'s guns finally began to elevate.

In the ready room on the *Kaga*, situated directly above an anti-aircraft gun, Ensign Yoshino, who was still waiting to report to his air officer, heard the firing begin. He ran out onto the walkway and at first saw only enemy torpedo planes being engaged by the ship's machine guns. Suddenly, Yoshino saw one of the gunners raise his baton to the sky, shouting. Looking up, he saw several American dive bombers "plunging down" on his carrier.[36] The nearest "hung like a spider on a thread coming right down at us."[37] To Ensign Maeda, the planes were diving so steeply that they looked as if they were "coming upside down."[38]

✪

LEADING SCOUTING SIX, EMBARKED on a 70-degree dive, was McClusky.[39] Just behind him was the rookie Richard Jaccard, who was so nervous that he initially lowered his landing gear rather than opening his dive flaps.[40] He was followed by Bill Pittman, who was also seeing his first action. Just after he pushed over, his radioman-gunner, Floyd Adkins, was horrified to see the twin .30-caliber machine guns come loose from their rack and begin to fall away from the plane. Normally, the guns, which weighed about 175 pounds, took three men to lift into place. Now the average-sized Adkins, who was on his back because of the dive, had to steady the guns as the aircraft plunged toward the *Kaga*.[41]

Dick Best, leading Bombing Six, also prepared to dive on the *Kaga*. He had just opened his dive flaps when McClusky and his squadron, which had been cruising at a higher altitude, came pouring in. Best realized that both squadrons were about to attack the same carrier, so he broke away, hoping that his men would follow. Only two joined him. The rest, now a total of twenty-six planes, sped after McClusky.[42]

Most of the *Kaga*'s crew were still unaware of what was about to hit them. Yoshino and Maeda had seen the dive bombers, but many others were below deck. In the hangars, the last of the torpedo planes were still being rearmed. And in the ready rooms, the pilots were making last-minute preparations for their strike on the

American carrier. Ensign Yuji Akamatsu, for example, was on his way to his ready room just before the attack began. The torpedo pilot Lieutenant Takayoshi Morinaga was also waiting for orders to launch.[43]

Because the Dauntless descended from such a high altitude, only one kind of gun aboard the *Kaga* was any use against it. This was the Type 89, a 5-inch gun that fired fourteen rounds per minute. Once raised, all sixteen of these barrels began sending their 50-pound shells into the sky.[44] Though this may sound impressive, there was only time for each to fire a few rounds.[45] McClusky recalled that the antiaircraft fire did not start until he was about halfway down; some pilots did not notice any at all.[46] The American attack had taken the *Kaga* effectively unawares. The best that its gunners could hope for now was a lucky hit or to put the enemy pilots off their aim.

After diving for about forty seconds, McClusky released his payload at 1,800 feet: one 500-pound bomb and two 100 pounders.[47] Shortly afterward, his two wingmen did the same. Jimmy Thach, who was busy grappling with Zeros in the sky above, turned to look at a "glint in the sun" and saw the plunging Dauntlesses with the light reflecting off their wings. To him they "looked like a beautiful silver waterfall."[48]

On the *Kaga* there was only terror. The planes screamed as they descended, a sound that became increasingly shrill. Sesu Mitoya, the communications officer, stood on the flight deck near the tower. Hearing the noise, he looked up: "Tiny black specks detached themselves from the planes," he said, and "the specks grew larger." Like Fuchida on the *Akagi*, Mitoya was able to watch these devices descend. "Quickly I dove to the flight deck," he recalled.

McClusky, Jaccard, and Pittman all pulled up within seconds of each other. This was in many ways their most dangerous moment. They were now in easy range of antiaircraft fire both from the *Kaga* and from the supporting ships of the *Kido Butai*. Worse, they were at sea level, the altitude that was filled with Zeros. Some of the Zeros turned their attention to the dive bombers, while others continued their butchery of Torpedo Three, either because they did not see the new arrivals or because they considered the Devastators worthier prey.

McClusky brought his plane down close to the waves and looked at the array of ships standing between him and the open sea. He picked a gap and went for it at top speed. So far, the Zeros had left him alone. Pittman, on the other hand, already had someone on his tail. He swore it was a [German] "Messerschmidt 109-F," though it couldn't have been anything other than a Zero. His gunner, Adkins, still had the 175-pound machine gun in his lap. Adkins heaved it onto the fuselage and, holding a barrel in one hand and the back of the gun with the other, waited for the Zero to swing past. When it did, he let off a burst and sent it into the sea.[49]

All the bombs that McClusky, Pittman, and Jaccard dropped fell wide, though not by much. Kleiss, who had a somewhat jaundiced view of McClusky's dive-bombing skills, said very wide. Dickinson, by contrast, wrote that they "grabbed at [the *Kaga*] like an ice man's tongs."[50] McClusky seems to have missed by only 10 yards or so. At any rate, the first bombs were close enough to wound men aboard the ship—Maeda was hit in the thigh by shrapnel—and to shower the bridge with splinters.[51]

The next blow was more accurate. It was the veteran Earl Gallaher performing what he later considered a "perfect dive," plunging downwind on the carrier with the sun at his back. Observing the previous misses, Gallaher adjusted his aim. He came down, as he recalled, "as low as [he] dared" before releasing his ordnance.[52] Then Gallaher did the very thing he always warned his men not to do: he stood his plane on its tail so that he could observe his handiwork. His 500-pound bomb struck a Zero on the flight deck, completely demolishing it, and penetrated into the hangar deck, where it detonated.[53] The two smaller incendiary bombs exploded among some fuel tanks toward the rear of the ship. "God damn," his gunner exclaimed, "That was a beauty Cap'n."[54]

For Gallaher, this was a particularly poignant moment. It was revenge for his fellow Scouting Six pilot Johnny Vogt, who had been shot down over Pearl Harbor. It was revenge for the destruction wrought on the battleship USS *Arizona* that day, the aftermath of which Gallaher had witnessed and would never forget. "*Arizona*," he said to himself as his bomb struck home, "I remember you."[55]

Mitoya still lay on the flight deck, near the tower. Lieutenant Morinaga was topside as well, farther aft, with a group of ten or so crewmen. He ducked and covered his ears. The blast knocked him over; he was one of only three of the group who survived.[56] Commander Yamazaki Torao met the grisliest fate of all. Running toward the bridge when the blast went off, he was torn to pieces.[57] Even those below deck were affected. Ensign Akamatsu, who was on his way to the pilots' ready room, blacked out from the shock of the explosions.[58]

Just behind Gallaher came Ensign Reid Stone. His bomb missed. Next in line was Ensign John Quincy Roberts, who had sworn he would fly his bomb into the enemy carrier himself if necessary. In the course of his dive, however, his aircraft was hit by antiaircraft fire and plunged into the sea. He either missed or did not release his bomb. Of all three air groups, his was the only Dauntless shot down prior to completing its attack that morning. Both pilot and gunner were killed outright.[59]

Meanwhile, Dick Best's three planes were heading full speed for the *Akagi* at about 14,000 feet. His gunner, Murray, rotated his seat backward to resume his watch for enemy fighters.[60] He could see none, perhaps because the Dauntlesses were hidden by clouds or, more likely, because the combat air patrol was distracted slaughtering Torpedo Three.[61] Nobody on the Japanese flagship saw Best approach either, so transfixed were they by the attack on their neighbor. Civilian cameraman Teiichi Makishima was emblematic of the distraction: standing on the *Akagi*, he was filming the attack on the *Kaga*, oblivious to the imminent fate of his own ship.[62]

Now it was Kleiss's turn. He went through his check-off list for diving. First, he prepared his engine for the recovery: adjusting his fuel mixture and supercharger to accept the richer air at sea level. Then he prepared his engine for the stress of the dive: setting his propeller speed to "maximum" and closing his cowl flaps and oil cooler scoop. The final item on the list was the dive flaps. With his right hand he set their selector to the "open" position.[63] As the hydraulic pump opened the flaps above and beneath his wings, Kleiss took out his ephedrine spray, snorting it one nostril at a time. The drug cleared his nasal passages so that the rapid loss in pressure would not burst his eardrums. He stowed away the ephedrine and cracked open his canopy, so that if he crashed it would not jam shut. Then he rocked his wings from side to side, signaling that he was about to dive. Finally, pushing his control stick away, nosing his Dauntless toward the sea, he entered the dive. "Survive," he said to himself. "Survive."[64]

The rectangle of the *Kaga* was sweeping clockwise. The rear half of the ship was "in flames 50 feet high," which was probably the fire caused by the explosion of Gallaher's incendiaries among the fuel tanks. Yet the other half of the ship was untouched. Kleiss remembered that "the bow with a big red circle was intact."[65] It was an enormous emblem of the rising sun. He envisioned the position of the red sun in forty seconds and aimed at that point. Antiaircraft fire was more intense now, the black smoke blooming about the sky. "Survive," Kleiss repeated, the wind rough on his face.[66] He passed 10,000 feet, the red circle continuing to swing into position. His plane accelerated to 240 knots. His adjustments—the trim controls at his left elbow, the rudder pedals at his feet, the control stick—were minor. At 4,000 feet, he leaned forward, peering into the bombsight and reaching for the release lever by his left knee. He passed 2,500 feet, the recommended release point, but continued diving. He was so determined to secure a hit that he waited until he was at 1,500 feet. With his left hand he moved the release lever to "salvo," releasing his 500-pound general-purpose bomb. A second later, he released his two 100-pound incendiaries.[67] Then, he drew back the control stick and pulled up from his dive.

What Kleiss had dropped from his Dauntless was a metal container filled with 264 pounds of trinitrotoluene, also known as TNT. It was a cylindrical shape with an ogival nose and a four-finned tail. Looped through the nose was an arming wire. As the container fell away from the plane, the wire was withdrawn, activating a vane at the tip of the nose. The vane spun in the wind and immediately, because the speed exceeded 300 miles per hour, the gears on the vane sheered, causing the fuse to fully arm. Three seconds later it hit the deck of the *Kaga*. The upper portion of the fuse telescoped into the lower portion, forcing the firing pin into the primer. One-hundredth of a second later, after the container had entered the hangar, the primer set off the detonator, which then exploded the TNT. In an instant, the TNT was transformed into a hot gas. The gas expanded violently, sending out a shock wave in all directions.[68]

Recovering, Kleiss was so low that the ocean sprayed his windshield. Looking over his shoulder, he could see "an explosion in progress on the big red circle, or rather a big one and a little one of greater intensity."[69] The main bomb had hit the forward elevator and blown out all the windows on the bridge.[70] The conflagration merged with the one Gallaher had started, so that "the entire ship was a mass of flames 100 feet high."[71] Mitoya, standing up from the deck, ran up the stairs to the bridge. There, at the map table, was Captain Jisaku Okada, obviously in shock, standing "half-dazed, like a man in a dream." Another man, the fire control officer, reported that fire was spreading through the ship. "Unless we abandon ship now," he said, "she will take us down with her." "The Captain shook his head vaguely," remembered Mitoya. Then he said, "I will remain with my ship."[72] Mitoya thought something should be done. He went below deck looking for a phone to call the engine room for a damage report. As he went down the stairs, he heard the scream of more Dauntlesses.

Bearing down on the *Kaga* was James Dexter and his gunner, Don Hoff. Dexter had waited too long to dive and so had to compensate by angling steeper than 90 degrees. Anything not tied down began to rise out of the plane and drift away. Hoff lifted from his seat, straining against his lap belt, and watched appalled as the ammunition from his twin machine guns came out of their cans, "like two cobras rising in a basket." He was now forced to call out the altitude to Dexter through the microphone while frantically trying to jam the belts of ammunition back into their cans. Then Dexter released his bomb and yanked back on the control stick to clear the water. Hoff, who blacked out for a moment when recovering from the dive, regained consciousness in time to watch the resulting explosion.[73] It completely obliterated the bridge, killing Captain Okada and all others on it.[74]

It was only after coming out of his dive that Kleiss saw his first Zero of the day. The fighter made a pass at him, but Kleiss was too quick. He turned his plane on its side and Snowden fired a burst from his machine guns. The Zero pilot broke away, either wounded or short on ammunition. Perhaps he had already expended himself on the unfortunate torpedo bombers. Kleiss now had to find a path through the Japanese supporting ships, which blazed away at him as he banked and swerved to avoid their fire.[75] Dexter, who had pulled up shortly after him, was also attacked by a Japanese fighter, perhaps the same one. In this case, too, the assailant left off after Hoff returned fire.[76] Dexter now headed for home.

The next division of Dauntlesses was already on its way down. Seconds after McClusky and Gallaher had commenced their dives, Dickinson had rocked his wings back and forth, signaling his men to begin the attack. He then put up his nose and, as the plane shuddered to a stall, opened his dive flaps. Once his nose tipped over, he led his division down on the carrier below. It was, as he later wrote, his "best dive ever." Hurtling toward the target, he could see the first bombs strike even as Zeros were zooming down the runway. He knew the shape of the yellow deck and starboard-side tower from training: the *Kaga*. As he put it, the ship "symbolized that which we had trained ourselves to destroy."[77]

As he passed 12,000 feet, Dickinson could see all the other planes ahead of him. The nine plunging Dauntlesses were spaced about 1,000 feet apart. Dickinson approached the *Kaga* from the left side, slightly astern. "The target was utterly satisfying," he recalled. "The squadron's dive was perfect. This was the absolute. After this, I felt, anything would be anti-climax." Like Kleiss, he aimed at the red sun near the bow. Shortly before release, Dickinson peered into the telescopic bombsight. Carefully, he made adjustments to his flight path, to keep the bead of the sight just short of the sun. As he prepared to release, Dexter's bomb hit, causing the deck to ripple and curl open, revealing a large part of the hangar beneath. A few seconds after that, Dickinson himself released. He held his course for a moment—to avoid throwing the bomb—and then pulled up.

Like Gallaher, Dickinson defied regulations to watch the result of what he had done. Holding back on the stick, he stalled out abreast of the *Kaga* as the 500-pound bomb struck to the right of the island while his two 100 pounders exploded among parked planes on the forward flight deck. The destruction caused him to think of his own survival. He closed his diving flaps to gain speed and nosed down to escape the area. Two Zeros passed under his Dauntless, but to Dickinson's surprise, they chased off after other planes rather than firing at him. A third Zero did attempt to engage him, but Joseph F. DeLuca, his gunner, quickly fired back in response. The Zero broke away.[78]

No more than two minutes had passed since McClusky had pushed over. In roughly the same length of time, another seventeen Dauntlesses dived on the *Kaga*. It is unlikely that any further hits were scored.[79] One observer said that even as the attack was underway, "you couldn't see aft of the island structure because of the black smoke pouring from it . . . [as] flame and debris shot hundreds of feet into the air."[80] Thach, who was still watching out of the corner of his eye, later wrote that he "had never seen such superb dive-bombing." To him it appeared, somewhat optimistically, as if "almost every bomb hit." His main preoccupation at this point, though, was dodging the Zeros and protecting the torpedo bombers of Torpedo Three, who were still crawling toward the *Kido Butai*.[81]

The impact of the American attack on the *Kaga* was immediate and shattering. Within a few seconds the carrier had been transformed from a refuge into a tomb. The planes on deck were destroyed; orange flames and black smoke, as Mitoya recalled, were "belching out of their tails like chimneys." The deck itself, wood planks over a thin sheet of steel, was now "a crazy jumble of torn metal" ruined beyond repair. Mitoya wept with anger, sorrow, and frustration.[82]

The jubilation of the morning—the strike on Midway and the cutting down of the torpedo squadrons—had suddenly turned to despair. On the *Soryu*, the loudspeaker sounded an air raid, and the crew on deck switched from tracking Massey's progress to watching the *Kaga* belch smoke.[83] Below, the torpedo pilot Juzo Mori was eating rice balls in the ready room when he heard the musical warning. Some of the airmen ran topside, but he carried on with his meal, knowing that his plane wouldn't be ready to launch anytime soon. "Better to eat something now," he said to himself.[84] The fighter pilot, Kaname Harada, by contrast, was having his ammunition reloaded when the alarm sounded. He immediately jumped back into his Zero and began to take off.[85] On the *Hiryu*, officers and crews were mortified by the agony of the *Kaga*. "It was like a horrible dream in slow motion," the ship's navigator recalled, "to see such a great carrier done in this easily."[86]

On the *Akagi*, Kiyoto Furuta was outside cooling off after his spell helping to load planes in the hangar. Seeing the bombs hit the *Kaga*, he thought to himself, "Oh my God," and then went for the nearest lavatory. He expected to be sent on a counterstrike and needed to urinate.[87] Another observer on the Japanese flagship remarked, simply, "She is beaten at last."[88] What these men did not know was that their own ordeal was about to begin.

✪

SUDDENLY A LOOKOUT ON the *Soryu* shouted, "Enemy dive-bombers—hole in the clouds."[89] Unlike the other two squadrons, Bombing Three from the *Yorktown* was spotted while approaching at altitude. It was only a matter of seconds, though, before the squadron commander, Max Leslie, pushed over. He himself had no bomb, having accidentally dropped it in the ocean, but he wanted to dive anyway to lead his men in the attack. Leslie and his squadron plunged into what he later described, in his after-action report, as a "veritable ring of flame" thrown up by the carrier's antiaircraft guns.[90] Another observer said the gun-fire looked like "light bulbs blinking all around the edge" of the Japanese flight deck.[91] But while the *Soryu* engaged the attackers coming from the right, those diving from the left and from the rear of the ship had not yet been seen.[92] Harada was now in the air, but it was too late to stop the Dauntlesses. "They fell like stones," he recalled, "straight for the carriers below. They flashed past us. There was no way to intercept them."[93]

At the front of the dive was Lefty Holmberg, the gunfire strik-ing his plane "like rocks on a tin roof."[94] Though he was a rookie, he was the first Dauntless pilot to actually release over the *Soryu*. His bomb landed right in the middle of the flight deck, just ahead of the forward elevator, and exploded in the hangar below. The Japanese planes spotted to the rear immediately erupted, as one ob-server put it, "into sheets of flame," and a fighter, which was in the middle of taking off, was blown over the side of the carrier. One second later, a third bomb struck the deck between the two aft elevators. The shock of the explosions caused the *Soryu*'s turbines to stop momentarily. Leslie's group's attack had lasted about three minutes in all. It was 1028.[95]

The blast from the first bomb knocked over the ship's execu-tive officer, Hisashi Ohara. Ohara was on the bridge and returned to his feet with relief; it felt like nothing more than a steambath. Other men, however, rushed to cover his face with towels. He had been badly burned. The gunnery commander, Ryoichi Kanao, was also burned, especially on his hands, which felt like they had been skinned. Ohara and Kanao were the lucky ones, however, because almost everybody else nearby had been killed outright. The real impact was felt below, where the bomb detonated about 40 feet from Juzo Mori. Jets of flame shot into the ready room where he was eating. He was forced to run for his life.[96]

At sea level, it was now swarming not only with American torpedo planes, and Zeros in hot pursuit, but also with Daunt-lesses trying to make their escape. Lew Hopkins was attacked by a Zero as he pulled out and hugged the water as closely as he could.

His gunner encouraged him, somewhat redundantly, to "get the hell out of here."[97] Similar conversations were happening across the melee. The Japanese antiaircraft gunners had also woken up. Under fire from a Japanese destroyer, Dickinson pulled up and then ducked down to the water after each shot in order to put the gunner off his aim. Luckily for Dickinson, the Zeros were still primarily focused on Torpedo Three. He saw one of them pass to his right and draw ahead, "stalking" a group of Devastators that were crossing his course.[98] Dickinson aimed at one of them but then hesitated. "If I miss him," he thought, "he'll be alive and awfully mad at me." But the temptation was too great. Dickinson fired a solid burst and caught him: the Zero spun out of control and crashed into the water.

Meanwhile, Dick Best's three planes had reached the *Akagi* undetected at 14,000 feet.[99] He had to slow his Dauntless down enough to open the dive flaps. In the back seat, James Murray once again rotated forward, preparing to call out the altitude. Best now pushed over into a steep dive, at 70 degrees, with Edwin Kroeger and Fred Weber trailing him on either side. The "V" formation was less accurate than diving in column, but it maximized the element of surprise. Below, Murray could see fighters launching from what looked like a "dirty yellow deck" dominated by a large red "meatball." Like other Americans that day, his mind went back to Pearl Harbor, and he wondered whether "the Japanese pilots ever thought this could ever happen to them on their ships."[100]

After a few seconds, they were spotted. A lookout on the *Akagi* shouted the warning: "Helldivers!" Fuchida looked up, just as Yoshino had two minutes before, and saw three black planes diving toward him. Once again, the Japanese antiaircraft fire was ineffective. Only a few rounds came toward Murray. He watched them pass over and beyond his port wing. He called out the altitude in 1,000-foot increments as they descended so that Best could concentrate on lining up the target. When they passed 2,000 feet, Murray switched to 100-foot increments. All three planes released their bombs more or less simultaneously somewhere between

2,000 and 1,500 feet.[101] Fuchida saw the bombs falling toward the ship and crawled to cover.

As they pulled up, Murray was drawn into his seat by gravity. Looking down as the Dauntless passed over the *Akagi*, he could see the crew "scurrying" about. He immediately rotated his seat back again to face potential attacks from Zeros, but none appeared. Nearby, Murray and Best could see two carriers burning, the *Kaga* and the *Soryu*. Below them, they saw Torpedo Three—which was still, as Best recalled, "in tight formation," making its slow approach—under heavy antiaircraft fire and being attacked by a "covey" of Zeros. Murray fired at one of them, causing the enemy pilot to veer off out of sight.[102]

Fuchida heard the scream of the dive bombers as they descended. Then came the crump of the first bomb penetrating the flight deck, followed by "a blinding flash." Almost immediately afterward there was "a second explosion, much louder than the first."[103] One observer saw "the orange-colored flash of a bomb" on the deck of the *Akagi*, followed by "an explosion at the midship waterline [that] seemed to open the bowels of the ship in a rolling, greenish-yellow ball of flame."[104] Fuchida felt a "weird blast" of warm air and then another, though less violent, shock. He got on his feet and looked up, but the sky was empty. The *Akagi* antiaircraft batteries, which had hardly fired, were silent. There was nothing more to shoot at. Best and his two wingmen were already on their way home.

Only one of the three bombs actually hit the *Akagi*, but the other two were very near misses, and one of them had produced the second, milder shock wave that rocked Fuchida. At least he had some warning. Those below had none. The unfortunate Kiyoto Furuta was still in the lavatory when he was jolted by a massive explosion on deck. Immediately afterward, he registered another one—actually one of the two near misses—toward the rear. Furuta finished his business and made for the flight deck. Petty Officer Kaname Shimoyama had a similar experience. He was in the torpedo-adjusting room below the flight deck and, while looking through a porthole, could see Torpedo Three making its run, but he had no idea that the *Akagi* was under attack from dive bombers.[105]

On deck, Fuchida was appalled by the destruction that the bomb had wrought. It had blown a huge hole just behind the middle elevator, which now "drooped," twisted completely out of shape "like molten glass," into the hangar below. Some of the planes on deck had been overturned by the blast. Others stood tail on end, "belching livid flames and jet-black smoke."[106] "Strewn here and there," wrote one Japanese historian, were "corpses with only torsos remaining, as well as scattered body parts."[107] The deck itself was wrecked. No aircraft would take off from it again. Like Mitoya, Fuchida was a hardened man, but he too was crying tears of despair.

On board the *Hiryu*, the only undamaged carrier, the Japanese watched in horror. Ensign Taisuke Maruyama, a pilot, was waiting in his ready room when he heard about the attack. Going up on deck, he was stricken: "I couldn't believe my eyes when I saw the terrible sight of our damaged ships."[108] His dismay was shared by the other pilots, who rushed to get a better view of the calamity that had just befallen the *Kido Butai*. On the bridge of the *Hiryu*, the ship's executive officer, Commander Kanoye, was almost struck dumb. "What will become of us?" he wondered softly.[109]

★

THE JAPANESE CARRIERS DIED one of two deaths that morning. The attack on the *Akagi* was simultaneous and brief: three planes diving together and retreating together. The attacks on the *Kaga* and the *Soryu*, however, were sequential and drawn out: many planes diving in a long column, each contributing to the mayhem, if not the murder, of the target. What the *Soryu* endured lasted about three minutes; the attack on the *Kaga* was about twice that long.

The Dauntless pilots accomplished this violence with skill, delivering not so much a bomb as what was effectively a guided missile. Twenty-seven pilots attacked the *Kaga*, and four scored hits. Three attacked the *Akagi*, and one scored a hit. Nine attacked the

Soryu, with three scoring hits. Together this amounted to an average success rate of 21 percent. One in five bombs struck home.

All the pilots who scored direct hits on the *Kido Butai* that morning had joined the US Navy before the war: Dick Best, Earl Gallaher, Dusty Kleiss, James Dexter, Clarence Dickinson, Lefty Holmberg, Harold Bottomley, and DeWitt Shumway.[110] All but one (Dexter) had graduated from the United States Naval Academy. All but one (Holmberg) were combat veterans. Lew Hopkins was one of those who missed. "It was the seasoned veterans," he recalled, "who did most of the damage against the Japanese carriers at Midway."[111] Dusty Kleiss was emblematic of their experience and training. By the time he climbed into his Dauntless for take-off that morning, he had spent 826 hours in the cockpit. And what he did to the *Kaga*, he had already done eight times that year, to say nothing of his other training. Dive bombing was his trade and he was good at it.

Within minutes, the ocean had been radically transformed. It was now dominated by three funeral pyres, with the *Kaga*, the *Soryu*, and the *Akagi* all belching smoke. For those who witnessed it—be they the crews of the *Kido Butai* or the American pilots in the skies above—the sight was unforgettable. The Japanese could see that the *Kaga* was already beyond redemption, and the *Soryu*, probably, too. The *Akagi* appeared to be the least afflicted, because it had not been attacked by incendiaries. But deep down, its internal organs had already suffered terrible damage. It was obvious that the battle was going against the Japanese. It was a terrible moment for them. "The scene," Fuchida remembered, "was horrible to behold."[112] "It seemed unbelievable," wrote Mitoya. "In seconds our invincible carrier force had become shattered wrecks."[113] Kleiss, who was now circling wide above the Japanese fleet, saw things differently. To him, the three crippled carriers "were beautiful sights."[114]

PART III

AFTER

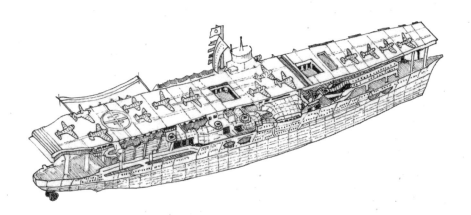

6

THE INFERNO

THOUGH NEITHER THE AMERICANS NOR THE JAPANESE KNEW IT yet, the Battle of Midway had already been decided. The fires that Wade McClusky's and Max Leslie's bombers started would be quenched only by the waters of the Pacific as the Japanese carriers sank. Over the next few hours, their crews fought the inevitable with the courage of desperation, but the Japanese fleet's battle against the three elements of air, fire, and water ended in failure and mass death. The arrival of the Dauntlesses had proved decisive. Their silver waterfall brought down an inferno that soon consumed most of the *Kido Butai*.

✪

INSIDE THE CARRIERS' HANGARS there was plenty to burn. The aircraft themselves were fully fueled (one Kate alone held about 180 gallons). But the blast had also broken the fuel lines. These broken lines steadily pumped fuel onto the hangar deck. Without ventilation, the fumes and the unsecured ordnance lying around created a potent fuel-air bomb. Ammunition, as one Japanese explosive expert wrote, "is an organic creature which, however we make it, insists always upon his own independence, betraying sometimes our selfish expectations."[1] The bombs and torpedoes piled up across the hangar decks of the *Kido Butai* had been assembled with a view to attacking the Americans; now they were about to demonstrate a mind of their own.

Ensign Haruo Yoshino, who was on the *Kaga* outside the pilots' ready room with several other men, was knocked unconscious by the blast of the first bombs. "When I came to my senses and looked around," he remembered, "everyone who was there just a moment ago had disappeared. Only a fellow one term junior to me and I remained there."[2] The others had been blown into the sea.

Lieutenant Yoshio Kunisada was also near the hangar. He had been making his way down a stairwell, leading a group of volunteers to help fight the fire, when a blast knocked him over. The lights went out. "I'm hit," said one of the men. Kunisada switched on his flashlight. He found the injured sailor, his foot turned at a strange angle. Kunisada gathered him up and began dragging him to a side room when there was a stronger blast, likely the result of the lethal fuel-air mixture. Like Yoshino, Kunisada was also knocked out.[3]

To escape the blaze, Yoshino and his companion continued on the walkway along the side of the ship. It brought them to a deck untouched by fire, but it still felt unsafe. Explosions could be heard from inside the hangar. For the past six months, the *Kaga* had been Yoshino's home. Now he wanted nothing more than to escape.[4]

Sesu Mitoya had been below deck when the secondary explosions began. He came rushing up the stairs to receive orders from the bridge. Climbing into the sunlight, he was shocked by what he saw: "There was no bridge. A direct hit had smashed the ship's nerve center." From the devastation it was apparent that the captain was dead and so were many of Mitoya's friends. "The *Kaga* was an inferno," Mitoya remembered, "with scorched, blackened men staggering about in helpless confusion."[5]

Ensign Takeshi Maeda was helped by a comrade to reach the rescue boat staging area near the *Kaga*'s stern. There he lay down to ease the pain from his wounds, feeling hungry because he hadn't eaten since breakfast. He was joined in the stern by others who were fleeing the fires. Through his shoulder blades it seemed as though he could feel the ship coming apart. The explosions caused "sudden jerks." Then came the most ominous sound of all. Silence. The engines had stopped.[6]

The *Soryu* was in a similar situation. One bomb had penetrated as far as the lower hangar deck, where it caused huge casualties among the maintenance crews. In the engine rooms below, the blast blew fire through the ventilation ducts.[7]

Down in the starboard engine room, the men who tended to the boiler fires found themselves immediately trapped, because the bolts on the hatches had melted together. One survivor remembered that "heat and smoke were everywhere." The men tried to cool themselves with water from the bilges, but that, too, had become hot. Some passed out; others went mad.[8]

On the bridge, Captain Ryusaku Yanagimoto found that all voice tubes, telephones, and engine telegraphs were out of action. He was unable to communicate with his staff, whether to receive information or to give orders; he had become a spectator aboard his own ship. His deputy, Commander Hisashi Ohara, was severely burned but insisted on setting up a new command on a lower deck. When Ohara ventured out, however, he found that it was no use— it was still impossible to raise other stations on the ship. Ohara descended to the flight deck, where he fainted with exhaustion.[9]

Senior Airplane Maintenance Officer Motoki Shigeo had been on the flight deck when the *Soryu* was hit. The second bomb knocked him down and he found himself surrounded by flames. Using a rope, he tried to climb down to an antiaircraft gun, but he lost his grip and fell about 10 feet, hurting his hip. Eventually he made his way to a lower deck, and, at this precise moment, there was a secondary explosion. "If I had remained where I was," he said many years later, "I would have been killed immediately."[10]

This was the start of a series of explosions, lasting several minutes, similar to what happened on the *Kaga*. Juzo Mori, who had finally escaped his ready room, arrived on the flight deck just in time to be caught by the blasts. "Pieces of airplane," he recalled, "were flying through the air." There was a "wall of flames rushing towards" him. Only a sudden change in the wind saved his life. Two more "thunderous explosions" from the hangar followed. Men were hosing the fire with seawater but it was little use.[11] Other crew members who had made it topside, such as Commander Ohara, were blown into the sea.[12]

The blast may have saved Ohara's life. The water revived him and, for the moment, separated him from the fire. Dozens of men were already in the ocean with him. In the distance he spied the blazing *Kaga*, the most afflicted of the three carriers, sending up black smoke. His moment of reflection was interrupted by a rope from the forward anchor deck. Remaining members of the crew were hauling men back to the ship even as the fire worsened. Groggy and badly burned, Ohara took their offer of the rope and then was laid out on his back on the ship. He overheard the gunnery officer order a signal to be sent to the flagship: "The captain is dead, the executive officer is unconscious. What should we do?"[13] The *Akagi* gave no reply.

Superficially, the *Akagi* was in better condition than the *Kaga* or the *Soryu*. The ship had been hit by only one bomb. It had exploded in the middle of the upper hangar deck, causing considerable damage, but it seemed that the fire could be contained. The staff flag secretary, a certain Lieutenant Commander Nishibayashi, was sent below to investigate.

The immediate problem on the *Akagi* was one of command and control. Damage to the communications channels prevented Admiral Chuichi Nagumo from communicating externally.[14] His chief of staff, Ryunosuke Kusaka, urged him to transfer his flag to the cruiser *Nagara*. This was essential, he argued, so that the admiral could continue to direct the entire force. But Nagumo's reactions were sluggish, perhaps indicating some kind of shock. He gave what a witness described as a "half-hearted nod." Kusaka repeated his entreaties. "Sir," he explained, "most of our ships are still intact. You must command them." But Nagumo remained on the *Akagi*.[15]

The situation looked different to many of the crew, however. Teiichi Makishima, the civilian cameraman, stood up from where he had been lying on the flight deck and found that "the elevator was torn and the iron plate was bent like candy. From everywhere, yellow and red flames were rising." In the hangar deck he could see airplane debris and dismembered body parts—scattered hands and feet. "Among them," Makishima said, he "heard the moaning of the injured and the cry of the devil."[16]

Makishima ran below into the crew waiting room. Mitsuo Fuchida and others had gathered there. "*Soryu* was also killed," one of the officers said. No one responded. An injured mechanic was brought in, bleeding from his head and stomach. His face had turned a deep blue, and he was having trouble breathing. His groans of pain were the only noise in the room.

Below deck many were trapped. Without power, there was no light, and without light it was difficult to navigate, undo hatches, climb ladders, and move between compartments. Petty Officer Kaname Shimoyama, inside the torpedo adjusting room below the flight deck when Dick Best's bomb struck, said the room went pitch black. Some men lost their composure; the hangar was close by, and secondary explosions were strong and frequent. "I thought that our carrier," remembered Shimoyama, "would sink at any moment." But he listened to his group leader, who kept yelling, "Porthole, porthole." Shimoyama found the porthole on the bulkhead and began unscrewing the covering. It was impossible to go fast enough. "Even today," he said more than a half century later, "I can't forget the helpless feeling that I had during this moment."[17]

Compounding the confusion was the unpreparedness of the Japanese damage control systems.[18] The attack had come as a complete surprise, so there was no time to purge the fuel lines of gasoline. As on the *Kaga*, the broken lines on the *Akagi* pumped fuel onto the deck of the hangar, feeding the flames. Another problem on all three carriers was that explosions had damaged the emergency generators. Without power, the pumps could not work. It was like *The Rime of the Ancient Mariner*: there was water everywhere except where it was needed. The ships were in the middle of the Pacific Ocean, but there was no way of bringing the water to the flames.[19]

The command structure aboard the Japanese carriers was also not suited for damage control operations. Unlike American ships, which appointed a senior officer in charge, Japanese ships delegated damage control to relatively junior officers. This made prioritizing men and resources difficult in times of crisis.[20] Moreover, the Japanese preferred to train only a quarter of their crew in damage control techniques, whereas the Americans tended to incorporate everyone but the aviators. Either way, it was hard work. If the fires didn't kill you, there was the smoke. Later in the war, Americans used a special mask to breathe and sealed beam lights to see in smoky conditions. But this equipment also had its limitations. The breather only generated enough oxygen for forty-five minutes, and the sealed beam lights could only illuminate several feet. At Midway, the Japanese lacked both types of equipment. They were burned by the fire and blinded and choked by the smoke.[21]

A chain of induced explosions spread across the Akagi. Many now feared that the ship was about to sink. Captain Taijiro Aoki immediately ordered the forward magazines flooded to prevent them from exploding.[22]

Dusty Kleiss, about 5 miles from the Kido Butai, turned for one final look over his shoulder and saw the carriers "flaming like Kansas straw stacks." The fires on the Akagi were already shooting 300 feet high, and its steel was "red hot." Then, on the Kaga, Kleiss saw a "catastrophic explosion that scooped out the forward part of the carrier." Its huge elevator was thrown into the air. "Rockets of flame, pieces of steel bolted upwards to about three or four thousand feet," Kleiss said. It was like "a roman candle with fire shooting up into the air." The whole carrier was blanketed by smoke.[23] Clarence Dickinson witnessed the same scene. "I saw her blow up at the middle," he wrote, as "a ball of solid fire shot straight up"; the ball of fire "passed through the fleecy lower clouds" about 1,200 feet above the water, and even higher. Some of this was powered by gasoline, but Dickinson, who was writing before the full story was known, thought the explosions were primarily caused by "their own bombs parked below on the hangar decks in readiness for planes to be rearmed."[24]

By around 1030, Kleiss and the other *Enterprise* pilots had completed the first part of their dogleg toward Midway, a move designed to hide the fact that they were carrier-borne aircraft.[25] It was time to turn northeast for home.

The pilots were on edge: most were flying alone, their formation having been broken up by the attack, and they were still within range of the enemy air patrol. Their concerns were not unfounded. Soon after they had set their course, several Zeros appeared. McClusky was shot in the shoulder, but his rear-seat gunner, Walter Chochalousek, gunned down one Zero and chased away the other. Kleiss also took fire but managed to escape unharmed. Ahead, he noticed several of his squadron members, but when he tried to join them, they sped off, likely mistaking him for another Zero. He eased off on his fuel mixture, hoping to save as much as he could for the flight home. The *Enterprise*, if he could find it, was nearly 100 miles over the horizon.

Shortly after, another Zero assailed Kleiss, and John Snowden once again drove it off. "If I had ever made a wise decision in life," Kleiss later reflected, "it was picking John to be my rear-seat gunner."[26] For those flying alone, with only their gunner, at best, for company, it would be a long ride back to the carrier. History, Kleiss later wrote, "would not much care which of the victorious pilots made it back to base," but to those individuals, of course, it mattered intensely.[27] Nursing their fuel gauges, anxiously scanning the skies, and often coping with battle damage and severe injury, the Dauntless crews slogged on.

None of the survivors of Torpedo Three recall seeing the explosion on the *Kaga*, but that is unsurprising, as they were still fighting their way to the *Kido Butai*. The squadron was largely intact.[28] Its twelve planes now prepared to attack the *Hiryu*, which lay between the blazing *Soryu* to the north and the burning *Akagi* and *Kaga* to the south.[29] In accordance with doctrine, the squadron split to carry out an anvil attack. This subjected the enemy ship to attack from two sides, so that it would be vulnerable to a torpedo spread whichever way it turned. Patrick Hart's division went one way, and Lem Massey's went the other, all the while under constant antiaircraft bombardment and passes from the Zeros.

Soon Harry Corl had his elevator controls shot away and was gliding toward the water. He desperately needed to regain altitude. After releasing his "tin fish," Corl succeeded in keeping his nose up enough to remain airborne. Oil was leaking from his engine, and one of his temperature gauges was shot, but he managed to control the aircraft and rejoin the formation.[30]

Then, to the horror of the squadron, Massey's plane exploded in a ball of flame about a mile from the *Hiryu*.[31] "Look at the skipper," Corl shouted. Glancing to the left, Lloyd Childers saw Massey hit the water.[32] By this point the Japanese combat air patrol had swelled to forty-three Zeros, and the *Hiryu*'s antiaircraft batteries were firing "away with full ammo." Torpedo Three continued on regardless.[33]

Lieutenant Nagatomo Yasukuni was responsible for six antiaircraft guns along the starboard side of the *Hiryu*. From his position, he watched the Devastators closing in. When they were just under a half mile away, they released torpedoes. Each was 13 feet long, their black shapes running about 30 knots (34 miles per hour). One tumbled into the water at an angle that rendered it useless; another sped along the surface "like a high-speed boat." Three traveled at the correct depth, passing close to starboard. "During this time," Yasukuni said, "I was sweating, hands clenched, and watching." According to one American pilot, only five torpedoes were launched. Yasukuni remembered eleven, an impossible number. "For a while," he said, "I was reacting instinctively and shouting." He was directing fire, attempting to kill the torpedo planes before they killed him. One of the Devastators came straight for the deck, as if intending "to self-destruct into the ship," before lifting up and soaring past.[34]

Had Wally Short's bombers been present, the *Hiryu* might have been dispatched there and then—but Torpedo Three had made a crucial contribution to the battle. Without so much as scratching a single Japanese carrier, Massey's men held the attention of the Japanese combat air patrol. Their torpedo attack, however faulty the torpedoes, meant that the Dauntlesses approached their targets with no opposition and were able to retire with greater freedom. But this distraction came at a price. Of the original twelve planes of Torpedo Three, only those piloted by Harry Corl and Bill Esders managed to escape.

Corl and Esders headed for home, still under attack from anti-aircraft fire and Zeros for the next fifteen minutes or so.[35] Jimmy Thach and his Wildcats mounted a strong defense, but they, too, were overwhelmed. Each time a Zero was shot down, Thach made a note on his kneepad, careful to mark only those that were engulfed in "real red flames." "Then I realized this was sort of foolish," he recalled. "Why was I making marks on my kneepad when my kneepad wasn't coming back?"[36] By this stage of the battle, Thach was convinced that no one in his squadron would survive. At any moment, it could be his plane in red flames, twisting toward the sea.

Corl's rear-seat gunner, Childers, was struck with two bullets in the thigh when a Zero strafed their plane. "The dirty bastard shot me," he said to himself. The blood turned his khaki uniform black, but for the moment, his leg was numb.[37] Several Zeros continued to trail them for the next fifteen miles, and Childers fired at them all the while. Once he had spent his .30-caliber ammunition, he used his sidearm, a Colt .45. One by one the Zeros broke off. The last remaining pilot eventually drew alongside and gave Esders a chivalrous wave before turning to his carrier.[38]

The pressure also eased on Thach and his four remaining fighters. Suddenly, the Zeros were gone. Thach, Ram Dibb, and Brainerd Macomber withdrew from the target area. Macomber's Wildcat was badly damaged, and Thach's was leaking oil. Only Dibb's machine remained in good order. Unknown to Thach, two more of his pilots, Tom Cheek and Daniel Sheedy, were still airborne; they had set course for home separately. On the way out, Thach saw a damaged Devastator crawling along, then another, and took up protective station above them until they were completely out of danger. Then he, too, sped away for home.[39]

✪

IT SOON BECAME APPARENT that the *Kaga*, the *Soryu*, and the *Akagi* were severely if not fatally wounded. On the *Kaga*, Commander Takahisa Amagai was at the air command post, a platform above the flight deck. Not quite twenty minutes after the attack, the heat was so intense that he had to leave. He decided to go below deck to help fight the fires. Across the ship, explosions were still going off as fuel tanks burned and ordnance cooked off, sending men and debris into the water. Amagai couldn't make it to the hangar deck; the heat was too intense. One of those who did was Chief Warrant Officer Takayoshi Morinaga. Because none of the water mains were operational, he organized a chain of buckets from the lavatories. It was a pitiful scene. Lieutenant Kunisada, who had been trapped there since the largest secondary blast, was also on the hangar deck. "Maintenance Officer is here," he shouted. "All section men come here to me!" He gathered the nearby survivors, a total of eight men. Half were seriously wounded. One said they should kill themselves in the fire. Kunisada restrained him and kept everyone together. As the fire spread, he led the men to a ledge outside the ship.[40]

Another blast rocked the *Soryu*, this one the largest of the morning. It may have been caused by fire reaching the torpedo magazine, ordnance cooking off inside the hangar, or a combination of both.[41] The explosion sent a gust of fire below deck that killed many crewmen who had yet to escape. Inside the engine room, sailors continued wrestling with the melted hatch. Finally, it gave way, and they groped about for a route topside.[42]

Mori was still on the flight deck in a "state of shock." With the recent blast, a "screaming jet of hot steam" shot out from the middle of the ship. Men began to jump from the deck into the sea. It reminded Mori of the British carrier *Hermes*, which he had helped sink months ago. This morning it was his turn to watch the sea from aboard a lifeless ship, contemplating his chances in the water or with the fire. It seemed to him like "Karmic retribution."[43]

On the bridge of the *Soryu*, the situation was grave. The steering failed at 1043, and two minutes later, Captain Yanagimoto gave the fateful order: "Abandon ship."[44]

Mori made his way to the lifeboat deck under the bridge. A crowd was gathering there, but the lifeboat wouldn't lower; there was a problem with the crane. Men began to leap into the sea. Mori thought it was a distance of some 60 feet. In truth it was about half that far, but he was still afraid. Looking south, he saw "the *Kaga* and *Akagi* were also burning fiercely. The sea was completely calm and the two ships floated unmoving, each under a boiling vertical pillar of thick black smoke." Eventually he was one of only several men left. "Finally, I screwed up my courage," he remembered, "took a deep breath and jumped."[45]

Mori entered the water feet first. By the time he surfaced, the lifeboat had fallen. He set to work dragging the wounded aboard; many were disfigured by burns or unable to swim.[46] High above, Captain Yanagimoto was seen limping to the semaphore platform to the right of the bridge. From there, he called down encouragingly to the men in the water: "Long live the emperor!" Then he appeared to plunge into the flames and was lost from sight.[47] To some of those watching, it seemed as if he had been killed, but others assumed that he was looking for a way through the fire.

On the *Akagi*, the situation still seemed under relative control. The explosions were now intermittent, and the engines still had power. The situation did not seem right to Makishima, however, who was still in the crew waiting room, deliberating what to do. Suddenly, the ship convulsed, as if hit by another bomb. More wounded mechanics began to arrive. "The torpedoes and bombs in the hangar have begun to explode," one of them said. Smoke billowed into the room, and Makishima looked for a gas mask but couldn't find one. He stumbled into the corridor, trying to escape the smoke.[48]

Overhead, there came the roar of several Devastators. They had released their torpedoes on the *Hiryu* and were turning homeward. Captain Aoki thought they were flying too close and ordered evasive action, throwing over the helm. Two minutes later, when he tried to turn the rudder back, he found that it was jammed. The earlier near miss off the starboard side must have damaged it somehow. Then the intense heat ignited Zeros that were parked on the flight deck, adding to the confusion.[49] The high temperatures also caused "rivets from the steel plates . . . to pop out like they were bullets," injuring crewmen.[50] The flames began to spread toward the bridge.

On the bridge of the *Akagi*, Nagumo still hesitated. Possibly he was like Mori had been at the guardrail—afraid. Or it may have been a question of honor: he did not want to be seen to abandon his post. Captain Aoki intervened. "Admiral," he said, "I will take care of the ship. Please, we all implore you, shift your flag to *Nagara* and resume command of the force." This was easier said than done, because Commander Nishibayashi reported that all the passages below were on fire. The only way out of the bridge was to use a rope. If they could reach the anchor deck, the admiral's party would be picked up by a boat from the *Nagara*. There was clearly no time to waste. At 1046, thirteen minutes after Dick Best had struck the *Akagi*, Nagumo took his leave of Captain Aoki, climbed through the window, and slid down the rope. It was some 20 feet to the flight deck below.[51]

Captain Aoki, Fuchida, and several other men remained on the bridge. Aoki tried in vain to contact the engine room. His navigator attempted, also unsuccessfully, to regain rudder control. Very soon, the situation on the bridge deteriorated further. The "unchecked flames," Fuchida recalled, were "already licking at the bridge." Ominously, the mattress material strapped to the side of the island for protection against shrapnel was beginning to burn. The air officer turned to his most senior pilot. "Fuchida," he said, "we won't be able to stay on the bridge much longer. You'd better get to the anchor deck before it is too late."[52]

Nagumo's exit from the bridge had been difficult enough, but Fuchida's was even harder. The heat was more intense, and he was still weak from his operation. With the help of some sailors, Fuchida made it through the window and took hold of the rope, which was "already smouldering" from the heat. He made it to the gun deck and went for the ladder. It was "red hot," as was the deck underfoot. All around him, explosions were going off. Fuchida half jumped and was half blown by another blast from the hangar.

Either the fall or the explosion briefly knocked him out. When he came to, he was on the flight deck with two broken ankles.[53]

So far Admiral Isoroku Yamamoto and the senior staff of the Japanese force were unaware of the seriousness of the situation. Throughout the morning, Yamamoto busied himself by playing shogi, a Japanese variant of chess, with another officer. His orderly, Heijiro Omi, was struck by the contrast between this relaxed mood and the "nervous atmosphere" that had characterized the attack on Pearl Harbor. Just before 1030, fire was reported aboard the *Akagi*. Moments later the same was said of the *Kaga*. "Oh, did they do it again?" Yamamoto muttered, still facing the shogi board. Then he said, "Nagumo will return." Omi remembered Yamamoto saying the same thing at Pearl; it had been a prediction that Nagumo would not carry out a second attack. Now it seemed like Yamamoto believed another withdrawal would take place.[54] At 1050, a printed message conveyed the seriousness of the situation: "Fires are raging aboard the *Kaga, Soryu*, and *Akagi*."[55]

✪

"ALL OUR PLANES ARE taking off now for the purpose of destroying the enemy carriers." That was the message sent by Tamon Yamaguchi, captain of the *Hiryu*, to the *Kido Butai* at 1050.[56] The *Hiryu* was the last remaining operational carrier. It launched eighteen Japanese dive bombers, nicknamed "Vals," and six Zeros. It was a pitiful band compared to the armada that had filled the skies that morning, but these were veteran pilots, perhaps the most experienced dive bombers in the Pacific.[57] If anyone could even the odds, they could.

Shortly after launching the counterstrike, the *Hiryu* came close to its stricken sister ship the *Soryu*. Flames surged along the 746-foot deck, sending up an enormous pillar of smoke. "She looked like a giant daikon radish that had been sliced in two," said one sailor. "It was possible to see right through her to the other side." On the bridge of the *Hiryu*, Rear Admiral Yamaguchi was astonished by the extent of the damage. "Can we contact her?" he asked one of his staff officers. "I will try," the officer said, taking up his position beside the signal lamp. But Yamaguchi couldn't think of any advice, only exhortation. He said, "Try to save your carrier!" The message was flashed several times on the lamp. But the result was similar to the *Kaga*'s signal to the *Akagi* earlier that morning. There was no reply.[58]

★

MEN ABOARD THE BURNING carriers began to think of nothing but escape. Aboard the *Akagi* it was similar to the *Kaga*: aviation fuel was feeding the flames, making them impossible to fight. Water was useless; it was heavier than fuel, and so whenever it was sprayed onto the flames, it sank underneath them, accomplishing nothing, or worse, causing the blaze to spread. Makishima said that "watering the gasoline would only make the fire even bigger."[59] Foam was the only weapon of any use. It was light enough to rest above the fuel and thick enough to smother the fire, starving it of oxygen. But the centralized foam system had been broken by the explosions. When the engine went out, so did the lights and the pumps. The best that the crew could do was to set up portable hand pumps on the anchor deck to feed water through the ship, but this was hardly enough to make a difference. "Gradually," Maintenance Lieutenant Hiroshi Suzuki recalled, "the blaze began to spread and everything was on fire."[60]

Those who were not fighting the fires, which by now had reached the lower hangars, began to huddle on the anchor deck.[61] "All kinds of sailors were gathered there," Makishima remembered. "The faces of these sailors were squeezed out by astonishment and horror, and none of them had a human-like face." Explosions broke through the upper hangar deck into the lower hangar deck. One of the officers ordered the use of a fire extinguishing pump, but the pump didn't work. Several men had portable fire extinguishers, but they made little difference. One man with a fire extinguisher ran away. Seeing this, a warrant officer drew his sword. "Extinguish the fire!" shouted the officer. "Anyone who runs away will be cut down." The man returned to the group but was killed by the next explosion. Wielding his sword, the officer herded a group of sailors toward the fire. But a torpedo exploded, turning both the soldiers and the warrant officer into "fine dust." The fire sank from the lower hangar into the living quarters, causing more men to come spilling out, seeking refuge on the anchor deck. Explosions continued, engulfing the upper hangar and spreading into the lower hangar.

Makishima turned away from the fire and looked at the sea. The *Akagi* had stopped. A nearby destroyer was spraying water onto the ship, but its arc of water fell short. Drawing closer was a cutter approaching from the port side. Nagumo and his senior staff officers came through the crowd and waited at the railing. Several men carried Fuchida. "Hey, newspaper reporter," shouted Captain Chisato Morita. "Get the newspaper reporter on board." The order saved Makishima's life. The men echoed the command, and when they found Makishima, he was brought forward and ushered aboard the cutter. Fuchida, still being carried, collapsed as soon as he was lowered to his seat. Minoru Genda came and sat down beside Makishima. "I wish *Shokaku* and *Zuikaku* were here," Genda said to no one in particular, referring to other carriers. "I wish this hadn't happened." Makishima heard these comments despite all the noise around them as commands were issued to organize the ship and prepare for departure. "What a pitiful thing to say," Makishima thought. On his other side was Captain Morita. Morita looked silently at Genda and then said, in a voice loud enough for Nagumo to hear, "This will affect Japan's national luck." No one spoke for a moment. Finally, a junior officer broke the silence. "Come on, row," he said. "Let's get to *Nagara*."[62]

The sailors began to row, drawing the cutter away from the burning *Akagi*. Makishima found it hard to believe: the destruction of such a proud ship. He looked at the bridge rising above the flames. The bridge from which battles from the Indian Ocean to the Pacific had been won. The bridge from which the Z flag had flown during the Pearl Harbor attack. With each explosion, another "piece of red-burnt iron splattered" into the sea. "Nagumo raised his grey-haired head and stared at the burning bridge without blinking, but eventually he quietly lowered his head," Makishima later wrote. He thought Nagumo might be praying. At the oars, a sailor kept repeating, "I'm sorry, I'm sorry," crying to himself as he rowed. On the *Akagi*, one of the high-angle guns continued to fire, flashing through the smoke. "There are sailors," thought Makishima, "who are fighting without leaving their station until the end."[63] But there were no American planes overhead. It was a wasted effort, an attack on empty sky.

Meanwhile, the heat on the bridge of the *Akagi* had become overpowering. Taking the same route as Nagumo and Fuchida had before them, Captain Aoki and his men managed to lower themselves to the flight deck. There they hovered near the bow, pondering their options. For now they could go neither forward nor backward. They were dying for a smoke, but there were only two cigarettes to go around. These were then shared between the men, everybody taking snatched puffs.[64]

At 1135, the *Akagi* was convulsed by another big explosion in the hangar.[65] The blast drove Aoki from the flight deck to the hangar deck.[66] His crew now split into two groups. One headed for the bow. The other, among them the dive-bomber pilot Kiyoto Furuta, headed for the stern. There Captain Aoki ordered all to gather around. He told the men that the pilots had to be saved and brought back to Japan, because they took so long to train. On a new carrier, he continued, they could fly again soon. If the other crew members expressed any objections to this hierarchy, none have been recorded. The order of departure mattered because there was only one boat available. It was lowered, and forty men, including the lucky Furuta, were transferred to a nearby destroyer. As the boat drew away, he could see that both the *Kaga* and the *Akagi* were completely ablaze.[67]

On the *Kaga* there were no more massive blasts, but the fires were spreading uncontrollably, setting off further secondary explosions. Commander Amagai did his best to direct damage control operations from his post on the starboard deck. As yet, there was still hope that the ship could be saved. Her engines were intact, and she was still moving. Many crewmen were already in the water, however, either because they had been blown overboard by the blasts or because they had jumped to escape the flames.[68]

One of them was Ensign Maeda, still suffering from the wound to his thigh incurred during the attack itself. He was too weak to jump, so a crewman had thrown him into the ocean. Yoshino, who was unhurt, jumped over the side of the carrier. From his vantage point in the water, he could see men gathering in the stern section. The ship itself was clearly done for. The enclosed hangar had broken open, and Yoshino could see inside, where it "was bright red" and "the series of explosions were still going on."[69]

✪

WHILE THE JAPANESE CARRIERS burned, the American aviators had a confusion of their own to deal with, concerning navigation. All morning, Stanhope Ring and the *Hornet* Air Group had flown westward, overshooting the Japanese fleet by a considerable distance. They had already lost their torpedo planes when John Waldron broke south to chart his own course to the *Kido Butai*. By 0915 the rest of the planes had begun turning back, individually or in small groups. By 0940 all were heading east, but none were certain about where to find the *Hornet*. At 1000 one of the fighters spotted the wake of the American ships on the horizon, but he misidentified them as Japanese. Keeping away, these planes began ditching in the sea. Ring himself managed to find his way back, landing aboard the *Hornet* with his bomb still underneath his Dauntless.

Historians have long speculated on the reason for Ring's course. Richard Nowatzki, an enlisted man aboard the *Hornet*, had overheard the moment that Ring reported to Captain Pete Mitscher after another mission in which he had returned with his bomb. "At our age," Ring said by way of explanation for his failure to press home his attack, "putting that plane in a dive with that bomb is like hitting yourself in the head with a baseball bat." Spotting Nowatzki, Mitscher had taken Ring outside to continue the conversation.[70] It was a brief exchange, but enough to reveal Ring's ambivalence about dive bombing and his keen sense of its physical costs. Unsubstantiated rumors about the air group commander continued to circulate for some time after the battle.[71]

Whether or not Ring's detour was intentional, navigation was a difficult skill. Many pilots who found the *Kido Butai* failed to return. Some took the wrong heading and were forced to set down in the water. If they were lucky, they would be rescued by patrols from Midway in the coming days. But others were never seen again.

Even if they picked the right heading, there was danger. Kleiss and Snowden traveled alone for miles. Then, at about 1130, Kleiss spotted Japanese aircraft. It was the *Hiryu*'s strike force, led by Lieutenant Michio Kobayashi, on its way to attack the American carriers. Kleiss counted eighteen Val dive bombers and six Zeros. They had also spotted him. Three Zeros peeled off to attack Kleiss. To his surprise and immense relief, however, they soon turned back, apparently to rejoin their formation.[72]

Kleiss's good fortune was Charlie Ware's bad luck. Ware was with another three Dauntlesses, a larger and more enticing target. But, as the Zeros came in, Ware's formation met them with accurate fire. The Japanese were forced to break off their runs early, and because Ware brought his group down close to the water, they were unable to attack the unprotected undersides of the American dive bombers. It was a textbook demonstration of the defensive capacities of the Dauntless. Two Zeros were so badly damaged that they were forced to head back to the *Hiryu*. The remaining four broke off and returned to escort Kobayashi's dive bombers. Sadly, only one member of Ware's group found his way home; the rest, including the intrepid Ware himself, were presumed lost at sea.[73]

A quarter of an hour later, Kleiss finally found Task Force 16. He touched down with 3 gallons to spare. McClusky could have insisted, as Ring had, on landing first, but despite his injuries and shortage of fuel, the commander of the *Enterprise* Air Group waited until all his pilots had safely touched down.[74] Only then did he begin his approach to the carrier. His plane had been hit no fewer than fifty-five times.[75] With the exception of Lew Hopkins, who returned "without a single scratch or hole," most of the aircraft had been damaged, some very badly. The maintenance crews greeted them with acclamation.[76] An armorer ducked under Kleiss's plane and held up the three arming wires in triumph to show that the bombs had been armed to detonate. Without this, all the heroics would have been for naught. Kleiss and Snowden had done their jobs, but so, too, had the armorers and the maintenance men.

✪

SO FAR, THE AMERICAN carriers had been unmolested, but that was about to change. Two minutes after Kleiss climbed out of his cockpit on the *Enterprise*, the *Yorktown* radar spotted an unidentified formation of aircraft. The formation was also climbing—something friendly aircraft would never do. Kobayashi's dive bombers had arrived.[77]

Radar meant that the Americans could prepare. They stopped fueling operations and drained the lines, charging them with carbon dioxide at 20 pounds of pressure. Gasoline tank compartments, which had already been filled with CO_2, were sealed and secured. There was also an auxiliary tank of 8,000 gallons of aviation fuel that was pushed overboard. Unlike the Japanese carriers, the *Yorktown* would not burn easily.

"Set material condition affirm," announced the loudspeaker aboard the *Yorktown*, meaning "assume the highest water-tight integrity of the ship." It was about 1220. Musician Second Class Stanford Linzey looked to make sure the nearby door was shut. Already he was wearing his flashproof clothing, a thick overshirt and trousers. He was also wearing a set of headphones. His job was to relay messages from the officer at Damage Control Central in the bottom of the ship to the leader of a nearby repair party. Another order came over the loudspeaker: "All hands lie down on deck." Linzey lay down on the deck. He was amidships in the galley compartment, between the keel and the flight deck, at about the waterline. If there was a torpedo attack, this is where it was likely to detonate. Bombs from dive bombers could also penetrate this far. Last month, in fact, that very thing had happened in the Battle of the Coral Sea, immediately killing forty-five men in the compartment next to him. Linzey did his best to think of other things—to listen to his headphones or to think of his wife in San Diego.[78]

Far above, the *Yorktown* Wildcats intercepted the Japanese strike group, and within minutes, they managed to shoot down eleven Vals and three Zeros. Antiaircraft fire—from the carrier and its destroyer and cruiser screen—clipped the wings of two more Vals. It was an exemplary defense, but five Vals still managed to get through.[79]

"Air Department, take cover," said the loudspeaker aboard the *Yorktown*. "Gunnery Department, take cover." Through the floor of the ship, Linzey could feel the engines revving. The *Yorktown* was building speed: a fast target was a difficult target. "Stand by for air attack." Linzey clenched his hands. There was the "plink, plink, plink" of the time-fused bombs as they passed through each deck before detonating.[80] Two explosions went off somewhere above Linzey; the ship lurched. "The whining of engines stopped," Linzey recalled. The *Yorktown* was dead in the water. Another bomb detonated, this time on the deck below him. Listening for reports to relay, Linzey had "an ominous and foreboding feeling."[81]

Executive Officer Dixie Kiefer organized a response to the damage. There had been three direct hits by 551-pound bombs. One punctured the flight deck, detonating inside the hangar and starting a fire. One fell inside the smokestack, snuffing out most of the boiler fires. And one crashed down into the fourth deck, the one below Linzey, starting another fire. Kiefer appointed Water Tenderman Charles Kleinsmith to lead a team to the engine room to restore power. Other teams were dispatched to fight the fires and to repair the flight deck. In contrast to the Japanese, the Americans were able to contain the fires and make repairs. By 1340 the *Yorktown* was underway again with steam and electric power. More importantly, it was able to launch aircraft. At the Battle of the Coral Sea, the *Yorktown* had been hit and still managed to survive. It looked like that would happen once again.[82]

The action had been witnessed not merely by the rest of Task Force 17 but also by much of Task Force 16, which was about

10 miles off. On the *Enterprise*, the ordnance man, Alvin Kernan, watched the display "as if it were a movie."[83]

✪

ON REACHING THE *NAGARA*, Nagumo began to plan a counter-strike from the *Hiryu* with two battleships, three cruisers, and five destroyers. A report arrived that the American fleet was 90 miles away. All remaining surface ships, Nagumo decided, would charge the Americans. His battleships and cruisers were manned by some of the best gun crews in the world, and they would be less vulnerable to dive bombing than his carriers had been. There was also doctrine: Nagumo wanted to impale the enemy even as he was impaled.[84]

But at 1220, Yamamoto sent orders to the fleet. His plan was to consolidate his forces northwest of Midway and then continue the battle. Ships would be drawn from the attack on the Aleutian Islands and the Midway invasion force, and Yamamoto himself would continue charging forward to join with the *Kido Butai*. Twenty minutes later, however, a Japanese search plane sighted an American force that was clearly withdrawing. The distance between the American and Japanese fleets was increasing. The surface action in which Nagumo had placed his hopes for revenge was no longer feasible.[85]

At about this time the Japanese destroyer *Arashi* picked up Ensign Wesley Osmus, a Devastator pilot who had been shot down while attacking the *Hiryu*. Under brutal interrogation, Osmus revealed details of the American fleet. There were actually three American carriers, Osmus said, not just one, and they were operating in two separate task forces. This information reached Admiral Yamaguchi at 1300.[86] It was now clear to him, and to Nagumo, that the Americans enjoyed an overwhelming superiority in carriers and aircraft.

Meanwhile, the survivors from the *Soryu* realized that their beloved captain was not among them. They thought he must have remained on the bridge of the doomed carrier in order to go down with the ship. A certain Petty Officer Abe, a navy wrestling champion, was nominated to go back on board. He was to rescue the captain, by force if necessary. On reaching the bridge, Abe saw Yanagimoto standing completely still, sword in hand, facing the bow. "Captain," Abe announced, "I have come on behalf of all your men to take you to safety." "They are waiting for you," he continued. "Please come with me to the destroyer, Sir." Yanagimoto ignored Abe. The wrestler took a step toward his captain, but seeing that he was determined to stay, backed off. Tears came to Abe's eyes and he left the bridge. Behind him, he could hear the captain singing "Kimigayo," the Japanese national anthem.[87]

At 1330, the *Hiryu* launched its second strike, a force of torpedo bombers nicknamed "Kates," commanded by Lieutenant Joichi Tomonaga, the same officer who had led the attack on Midway that morning. Though his aircraft still had a leaky fuel tank from that mission, making his return very unlikely, he refused all offers to exchange planes with more junior pilots. Meanwhile, the first-strike group returned. It reported leaving an American carrier on fire. There was therefore hope that the Japanese could even the score.

Makishima watched all of this unfold from the *Nagara* with Nagumo and the rest of the command staff. He was still awestruck by the event. "With a mysterious calm associated with absent-mindedness, I went around," he said. Above the *Kaga* there was "smoke that looked like a cumulonimbus cloud as if a volcano had exploded, swirling and rising." The red flames aboard the ship were reflected on the blue surface of the sea. "The same was true for *Soryu*," he said, which "had already stopped on the horizon." In comparison, the *Akagi* still looked like it would survive. "The bow wasn't on fire yet," noticed Makishima, "and sometimes high-angle guns were fired."[88]

The *Soryu* had abandoned ship at 1045, the *Kaga* at 1340. The *Akagi* had not, but it had transferred the command staff, and it was also decided to transfer the emperor's portrait, a sure sign that the ship was doomed. An officer bowed before the portrait and carefully took it down from the bulkhead. After wrapping it, he found a way through one of the passageways that was not blocked by fire down to a lower deck. To the accompaniment of the bosun's pipes and salutes from the surviving crew members, the portrait was taken to safety to a nearby destroyer.[89]

✪

TEN MINUTES AFTER THE *Yorktown* regained engine power, the radar picked up another enemy air group. Again the fuel lines were drained and charged with CO_2; again Wildcats were sent out to intercept. And again, the Japanese fought their way through. Linzey was still at his battle station below deck. "Stand by for torpedo attack," announced the loudspeaker. Inside the galley compartment, Linzey was blind. He could only lie on his back with his eyes shut, listening to his headphones. The bridge announced that two enemy planes had launched torpedoes. Linzey clenched his hands as before, waiting. This time there was nothing. The torpedoes ran deep, passing underneath the ship. Then two more were launched. Both struck with a "sickening thud." There was "a tearing or wrenching sensation." The lights went out and the ship began listing to port. As the floor tilted beneath him, Linzey felt cold seawater flow across his body and the room filled with smoke. "Below decks," Linzey said, "eerie darkness prevailed throughout the ship."[90]

They had been attacked by Tomonaga's ten Kates, each armed with a 1,700-pound torpedo. Tomonaga was quickly downed, but two other pilots scored hits, and this time it was fatal. More than fifty men were killed instantly in the explosions. The rudder was jammed; the ship was dead in the water again. The Japanese torpedoes were a more deadly weapon than the bombs. Within minutes, the *Yorktown* was listing 27 degrees. Captain Elliott Buckmaster ordered the men to abandon ship. In the smoky darkness, those in the galley compartment formed a line, each taking hold of the man in front of him. The door had been warped shut, but to their relief, the scuttle, an emergency hatch in the center of the door, loosened. Soon the hatch was open and they climbed through into the next compartment. "I remember the hope that rose inside me," Linzey said years later, "as my hands grasped the first rungs of the ladder that led me up to the next compartment on the second deck." His elation soon came crashing down when he reached the hangar. "I saw twisted metal, gaping holes in it, and debris scattered everywhere," he remembered, "the lower edge of the hangar deck often dipping into the water." He feared that the ship might capsize at any moment. This prevented him from sliding down the floor into the water. Instead, he climbed up the incline to the high side. Along with the other men, Linzey stripped off his clothes and slipped a life jacket over his head. There was a rope from the hangar into the water. Linzey took hold of it and lowered himself down into the Pacific, which was now covered with several inches of thick oil.[91]

✪

THE TRAGEDY FOR THE Japanese worsened as the day drew to a close. Within an hour, twenty-four Dauntlesses returned to attack the one remaining Japanese carrier, the *Hiryu*. This time the Japanese combat air patrol and antiaircraft defenses were better prepared, but in all other respects it was a repeat of the morning. The Dauntlesses were accurate—at least they were accurate enough. Four pilots, one of whom was Kleiss, scored hits. Fire broke out immediately and proved impossible to bring under control. Ensign Taisuke Maruyama, a pilot aboard the *Hiryu*, found himself surrounded by violence. On the rear deck, a doctor was performing surgeries without anesthetic. Men had lost limbs from burns or explosions. Through the billowing smoke, Maruyama noticed a red light near the horizon: the sun. It was going down. As if to echo Kleiss, Maruyama found himself being swept along. "There was nothing we could do to extinguish the fires," he realized. The current of the moment was too strong to resist; it was too late to avoid what seemed to be the predetermined outcome. Maruyama looked at the dying sun. "I felt it was like a castle being burned, once the battle was lost," he said, "back in samurai days."[92]

Juzo Mori was rescued along with hundreds of other survivors by the destroyer *Makigumo*. From the deck he could see his old ship, the *Soryu*, "burning fiercely." The sight threw him into a "deep depression," and he tried to occupy himself by going through the crowd, looking for his friends. Many were badly burned or were reported dead. "I knew what was done was done and there was nothing we could do about it now," Mori said, "but I couldn't stop thinking about it." He was struck by the apparent randomness of it all, including how he survived and others had not. After the sun went down, only a few clouds were left in the sky. "Transfixed by the grandeur of the scene we gazed on wordlessly like little children as the sky slowly faded through the hues of sunset. Were it not for the horror of the *Soryu*'s burning hulk," he later wrote, "it was just another beautiful Pacific evening." At about this time, probably, Nagumo ordered the ship scuttled. At 1912 it was hit by torpedoes from the destroyer *Isokaze*. By 1915 it was gone.[93]

Survivors of the *Kaga* had a similar experience. After leaping overboard, Yoshino floated in the water for hours, clinging to a piece of driftwood. He was rescued by the destroyer *Hagikaze*, which then left the area, perhaps because it was preparing for Nagumo's surface attack. By sunset, when the *Hagikaze* returned to the *Kaga*, Yoshino didn't recognize it, because "the hangar between the bridge and stern was burnt down." The once proud silhouette had withered away to half its size. The *Kaga*, too, would be scuttled. When the men learned what was about to happen, they gathered on the deck of the *Hagikaze*. Ensign Maeda had received twenty-eight stitches in his leg without anesthetic, but he insisted on being carried up with the others. While the men held a silent salute, torpedoes streaked from the *Hagikaze* into the *Kaga*. "Tears started to run down my cheeks," Maeda said, "and everyone around me was crying; it was a very sad sight."[94] Many others, including Mitoya, were weeping openly.[95] At 1925 the *Kaga* went down.[96]

At the same moment, Captain Aoki of the *Akagi* gave the order to abandon ship. The injured were lowered into boats to be taken to nearby destroyers. Those who were still able-bodied, such as Hiroshi Suzuki, made their way to the lower decks, where they jumped into the ocean and swam away. Survivors were rescued by the destroyers *Arashi* and *Nowaki*.[97] Suzuki watched the *Akagi* as he was drawn away. "It looked fine from the side," he recalled.

"But the flight deck and the centre of the ship were burning out of control." Dick Best's single bomb had been enough to light an unquenchable fire.[98]

Captain Aoki was one of the survivors. He radioed Nagumo for permission to sink the *Akagi*, but the admiral seems to have taken his time about responding, because nothing was done to carry out the request. Three hours later, the *Akagi* was still afloat. At 2225, Admiral Yamamoto ordered her sinking delayed. Aoki, who may have interpreted this as a slight on his honor, by suggesting that he had abandoned ship too soon, returned to his burning carrier. He went to the anchor deck, which was not yet engulfed by flames, and lashed himself to an anchor. Clearly, he was, like the late Captain Yanagimoto, planning to go down with his ship.[99]

Finally, at 0350 on June 5, 1942, the day following the attack, Yamamoto ordered his men to sink the *Akagi* to prevent her from falling into American hands. This posed the problem of what to do about Captain Aoki, who was still tied to the anchor on the burning vessel. The first navigator, Commander Gishiro Miura, went back to the ship. He managed to persuade Aoki to return with him, and both men lived to fight another day.[100] The end was witnessed by Hiroshi Suzuki. He reported that the torpedo officer assigned to administer the final blow was crying. A young officer, he had never fired torpedoes in combat before. His first would be sent toward the *Akagi*, one of his own.[101] At 0450 he carried out his orders. Twenty minutes later, at 0510, it was the *Hiryu*'s turn.

✪

BEFORE SUNRISE ON JUNE 5, Yamamoto canceled the Midway operation. He spent the next few days trying to consolidate his forces and retire in as orderly a fashion as possible. Meanwhile, the American pilots from Midway and the carrier task forces continued patrolling, looking for the Japanese and survivors alike. When Japanese ships were spotted, squadrons of dive bombers and other planes launched to attack. What was left, however, made for difficult hunting. Because of their speed and agility, destroyers were much harder to hit than carriers, and because of their thicker armor, battleships and cruisers were much more difficult to sink.

Survivors were often in a helpless state. After his Devastator went down, the pilot George Gay hid under a seat cushion, hoping that the nearby Japanese ships would mistake him for debris. His camouflage worked, and by nightfall he was alone and able to inflate his life raft. There was plenty inside his pack of survival gear—a hand pump, a safety knife, flares, even a prayer book—to keep him occupied. He spent a cold and wet night humming "Violets for Your Furs," a Frank Sinatra song about Manhattan in winter. Anything to keep his mind off the burn on his leg, the shrapnel in his hand, and the gunshot wound in his arm. In the morning he was rescued by a Catalina from Midway.

Others were not so lucky. Ensign Tony Schneider, who had run out of fuel before the attack began, had to spend three days in a raft with his gunner before they were rescued. Norman Vandivier and his gunner, Lee Keaney, of Sandusky, Ohio, dived unsuccessfully on the *Kaga* and then ran dry. After ditching in the ocean, they were never seen again.[102]

Those rescued by the Japanese were executed. Wesley Osmus, another Devastator pilot, was killed with an axe after his interrogation was complete. Ensign Frank O'Flaherty and the aviation machinist's mate Bruno Gaido were captured by the *Makigumo*. They were interrogated as well and then, with weights tied around their legs, pushed overboard.[103]

On June 6, Captain Buckmaster returned to the *Yorktown* with a skeleton crew. By harnessing electricity and steam power from a nearby ship, it seemed that it might be possible to rescue the damaged carrier. The crew was taking a break for lunch when several ominous wakes were spotted. A Japanese submarine, after hours of careful maneuvering, had launched four torpedoes—and all but one struck home. The *Yorktown* was finished.[104]

That night, on the *Enterprise*, Dusty Kleiss wrote his first letter to Jean since the eve of battle. "Just have a second to let you know I'm OK but am tired as the dickens," he told her. "If anything should get me now I just want you to know . . . that recently I've had more than my share of luck and that [Prime Minister Hideki] Tojo is most unhappy about it all." Like Mori, Kleiss was astonished by what had happened and grateful to be alive.

✪

"SO ENDED THE DREAM of Japanese Empire," Mitoya recalled. "The peak of Japanese power had been reached and passed." "The catastrophe of Midway," he concluded, "had been the turning of the tide—and deep in our hearts, we Japanese knew it."[105] This was also the view of the Dauntless pilot Cleo Dobson, who wrote in his diary, on June 4, 1942, "We have won the biggest naval engagement in the world." "The Japs," Dobson continued, "were taken by surprise and had the hell beat out of them. I predict this as the turning point of the war."[106]

7

THE LEGACY

THE BATTLE OF MIDWAY WAS A VICTORY NOT MERELY FOR THE US Navy but also for American innovation and ultimately American society. How this triumph was achieved and should be interpreted has been a matter of contention for eighty years and will likely remain so. Today, as war once more looms in East Asia, the battle has taken on renewed importance, both in popular culture and in elite discourses on both sides of the Pacific Ocean. But the world has moved on from 1942, and unless the United States wakes up to the steady erosion of its naval power, it risks another Pearl Harbor—without any guarantee of another Midway.

MIDWAY DID NOT DECIDE the war in the Pacific, whose ultimate outcome was clear well before the first shots were fired. Even if Japan had won the battle, the sheer economic might of the United States would have eventually told against her.[1] Nobody knew this better than some of the Japanese leaders themselves, who thought the contest hopelessly one-sided from the start, but were driven to war by a feeling of desperation.[2] Moreover, the whole concept of a decisive battle in World War II—that is, a battle that decided the outcome of the entire conflict—is a mistaken one. It was a war decided not by the fortunes of battle on a particular day or set of days but by a steady process of attrition.[3] The battle was a turning point, to be sure, but if it had not been fought, or if it had been lost, the tide would probably have turned against Japan at a later moment.

Nor did Midway spell the end of Japanese naval aviation. Yes, the battle was extremely costly in terms of ship losses and casualties among the maintenance crews. But the pilots themselves—who were prioritized during the evacuations—got off relatively lightly. It was the subsequent meat grinder of the Solomons and the Marianas that eventually wore down Japanese airpower.[4]

But if the United States had lost at Midway, the war would have taken much longer, with serious political and human consequences.[5] The Japanese might well have tried to take Hawaii, and would probably have launched attacks on the West Coast of the continental United States.[6] The Japanese would also have been able to move west. Admiral Chuichi Nagumo could have returned to the Indian Ocean and done fearful damage to the British position there, even if the Germans and Italians advancing across North Africa had little chance of actually making a rendezvous with him.[7] Australia would probably have been subjected to sustained attack, and while it presented a costly target, it probably would have been cut off from the United States for some time. The highly successful American submarine campaign against Japanese shipping, much of which was mounted out of Midway, would have been set back.

All this would have put severe strain on the "Germany First" strategy agreed between the Allies. It would also have caused the diversion of vital American-produced war materiel from Britain and the Soviet Union to the Pacific. Japan would have been defeated eventually, but a lot might have happened in Europe in the meantime: the murder of the Jews would have been prolonged, the Allied landing in Europe delayed, and the complete occupation of continental Europe by the Red Army made more probable. So even if Midway was not decisive, it was highly consequential.[8] Without the American victory there, the world would have been a very different place.

In this sense, the veterans of the Pacific War, and especially those of the battle itself, can be forgiven a little hyperbole. Many, including John Waldron and Cleo Dobson, thought it was the "turning point" of the war for the Pacific.[9] Kleiss thought it determined the outcome in Europe as well. "If we had lost the Battle of Midway," he said, "there would probably be a lot of Japanese and German being spoken in the United States and London."[10] Robert M. Morgenthau, an attorney who served in World War II, and Frank Tuerkheimer, a professor of legal history, also thought the implications were enormous: "Had the US lost Midway," they wrote in *Newsweek* in 2007, "the state of Israel would have remained a dream."[11]

Midway was also distinctive. No World War II battle of such global importance hinged so much on decisions made by so many relatively junior officers.[12] If Wade McClusky had not decided to continue his search or Richard Best had simply joined the general onslaught on the *Kaga*, leaving the *Akagi* to escape, then the outcome of the battle would probably have been very different. Nowadays, we all know about the importance of the "strategic corporal"—a relatively low-ranking soldier whose judgments in the counterinsurgency in Northern Ireland, in Iraq or Afghanistan, or in peacekeeping operations in places such as Bosnia—and how his or her decisions can have major political consequences. But this was not a familiar concept in 1942. The importance of the individual at Midway is redolent of an earlier—or perhaps a later—age: it was unusual for the mid-twentieth century, when battle tended toward massed confrontation between conventional armies.

Junior officers were important, however, because they were executing a specific plan. "The ocean," said Herman Melville in his novel *Israel Potter*, "is one hammered plain. Stratagems—like those of disciplined armies, ambuscades—like those of Indians, are impossible. All is clear, open, fluent." Alvin Kernan, a participant of the Battle of Midway, quoted this passage with approval.[13] He thought that the battle was characterized by the openness and fluency of the sea. But there was stratagem at Midway: Admiral Chester Nimitz planned an ambuscade, or, to use the more contemporary term, an ambush. Northeast of Midway was the kill zone. The atoll itself was essentially a support-by-fire position; it was used to fix the *Kido Butai* in place. Meanwhile, the assault element—that is, the Dauntless dive bombers—attacked from the eastern flank.

The Japanese had planned a similar stratagem of their own: attacking Midway would draw out the American fleet so that it could be ambushed. In fact, the opposite occurred. What the Japanese expected to do to the Americans was done by the Americans to the Japanese.[14]

Nimitz's plan also produced a clear result, unlike the Japanese attack on Pearl Harbor, or the Battle of the Coral Sea. In one respect, this is because the Japanese did not accomplish their objectives. They never captured Midway; nor did they ambush the American fleet. But the main reason that the outcome was apparent was the imbalance in losses. Japan lost four carriers, America only one.

For many of the Dauntless pilots, this was a story of revenge. Clarence Dickinson published a condensed version of his memoir in the *Saturday Evening Post* in October 1942 under the title, "I Fly for Vengeance."[15] But every single pilot who dived on the *Kido Butai* had joined the navy prior to Pearl Harbor. They volunteered to fight long before it had anything to do with revenge.

Midway was so named because it lay in the middle of the north Pacific Ocean; it was midway between North America and Asia. An entomologist who visited in 1941 thought the name apt in another sense: "It is also halfway around the world from Greenwich," he said, "at which point our time begins."[16] The battle took place in June, near the middle of the year. What these observations amount to is that Midway is a place defined in relation to other things; it does not seem to exist on its own. There is no one to speak for Midway, no ruler or representative.

Other battlefields of World War II were different. They were places of life, people, and history—and in many respects, the battles were an attack on these things themselves. Consider the vast damage that resulted from the Blitz over London, the D-Day invasion of Normandy, the firebombing of Dresden, or the atomic bombing of Hiroshima and Nagasaki. By contrast, Midway was a nowhere place, the crown of a dormant volcano, a way station, an outpost.

No fight is clean, but Midway—inhabited by no one but sailors, marines, and airmen—was much less dirty than the rest of the war. Even battles in the Western Desert, another seemingly remote place, affected the inhabitants of North Africa. But at Midway, the only men who fought and died were men who had traveled thousands of miles for that purpose. Aside from a handful of exceptions, such as Teiichi Makishima, the photographer, no civilians witnessed the battle, and today, none live among the wreckage. As the writer and broadcaster Michael Medved put it, "No ghosts cling to this meager territory."[17] On the sand dunes nowadays there is only a weathered airstrip and more than a half-million gooney birds. The violence that happened there is forgotten.

Midway was pure in another respect as well. It was won by relatively low-grade technology. V-2 rockets and the atomic bomb were developed as the war unfolded; they seemed to have been forged by the enormous pressure for survival and victory. But the Dauntless was a plane of the 1930s, and it performed a mission conceived in the preceding world war. To be sure, the pilots were courageous and disciplined. But many powers developed dive bombers and used them effectively in combat. The strength and vulnerability of the carrier, as well as the importance of drawing first blood, were also understood by the Japanese and American navies alike. If there is such a thing, and we believe there is, Midway was a fair fight.

All these qualities meant that Midway astounded those who witnessed it. In advance of the battle there were some who had premonitions of its importance. George Gay remembered Waldron's admonition that "the approaching battle will be the biggest of the war, and may well be the turning point."[18] There was also an epic scale to the way events unfolded. Most famously, this was expressed by Mitsuo Fuchida's exclamation that "the tide of battle" had shifted in a mere "five minutes."[19] Tom Cheek, a Fighting Three pilot, said something similar when he saw the carriers aflame: "Awe-struck; my mind trying desperately to grasp the full impact of what I had just witnessed, and the scene still in motion."[20] Part of what impressed Fuchida, however, was the synchronicity of so many different events: the convergence of the *Enterprise* and the *Yorktown* dive bombers, the eruption of flame on three carriers. It was the same with Gay in his attack on the *Hiryu*. "I cannot tell you the sequence in which the planes went down," he said. "Everything was happening at once, but I was consciously seeing it all."[21] The intensity of life, or in this case the loss of life, was too much to comprehend.

Such a dramatic scene demanded to be shared. Dickinson had this urge immediately after his successful dive. "As I flew on," he said, "more and more I wanted to get back to the carrier and live through this day's work again. I was greedy for details of what others had seen. With each mile my eagerness to get back increased."[22] Dusty Kleiss wanted to remember it in writing. That was the only way to make sense of what had happened. "Meticulously, I wrote down every detail I could remember," he said. "I knew I had just been part of a battle that would be forever remembered. I wanted to get every detail right. . . . I wanted to narrate what I had done, commit every anecdote to paper."[23]

Victory was down not so much to luck as to the skill of the dive-bomber pilots and the quality of their equipment. To be sure, they were fortunate that the torpedo squadrons had diverted the Japanese combat air patrol. Not a single plane was lost to enemy fighters before the attack, and only two were shot down overall (Ensign Joe Penland is thought to have been hit by a Zero, Ensign John Quincy Roberts by antiaircraft fire).[24] The reason for most Dauntless losses was fuel: on the return leg they ran out before reaching the carriers and crashed into the sea.[25]

But the Dauntlesses would probably have prevailed even if the Japanese combat air patrol had been ready for them; the sacrifice of the torpedo bombers may not have been necessary. Repeatedly in the course of 1942, Dauntless planes brushed past Zeros to carry out deadly attacks.[26] The apparent exception was the Battle of the Coral Sea, but this was due to circling over the target for half an hour while waiting for torpedo bombers to arrive. Under normal conditions, the Dauntless arrived unnoticed or, if intercepted, would fight its way through. It proved to be not merely a battle-winning but a war-winning weapons system.

This was certainly the view of the Japanese. In postwar inter-rogations, they were asked which of the American attack aircraft had been effective against them. The air officer of the *Akagi*, Taka-hisa Amagai, said he most "feared" the dive bombers, because he "could not dodge" them.[27] Captain Susumu Kawaguchi, the air officer of the *Hiryu*, agreed, saying that you couldn't "avoid" dive bombers, whereas torpedoes could be evaded, at least at longer range.[28] This assessment was echoed by Captain Taijiro Aoki of the *Akagi*. "You can swing away from torpedos," he told his question-ers, "but the worst is dive-bombing."[29] The executive officer of the *Soryu*, Hisashi Ohara, said, "The dive-bomber was the most effective because it was much more accurate and hard to hit by gun fire because of the speed and high angle of fire"; it was also "difficult to avoid the bombs."[30] Though Ohara had some regard for torpedo bombers, he was unconcerned by "high horizontal bombers because we could watch the bombs fall and avoid them." They all knew what they were talking about.

Like all battles, Midway has spawned its share of counterfac-tual ruminations. What if Nimitz had not believed the intelligence? What if the Japanese had acted on the problems thrown up by their pre-Midway war games? What if Nagumo had attacked the Amer-ican task forces right away with at least some of his aircraft? What if McClusky had turned back? These are all useful questions, and thinking about them helps us to understand the battle.

But it would be worth widening the scope of these counter-factuals, at least for a moment. What if interwar California had not been such a hotbed of aeronautical innovation and experi-mentation? What if the Japanese had bought a license to produce Dauntlesses, which had seemed a possibility in the 1930s? What if congressional cost cutters had scrapped the Dauntless program? What if there had been no mass German immigration to produce a Chester Nimitz, or engineers of the quality of Ed Heinemann? What if navy intelligence had weeded out Kleiss on grounds of suspect loyalty? What if the navy had thought fit to make Doris Miller a pilot rather than a mess steward? Or Jean Mochon, for that matter? Or made Neta Snook an admiral? In asking this, we are not trying to apply the standards of the present to the past. Our point here is simply that the US victory at Midway was a product not just of American arms and engineering but also of American society, with all its strengths and some of its weaknesses.

✪

THE STRUGGLE FOR THE interpretation of the battle in the United States began well before it was over. First out of the blocks were the B-17 "Flying Fortress" bomber pilots, who returned to Midway on the morning of June 4 with tall tales of ships sunk or left ablaze. These reports quickly found their way into the newspapers, and for a while it was widely believed that high-level bombing had won the day. In Washington, DC, the *Evening Star* reported that "Army heavy bombers—Flying Fortresses—attacked the Japanese battle fleet from a high altitude, hitting one carrier," and possibly more.[31] When Kleiss and some of the other *Enterprise* pilots, who knew better, heard such boasts from B-17 crews at the Royal Hawaiian Hotel in Pearl Harbor, the result was a brawl that took the Shore Patrol twenty minutes to sort out.[32] Months later, misreporting about B-17s and B-26s persisted. In September 1942, *Aviation* magazine claimed that "the score for the Army Air Force in this battle was: 3 carriers, 3 battleships, and 2 transports sunk or damaged severely during a two-day attack."[33] None of this was true.

The episode epitomized the great debate over the best form of bombing, which pitted dive bombers against high-level bombers, who in turn were divided between those who favored "pinpoint" accuracy and those who swore by "saturation" bombing. The argument rumbled on among the high-level flyers until "carpet bombing" was finally accepted, after the extreme inaccuracy of high-level bombing could no longer be mitigated or concealed.[34] As far as naval aviation was concerned, however, the matter was settled much earlier.

In the after-action reports written by the task force commanders, there was clarity that the battle had been decided neither by the high-level bombers nor by the torpedo bombers, but instead by the dive bombers. These reports did, though, stress the importance of luck and the contribution of the torpedo bombers. According to Ray Spruance of Task Force 16, the Dauntlesses had arrived "in the nick of time," caught the enemy with "his planes on deck," and burned him just before he could launch. The torpedo bombers, Spruance explained, had contributed to the victory by "preventing him from launching" and by "pulling" the enemy combat air patrol down to sea level, leaving "the air clear for our dive bombers." The main elements of what would become the traditional narrative of the Battle of Midway were thus put in place very soon after the event.[35]

For Nimitz, the real victor of the battle was also clear: the dive-bomber pilots and their Dauntless planes. Shortly after the battle, he sent Ed Heinemann a private telegram. "Thanks for building the SBD," Nimitz wrote. "It saved us at Midway."[36]

Yet victory brought its own challenges. Nimitz sought to celebrate and explain it without offending any of the participants. He also had to find a way of recognizing the contribution of the torpedo bombers, whose martyrdom was obvious. Shortly after the battle, Nimitz went to see George Gay, the *Hornet*'s only survivor from Torpedo Eight, in the hospital. It was not just a sympathy call. The admiral had a new mission for Gay: he would be taken out of active service and sent on a morale-raising tour instead.[37]

If the Americans sought to exploit their victory, the Japanese were determined to disguise their defeat. The battle was initially reported as a victory in Japan. On June 11, *Tokyo Asahi Shimbun* reported that "with this one operation, American aircraft carrier power has been reduced to zero and dominance in the Pacific is conclusively ours." "The fact that the crew on our carriers were practically all rescued," continued the paper, "should be called divine protection."[38] This sparked celebrations not only among the Japanese public but also elements of the military. The political leadership, too, was initially kept in the dark about the real outcome;

the members of the cabinet were not informed. It took several days before the Imperial Navy confessed the truth to Prime Minister Tojo. He, in turn, delayed telling the emperor, who was devastated by the news.[39] The names of the four carriers sunk at Midway were only struck from the navy register in August, two months after the battle, and it took over a year for the losses gradually to become public knowledge.[40] It was not least for this reason that Midway did not, at first, seem like a turning point to the Japanese people.

For the survivors of the battle, the Imperial Navy's attempts to bury the defeat added insult to injury. "To conceal the loss of our four carriers," Ensign Takeshi Maeda recalled, "wounded men from the battle stayed in virtual isolation in the same building for over a month." Able-bodied pilots were confined to base. Like Nimitz, Admiral Isoroku Yamamoto visited the wounded in the hospital. Takayoshi Morinaga, a *Kaga* aviator, remembers the admiral as "kind and dignified," but Moringa was upset at being "quarantined" in the hospital. Another pilot felt he was being treated like a "prisoner of war." Many of these survivors had no money—they could not even afford cigarettes. Some were kept in isolation for three months. Their distraught relatives, who had heard rumors of great losses, sometimes gave them up for dead.[41]

One of the wounded was Shigeo Motoki, a senior airplane maintenance officer from the *Soryu*. He had been severely burned and his condition only worsened when he reached mainland Japan. "It especially hurt when my bandages were changed," Motoki said. "No words could possibly describe that level of pain." His condition, along with his confinement, was too much to endure. One night Motoki snuck out of his room and, in a weapons locker, found a pistol. He was preparing to kill himself when he was discovered and stopped by a guard. It was not the first time that Motoki resented his survival.[42]

In mid-September 1942, the Midway story acquired a new dimension with the release of John Ford's celebrated documentary, or, if one prefers, propaganda newsreel.[43] At only eighteen minutes long, it would be broadcast as a prelude to feature films throughout the United States. The opening scenes portrayed the quirks of island life and the gooney birds. But soon the camera was under fire from Joichi Tomonaga and the rest of the Japanese striking force. Explosions went off nearby; Ford himself was hit by a piece of debris. Aside from several exclamations, the only sound is the rumble of airplane engines, the crack of machine guns, and the whisper of flames. Then a voice says quietly: "Yes, this really happened." The final scenes are a burial at sea. When President Roosevelt saw it, he declared, "I want every mother in America to see this film." It chronicled a moment of personal as well as national sacrifice: one of the Marines shown on the island was Roosevelt's eldest son, James. Ford agreed with the president. "This is a film for the mothers of America," he said. "It's to let them know that we're in a war, and that we've been getting the shit kicked out of us for five months, and now we're starting to hit back."[44] Thanks to Ford's documentary, the island itself and the terrifying Japanese attack would loom large in the American historical memory of the battle.

John Ford also began the canonization of Torpedo Eight. One of his cameramen had filmed the squadron before the battle, and Ford subsequently made an eight-minute tribute out of the footage.[45] This was suitable for home projectors and sent to the families of the men. A somewhat mawkish but nevertheless affecting film, it brought the crews, including John Waldron, back to life before depicting their solemn funeral on the hangar deck. The opening titles announced that these men had "written the most brilliant pages in the glowing history of our Naval Air Forces." Later in the war, Henry Hathaway's Hollywood blockbuster *Wing and a Prayer: The Story of Carrier X* (1944) described a torpedo squadron, widely understood to be based on Waldron's men, sinking the Japanese fleet at Midway. The martyrdom of Torpedo Eight increasingly resembled the British cavalry at Balaklava during the Crimean War, as immortalized in Alfred Tennyson's poem "The Charge of the Light Brigade." Its sacrifice was given meaning through transfiguration.

✪

MEANWHILE, THE WAR CONTINUED. Largely a spectator at Midway, Richard Nowatzki nearly ran out of luck in the Solomons.

At the Battle of Santa Cruz in late October 1942, the *Hornet* was sunk by Japanese aircraft. Nowatzki went over the side into shark-infested waters and was fortunate to have survived. In June 1943, the Dauntless piloted by Marine Daniel Iverson at Midway went down in Lake Michigan by accident. Iverson himself was not on board, but he was killed during a training exercise the following year. Of fifty dive-bomber pilots attacking the *Kido Butai* on the morning of June 4, at least seventeen had been killed by the end of the war. There was often no time or inclination to mourn them. "You cannot afford to brood when your friends are killed," Dickinson wrote while the war continued. "It is my habit simply to think of them as if they had been transferred to another ship."[46]

It was not that easy for many others. The family of Norman Vandivier, for instance, received a telegram on June 17 informing them that their son had been killed in action. But the next day, they received another telegram "correcting the first, indicating that he was missing in action." Lieutenant Lloyd Smith, commander of Bombing Six, also wrote to say that Vandivier was not dead but missing. "Your son," he said, "was forced down at sea," and had "good chance of . . . rescue." Unsure of what else to do, the father wrote to Smith, hoping for "information which will help ease our pain." Near the end of October, Tony Schneider, another Dauntless pilot who participated in the battle, wrote to offer his condolences. "Enclosed is $8.00," he said, "the sum of which I was indebted to your son." It would have been a difficult letter to write. He finished by saying, "Norman was my best friend and room mate on our ship and I share your grief over his loss. I was forced down at sea on that date myself and though I was fortunate enough to be rescued on the third day, the news I have been able to get about other friends less fortunate than I has been very sketchy and incomplete. I'm sorry I cannot relieve your mental anguish."[47]

Most of the main protagonists at Midway, like Schneider, survived the war. Schneider earned three Distinguished Flying Crosses, leading bombing squadrons from the *Lexington* and the newly built *Yorktown*.[48] Earl Gallaher also continued flying combat missions.

What they experienced at Midway became the basis for more of the same.

Many others, however, were rotated into staff and instructor roles back home. Kleiss became an instructor pilot, teaching the basics of flight to a new class of dive-bomber hopefuls. He was stationed in Florida, the same place where he had learned to fly, but his situation had changed dramatically. Weeks after returning to the United States, he and Jean eloped in Las Vegas. Now she was pregnant with their first child, but adequate medical care was difficult to find. The military hospital was overcrowded, and Kleiss couldn't afford a private doctor. Finally, Kleiss made informal arrangements with a navy doctor, but when Jean went into labor, the doctor couldn't be reached. The baby ended up being delivered by an intern who had never performed the procedure before. Soon afterward, the poor facilities meant that both Jean and the baby developed an infection. Eventually both recovered, but it was a harrowing experience for the family. Kleiss said, "The Navy had failed me."[49]

About Midway, Kleiss said very little. His rear-seat gunner, John Snowden, sent him a letter near the end of the war. "I've often wondered how you felt on those attacks," he wrote, guessing that Kleiss was "probably as scared as I was." Apparently Kleiss never spoke about his feelings with Snowden. He was also silent with strangers. Three weeks after the battle, he arrived in San Francisco. There was "a patriotic crowd" eager to buy veterans of Midway a drink. Kleiss avoided them. It was the same with his family. When he returned to Coffeyville, Kansas, his hometown was enthusiastic. The locals knew he had earned a Distinguished Flying Cross for something that had happened in the South Pacific. But about the events of June 4, Kleiss said nothing, at least then. "I made no mention of the fact that I had participated in the Battle of Midway," he said, "not even to my father."[50]

George Gay was different. He spent the rest of the war on tour, feted by society and often pursued by female admirers. Although this may sound like an enviable fate, the psychological cost to him was considerable. Gay, known as the "sole survivor" of his aircrew, suffered from survivor's guilt as well as from the reproaches of those who could not understand why he had returned when their own loved ones had not. He struggled with his celebrity status and the repetition of a story that both lionized him and alienated him from others.

Gay's post-Midway work was hugely important, however. The direct military contribution of Torpedo Eight at Midway was not insubstantial, as we have seen. But the effect of its work that it delivered after the battle—through Gay's efforts—was perhaps even more significant, though it is also unquantifiable. The sacrifice for the US war effort surely inspired hundreds of thousands, perhaps millions, of people as the conflict continued.

As for Nimitz, he served as commander of the Pacific Fleet for the duration of the war. After the Japanese surrendered in August 1945, Nimitz arrived in Tokyo, where he visited the *Mikasa*, Admiral Togo Heihachiro's flagship during the Battle of Tsushima. The *Mikasa* had been preserved as a national monument, and Nimitz, who had met Togo and attended his funeral, stationed a Marine guard permanently aboard the ship to protect it from looting.[51] The battleship might have been eclipsed by the carrier, but it was still worthy of respect. In November, Spruance succeeded Nimitz as the Pacific Fleet commander.

On the Japanese side, the rest of the conflict also took its toll on the Midway veterans. Juzo Mori lost his right hand; it was mutilated by an American .50-caliber round over Guadalcanal. Yamamoto was killed in the air; in April 1943, US fighters gunned down a plane carrying him from Rabaul to the Solomon Islands. Nagumo chose suicide; in 1944, US forces were poised to overwhelm his position at Saipan, so he shot himself in the head rather than face capture. Maeda flew torpedo-bombing missions for the next two years, until August 1945. Then he was ordered to load his plane full of explosives and wait for the order to become a kamikaze. Within weeks the war ended, and he was spared. Fuchida, never to be outdone, claimed to have been present when the Japanese government signed the surrender document on the USS *Missouri* in Tokyo Bay.[52]

Like the Americans, the Japanese also needed stories to sustain themselves both during and after the war. Tomonaga surely had an eye for posterity when he gamely waved aside the concerns of his maintenance crew over the damaged fuel tank. Likewise, Captain Ryusaku Yanagimoto's decision to go down with the *Soryu* was surely not an act of nihilism, despair, or even expiation, but a gesture designed to inspire future generations. For Shigeo Motoki, solace was found in music. After his suicide attempt, he was transferred to Kasumigaura Navy Hospital in the city of Tsuchiura, about 40 miles north of Tokyo. There, he heard two pieces of classical music that caused him to reconsider his situation. It was a performance of "Andante Cantabile," the second movement of Tchaikovsky's String Quartet No. 1, and Riccardo Drigo's "Serenade." "To this day," Motoki said years afterward, "those two pieces are 'mine.'"[53]

The man who made the US victory at Midway possible eventually made it to the Pacific himself. Heinemann was sent there by the Douglas Corporation and the Bureau of Aeronautics in October and November 1944 to study combat operations at firsthand.[54] By then, the navy was phasing out the Dauntless. Just as Midway was decided in a few minutes, the battle-winning weapon had only a relatively brief life span before being superseded by further innovation. In July 1944, the last of 5,936 Dauntlesses rolled off the production line at El Segundo. Rear Admiral John McCain, the father of the famous Vietnam War navy pilot and US senator John McCain, claimed that the Dauntless had "sunk more enemy combatant tonnage than all other arms of the service combined."[55] Even if this was something of an exaggeration, it was certainly true that the Dauntless had sent the most Japanese ships to the bottom during the critical year of 1942.[56]

The Dauntless's status as a battle-winning weapon was therefore secure. The Office of War Information stated simply that "the Navy's carrier-based standard dive-bomber [the Dauntless] is the best in the world in its category."[57] As one chronicler added, this was but "half the story." "The other half," the writer continued, was that "it was ready in quantities on the decks of our carriers, and our Navy flying personnel was thoroughly trained in its handling, when we entered the war."[58] In other words, it was peacetime procurement that had enabled the United States to turn the tide in the Pacific War.

This truth about the Dauntless was recognized by the pilots themselves. Kleiss later wrote, "Our planes were the newest, most accurate of naval weapons," the only ones capable of sinking "a fast-moving swirling ship." He believed that credit for the victory at Midway should go not merely to the pilots but to the designers and builders of the Dauntless as well. "Our nation," he insisted, "owes a great debt to Ed Heinemann and his brilliant team at the Douglas Aircraft Plant in El Segundo, California."[59]

Of the seven carriers in action on both sides at Midway, only one survived the war. The *Enterprise* led an eventful but charmed life. It was badly damaged in the Solomons, but repaired. This was followed by service in the Marianas and the Philippines. It was very seriously damaged again, this time off Okinawa, in May 1945, but made back it to port, where it saw out the end of the war while under repair. The *Enterprise* had been in the thick of it from beginning to end and was thus christened the "fightingest ship" in the US Navy.[60]

The American memory of Midway was promoted through the naming of ships and bases, the classic navy method of establishing and maintaining traditions. This began during the war itself. A new USS *Hornet*—the ninth US Navy ship of that name, both bigger and faster than its namesake at Midway—was commissioned in 1943. The USS *Midway* came into service shortly after the war ended. The battered *Enterprise*, the last surviving carrier from the battle, was taken out of service and eventually scrapped. Its name was passed on to the first nuclear-powered US aircraft carrier. There were also several smaller ships christened with the commemoration of the battle in mind. For example, Severin Rombach of Torpedo Six was remembered through a destroyer escort. So was John Waldron, who also had an auxiliary naval air station in

Texas named after him. Another was Lofton Henderson, a Marine Corps pilot who died leading the squadron of Dauntlesses from Midway. His memorial became Henderson Field, an important airfield on Guadalcanal.

At the same time, the memory of Midway received its first challenge. In August 1945, atomic bombs detonated in Hiroshima and Nagasaki. Suddenly it seemed as if the war, if not the world, had been won by a new type of weapon. Nimitz arrived back in the United States hardly two months later, concerned that the wrong lesson had been learned. "New weapons such as the atomic bomb," he said at a public event in California, "may change the character of warfare but it will not change the fact we must have control of the sea." He brought the same message to a joint session of Congress. At stake was the story of December 1941 to August 1945. Was it a loud opening—a seven-month naval battle, won by talented pilots and relatively old airplanes—followed by a nearly three-year diminuendo as Japan resisted the inevitable? Or was it a gradual crescendo, a drawn-out contest of industrial production, epitomized by the arrival of a new but dissonant technological age? Nimitz thought it was the first. Victory, he said, resulted from the fact that Japan, "a maritime nation, dependent on food and materials from overseas, was stripped of her sea power."[61]

✪

MOST OF THE MIDWAY veterans who survived the war were demobilized in 1945. Dick Best, fittingly, took a job with Douglas Aircraft Corporation. Quite a few, though, stayed in the navy. Stanhope Ring—his "flight to nowhere" now firmly behind him—continued his meteoric rise. He was an observer at the atomic bomb tests at Bikini Atoll and then commanded the USS *Boxer*, the first American carrier to fly jet aircraft. Dickinson also took command of a carrier, the USS *Franklin*. Kleiss took a staff job at the Bureau of Aeronautics, the navy's office for aircraft strategy and design.[62] Spruance was appointed president of the Naval War College in Newport, Rhode Island. He brought McClusky along with him to help run the officer postgraduate program.[63]

Nowatzki also reenlisted; he was later injured serving on a destroyer in the Korean War. During that conflict, his crew adopted a destitute Japanese schoolgirl who had been orphaned by the atomic bomb at Nagasaki. Nowatzki wrote up his experiences in a self-published memoir titled *The Compassionate Destroyer*, the ship that could heal as well as wound.

Japanese Midway veterans also went their separate ways. After an interval, Minoru Genda rejoined the Japanese military, which became known as the Japanese Self-Defense Forces. He chafed at the restrictions on Japanese rearmament and upon retirement went into nationalist politics. Genda stirred controversy in 1969, when he stated that the Japanese Empire would have used the atomic bomb if it had possessed one. His former classmate Mitsuo Fuchida had a very different experience that included a road-to-Damascus moment a few years after the war. He became a Christian, a pacifist, and a regular visitor to the United States, where he eventually settled. Kaname Harada, who also became a pacifist, opened a kindergarten. "I realized the war had turned me into a killer of men," he said, "and that was not the kind of person I wanted to be."[64] Kiyoto Furuta went into farming; Juzo Mori ran a bar.

Ed Heinemann's career really took off after the war. The growing confrontation with the Soviet Union gave him plenty of business. Already famous on account of the Dauntless, he designed several other remarkable aircraft, including the iconic Douglas A-4 Skyhawk, a mainstay of carrier operations during the Vietnam War that was also flown by many other air forces. Within the industry, he became known as "Mr. Attack Aviation."

One result of the Cold War was the US-Japanese cooperation in the face of the new Sino-Soviet threat. Heinemann and Douglas, who had formerly been the scourge of Japanese shipping, now collaborated on aircraft production with the Japanese manufacturer Mitsubishi, which had built the Zero.[65] Thanks to the Cold War, the two companies were now on the same side.

There is something about Heinemann's trajectory, and the rise of the US aviation industry generally, that epitomizes the American dream and the roots of American greatness. He certainly thought so himself. "The growth of aviation in the short span of fifty years is symbolic of the American character," Heinemann said in 1953. "It has been the result of our inherent atmosphere of freedom," he continued. "That atmosphere where the curious, enterprising American can aspire and grow best expressed as the pioneering spirit."[66] One might add that Heinemann and the Dauntless also encapsulated the dynamic partnership that characterized the growth of what President Dwight Eisenhower would soon decry as the "military industrial complex," without which the global dominance of the United States, even today, would have been unthinkable.

Despite his outward exuberance, Heinemann had some ethical qualms about his work. In a letter to a friend, he shared a brief autobiography, written in the third person, which revealed that "during his entire design career, he was constantly nagged by pangs of conscience regarding the diabolical devices he was developing, such as bombs and aircraft." This, Heinemann said, "often caused a great deal of soul-searching." He was particularly concerned by "high-altitude bombing against cities and villages which becomes inevitable in any war." In this context, Heinemann explained, his conscience was "eased" by the knowledge that he had designed the airplane that had "stopp[ed] the Japanese at Midway Island."[67]

The tension between Heinemann the engineer and Heinemann the man continued after he designed the Skyhawk, which the Argentine Air Force used to send several British ships to the bottom of the sea during the Falklands War in the South Atlantic. After that conflict, Heinemann wrote to the Argentine ambassador in Washington to ask for pilots' impressions of the aircraft. It was now rather old, Heinemann conceded, "but it is still a good attack airplane and I am still being asked to advise various countries on its use."[68] The answer clearly both pleased and disconcerted him. "I am sorry to see the fighting on so many fronts," he told the Argentine air attaché in Washington. "But after all, that is how life goes. As we design a new aircraft, we unfortunately cannot predict how they will be used."[69]

✪

IN THE FIRST TWO decades after the war, Midway became established in American popular culture. The 1949 Hollywood movie *Task Force* led the way. Beginning with striking original footage from the early days of naval aviation, it switches to glorious color toward the end, tracing the story of a navy pilot, Jonathan Scott (played by Gary Cooper), before and during World War II. The centerpiece is a dramatic reconstruction of the Battle of Midway featuring Wade McClusky in a supporting role. But the moment of greatest interest is the hero's early role in "making people air-minded"; he even considers a career in the defense industry but is brought up short by the thought of "selling planes to Mussolini." (One wonders whether he knew of the sale of the Dauntless prototype to the Japanese in the 1930s.) When faced with a congressman skeptical of the cost of naval aviation, Scott tells him that without carriers, "the West Coast papers" would have been "printed in Japanese"; there were resonances of this phrase in Kleiss's later remark that without Midway, "there would probably be a lot of Japanese and German being spoken in the United States and London."[70] The US Navy made its facilities available to the studio, so the movie enjoyed official imprimatur. Perhaps unsurprisingly, Radio Moscow condemned the film as one "which glorifies war and calls for the militarization of the country's whole life."[71]

The Battle of Midway also featured strongly in Japanese postwar cinema. Though it was a defeat, the engagement did not raise the same uncomfortable questions around atrocities as did—for example—the war in China, and thus it was a relatively safe topic. Despite the pacifist political ethos of the new democracy, these films were often quite patriotic and suffused with soft militarism. Some, such as *Eagle of the Pacific* (1953)—which included spectacular scenes of Midway—were commercially very successful. One leading reviewer said he had learned of the battle for the first time by watching the film, further evidence of the extent to which news of the defeat had been kept from the Japanese public.[72]

More Japanese films followed over the next two decades. The largest-scale film in this genre was *Storm over the Pacific* (1960), which included dramatic reconstructions of the fatal attacks on the *Kido Butai*. Eight years later, *Yamamoto Isoroku, Commander in Chief of the Combined Fleet* appeared, a sympathetic treatment emphasizing the hero's reluctance to go to war with the United States.[73] The battle itself was portrayed as a very close contest in which the American dive bombers surprised the Japanese counterstrike just before it was about to be launched. There were also screenings of American movies in Japan. In a neat symmetry, the Japanese release of Gary Cooper's *Task Force* ran under the title of *Kido Butai*.

Meanwhile, the traditional interpretation of Midway was taking shape. In the 1950s, Fuchida cowrote a memoir of the battle—subtitled *The Battle That Doomed Japan in Five Fateful Minutes*—that insisted that Nagumo had been on the verge of launching his strike on the American carriers when the Dauntlesses struck. "Five minutes," Fuchida famously wrote. "Who would have dreamed that the tide of battle would shift completely in that brief interval of time?" The five minutes he was referring to were not just the genuinely decisive moments when the Dauntlesses wrought their destruction, but the completely fictitious five minutes that allegedly separated Nagumo from the launch of his counterstrike. Fuchida went on to blame the failure not just on bad luck but also on national arrogance brought on by succumbing to the "victory disease" after the triumphs of the previous six months.[74] Japan, in other words, lost the battle; the Americans did not win it.

Other assessments in Japan were more nuanced. In 1946, Masataka Chihaya recorded his thoughts on the "bottomless defeat" of the Imperial Navy. He criticized Japanese strategic fascination with a decisive battle, military leadership that failed to accurately perceive its enemy, the action of Germany in Europe, and the interservice rivalry between the Imperial Japanese Army and Navy. But Chihaya also praised his opponents. "After Pearl Harbor," he said, "the recovery of American sea power was astoundingly rapid." "Stupendous industrial efficiency" and a willingness to fight, he continued, allowed the American navy to develop into "an institution invincible in defense, irresistible in offense."[75] A similar appraisal of the war was published in *Sensi Sosho*, the official military history of Imperial Japan's war in the Pacific, which began publication in 1966. It said the war was a problem of strategy, logistics, alliances, and spirit.[76]

But it was Fuchida's perspective that won out, at least for a time. Much of his view made its way into the first major Midway book in the United States, Walter Lord's *Incredible Victory*. Superbly written and based on extensive primary research, it is still worth reading today. Next to intelligence, Lord stressed the role of the torpedo bombers in creating a narrow window for the dive bombers in which to strike before Nagumo's forces got into the air. His most potent message, though, was the sheer improbability of the victory. The American pilots were not only outnumbered, Lord wrote, but "knew little of war," and they were beset by "equipment problems," including some that prevented dive bombers from being able to dive. By contrast, the "enemy was brilliant, experienced and all-conquering." The Americans, he concluded, "had no right to win," and "yet they did," showing that "every once in a while 'what must be' need not be at all."[77]

A more scholarly version of the same argument was presented by Gordon Prange, who was also the author of a legendary book on Pearl Harbor titled *At Dawn We Slept*. Although *Miracle at Midway*, the second book of that title to appear on the battle, was published posthumously some time later, Prange had conducted most of his research for the book in the 1970s. There was already the first hint of skepticism about the contribution of the torpedo bombers, especially Waldron's squadron, but in broad terms, Prange followed Lord. He, too, relied heavily on Fuchida as a "prime source," stressing the importance of American luck and concluding the victory was a "narrow squeak." It was the title, though, that said it all: victory had been a "miracle."[78]

Although both men acknowledged the critical role of the dive bombers, neither Lord nor Prange looked at the Dauntless in detail or made any mention of Ed Heinemann's role in the victory.

✪

THE HOLLYWOOD BLOCKBUSTER MOVIE *Midway*, released in 1976, defined the popular image of the battle for a generation.[79] The portrayal of the Japanese was largely sympathetic; there was no mention of the murders of Bruno Gaido, Frank O'Flaherty, and Wesley Osmus. Though set in a world convulsed by hate, the film was remarkably temperate. There was no talk of "vengeance" for Pearl Harbor. The characters were battling purely personal demons, such as fear of failure or a generational conflict between a (fictional) father and son. There was even a scene drawing attention to the unjust internment of Japanese Americans during the conflict. This restraint may have been partly driven by the Cold War imperative to maintain good relations with economically prosperous Japan in order to present a common front against the Soviet Union. No narrative device, however, was capable of softening the destruction of an aircraft carrier. In the cinema, the sister of the Japanese American film critic J. K. Yamamoto was so upset by the loud audience cheers every time a Japanese ship blew up that she considered covering her face as she left the movie theater.[80]

Some of the characters in the film were fictional, but most were historical figures. Henry Fonda, who had done some of the narration in John Ford's documentary thirty-four years earlier, was cast in the role of Chester Nimitz. There were other efforts made to ensure verisimilitude. Max Leslie, who had commanded Bombing Three during the battle, served as a technical adviser. The supposed role of the torpedo bombers, and especially of George Gay's squadron, in pulling the Japanese fighter cover down to sea level was heavily emphasized. In case anyone did not get the message, it was even verbalized by the Japanese characters. Unsurprisingly, perhaps, Gay—who also advised on set—loved the film. Dusty Kleiss's view is not recorded.

Over the past forty years or so, *Midway* has been widely criticized for its inaccuracies. Early on, the *New York Times* described it as a "kamikaze attack against one of the greatest sea battles of modern times."[81] Despite the claim in the preamble that it was a true story using original footage, much of the film was shot later, as any aviation buff would notice immediately. Most of the Japanese material was lifted from *Storm over the Pacific*. There were also borrowings from the lavish Pearl Harbor movie *Tora! Tora! Tora!* (1970), and even dogfights from the British epic *Battle of Britain* (1969).[82] One of the central tensions in the story is a fraught romance between an American naval officer involved in the battle and an American-born daughter of Japanese immigrants—something that had more to do with later perceptions of the war than actual events.

That said, the film more or less reflected the prevailing scholarly interpretation of the battle at the time. Central to its narrative was the concept of luck, as elaborated by Walter Lord. "Were we better than the Japanese," wonders Nimitz at the end of the film, "or just luckier?"

The influence on American popular culture was considerable. *Star Wars*, which debuted in 1977, was hardly more than the Battle of Midway set in space. It portrayed a battle between an "Empire" and "the Rebels," not unlike the Empire of Japan and the United States, itself a rebellious British colony. The first was motived by hatred and imperialism, the second by righteousness. Success was accomplished by means of "the Force," something as mysterious and vital as luck had been in the Midway accounts of Prange or Lord. Victory resulted from one's essence and piety, not training or equipment. Moreover, the dramatic dialogue of the starfighter pilots as they attacked the Death Star (in effect the imperial *Kido Butai*) borrowed heavily from that used between the carrier pilots in the Midway film the year before.

✪

WORLD WAR II WAS waged by the Democratic president Franklin Delano Roosevelt, and Midway was fought by supporters of both parties and none. Yet as the country became more embattled at home and abroad after the Vietnam War, there was a widespread feeling that the legacy the "Greatest Generation" had left the nation through its service in World War II was in peril. The US Navy was stagnating. The smell of "dope" was once again abroad in California—this time not the banana oil fragrance used by aircraft developers but the waft of illegal narcotics. Perhaps this was an unfair perception, but it was how many people at the time, particularly those who had served in the war, saw things. It prompted some of our protagonists to look for national renewal.

Most vocal among them was George Gay, who fretted throughout the late 1960s and 1970s that the Soviet Union was stealing a march in the Cold War. Remarkably, given that President Richard Nixon's opening to China was in full bloom, Gay was also worried about Beijing. "The [Red] Chinese," he wrote, "are the only ones who think they can kill everyone else, lose an equal number and still have millions left." "Why do we encourage and help these people," he wondered. "We have known since before the end of World War II what their intentions are and they have never once given us given us a reason to trust them."[83]

Central to Gay's concern was restoring America's strength and preparedness. Our copy of his memoir is inscribed by him with the words, "Keep America strong." In Gay's mind, this was the same struggle he had waged at Midway and afterward. "I can still hear Admiral Nimitz saying: 'Go back and tell the American people that we need their help,'" he wrote.[84]

Ed Heinemann broadly shared these views and contributed to the Republican "1976 G.O.P. Victory Fund."[85] A year later, he received a "Certificate of Appreciation" from the Republican National Committee, thanking him for his support for the "principles of individual freedom, limited government and free enterprise."[86] Seven years later, Heinemann received a signed form letter from Ronald Reagan thanking him for his help in the forthcoming presidential election. This was followed by another missive from the president extolling his policy of "peace through strength" and criticizing the "liberal architects of a defense policy based on weakness."[87]

From this perspective, Heinemann would have seen the election of Ronald Reagan in 1980 as an opportunity to restore American power. It was followed by the reinvigoration of the US Navy under its new secretary, John Lehman, himself a naval aviator (and, incidentally, a German American). Lehman embarked on the creation of a "600 ship navy," overseeing a huge program of construction and development. Accompanying this investment was the "microchip revolution" led by Silicon Valley. These developments underpinned the "revolution in military affairs" driving the renaissance of US power. By the end of the decade, the US Navy once again completely dominated the globe, overshadowing the Soviet fleet and threatening to attack Moscow's exposed position in East Asia if it attempted any aggression in Europe.

By this point, a considerable amount of time had passed since World War II. With the passage of time, there was forgiveness. Heinemann was contacted by the "Wings of Friendship," a group of aviators who hoped to improve US-Japanese and Pacific Rim relations by means of "the dynamic display of vintage— and legendary—[World War II] aircraft." Supporters of the initiative included Jimmy Doolittle, who was then in his nineties.[88] At around this time, George Gay was invited to Paris for the debut of the film *Tora! Tora! Tora!* Many Japanese veterans were invited as well, including Mitsuo Fuchida. "He kept repeating how sorry he was for it all," said Gay of Fuchida, "and every time he said it, I could not help wondering if he didn't mean that he was sorry they lost."[89] As if to make history even stranger, soon all of Fuchida's children were living in the United States. The man who had led the attack on Pearl Harbor had adopted the faith of his enemy and sent his children to live among them.[90]

In old age, Heinemann's place among the pantheon of American defense engineers was assured. He had time to return to his childhood interest in shipbuilding and designed various smaller craft. This brought him into contact with the China Shipbuilding Trading Company, based in Beijing, which was interested in one of his patrol boats. In early 1983, Heinemann visited Beijing and met with, among others, Sun Fang, the head of the military product department at the company.[91] While there, Heinemann visited their "Air University" and said he was "quite impressed" by its five hundred students, who were learning "aircraft design from the ground up."[92] Later, when attending the graduation ceremony at Northrop University at Inglewood, California, he was "surprised at the large number of Asians" studying aeronautics and electronics.[93]

Heinemann stayed in touch with China Shipbuilding through-out the decade.[94] He also offered to help the Chinese with acquiring an F-16, which he described as "the ultimate fighter presently avail-able," though "perhaps a little too advanced for your purposes."[95] At that time, during the mid-1980s, collaborations with People's Republic of China (PRC) bodies, even in sensitive areas such as military technology, were encouraged for Cold War reasons, in order to contain the Soviet Union. "Now that the President and others have visited China and have indicated a more liberal attitude towards them," Heinemann wrote, he looked forward to greater latitude in technology transfer.[96] This was a reasonable expectation, as the Reagan administration sent a delegation to Beijing in Au-gust 1984 to conclude a formal agreement of cooperation with the PRC's navy. As John Lehman, who led the delegation, recalled, this agreement was designed to "modernize their air force and navy planes up to an F-16 standard, to cope with state of the art Soviet fighters and bombers."[97]

Meanwhile, the US government decided to recognize the unique contributions of German American citizens to US aviation. In 1983, three hundred years after the first German immigrants had landed in America, a German-American Day was instituted. The National Air and Space Museum in Washington, DC, put on an exhibition to mark the fact that "aviation and space technologies, and their applications, have been especially enriched by Americans of German extraction." High on the list of those being honored, of course, was Ed Heinemann, who was described as having "an intuitive facility for aeronautical engineering."[98] For the boy whose childhood use of German had been drastically curtailed by the outbreak of war in 1917, it was a sign that the wheel had turned full circle.

✪

IN 1982, *MIRACLE AT MIDWAY* incautiously suggested that "little genuine controversy remain[ed]" about the battle.[99] The consen-sus was not to last. Instead, from the 1980s onward, the traditional view of the Battle of Midway was increasingly subject to revision.

John Lundstrom's *First Team*, though primarily a granular study of fighter tactics in the opening six months of the Pacific War, showed that Torpedo Three's attack did not take place, as hitherto believed, before that of the dive bombers, but was simultaneous, and had actually been completed after the Dauntlesses had departed.[100] Other matters were also cleared up, especially the vexed question of who had attacked which carrier; it is now agreed that McClusky struck the *Kaga* and Best struck the *Akagi*.

The new millennium brought a fundamental shift in our understanding of the *Kido Butai*'s behavior at Midway and the course of the battle more generally. Thomas Wildenberg, one of the world experts on US dive bombing, in 2004, attributed the success of the Dauntlesses to superior skill and doctrine rather than pure luck.[101] In 2005, Jonathan Parshall and Anthony Tully published their groundbreaking *Shattered Sword*, which showed that, contrary to Fuchida's claims, Nagumo was nowhere near ready to launch his own strike when the Dauntlesses appeared. This was also the conclusion of Dallas Woodbury Isom in 2007 in *Midway Inquest*.[102] The famous "five minutes" between victory and defeat—a staple of most accounts up to that point—was now no longer tenable. It took five minutes to cripple the *Kido Butai*, to be sure, but if the dive bombers had struck a bit later, the outcome would have been much the same.

One feature of the Midway debate was the pioneering use of the internet to bring together veterans and students in the famous "Battle of Midway Roundtable," or BOMRT. The editor, Ronald Russell, brought its work to wider attention in his book *No Right to Win: A Continuing Dialogue with Veterans of the Battle of Midway*. One of the myths he dispensed with, thanks to contributor Will O'Neil, was that a Japanese amphibious invasion likely would have been a monumental disaster for them, a total reversal of what happened at Wake Island.[103] At the same time, the title of Russell's book reflected an enduring belief in the American victory as an unexpected and almost undeserved outcome.

Another issue was the approach of the *Enterprise* Air Group and the way that Wade McClusky had apportioned targets. Did he follow doctrine? Did he make a mistake? Did his radio malfunction? The question of doctrine matters, because it reveals what participants of the battle intended to accomplish, what they expected of themselves, and what they thought the enemy was capable of doing. Some believed that McClusky had been hasty, that he had given vague commands to his pilots and compromised their effectiveness, a mistake rectified only by Dick Best's impulsiveness. Others thought McClusky had performed admirably, applying an outdated manual to a unique challenge.

The debate over McClusky's actions has proved intractable, not unlike George Gay's claim that he floated in the water under a seat cushion, watching the Japanese fleet steam back and forth. Considering that the carriers were separated by a distance of several miles, this part of his account is somewhat hard to believe. Like many stories, it reduces to a contest of testimony against reason. And Gay, like all witnesses, is biased. "When we tell war stories," Kleiss ruminated, "we veterans unconsciously leave out all the details that embarrass us." He explicitly incriminated himself in this observation, adding, "I wonder what I've unconsciously left out now." All narratives are suspect in this sense, because they serve to justify the speaker as well as inform the audience.

Along with these factual debates there are two other aspects of the battle that have attracted attention. The first is the sense that something miraculous had taken place that day, that "God was at Midway." This was the title of Stanford Linzey's personal account of the battle, published in 1996. Upon closer inspection, however, one learns that Linzey was convinced of divine aid not because America successfully ambushed the Japanese fleet but because all but one member of his Bible study group survived the sinking of the *Yorktown*. Still, this idea has persisted in varying degrees throughout nearly every account. Even historians who cite Japanese hubris as the reason for the battle's outcome are appealing to a universal moral standard, a kind of divine judgment. Either America deserves to win or Japan deserves to lose. Both views regard the outcome as just and foreordained.

Midway has thus always made for good sermons. Fuchida used it to warn against Japanese hubris, Lord and Prange to praise American fortune. We preach our own lesson, of course. It was better for the world that Roosevelt and his navy won their contest against Emperor Hirohito, but, as we have shown, the American protagonists who brought about this result did not regard it as inevitable, at least as events unfolded.

The other important theme is an increased emphasis on the Douglas Dauntless and the men who flew it. In 1991, Barrett Tillman published the definitive biography of the plane. Three years later, Daniel Iverson's Dauntless was discovered at the bottom of Lake Michigan, raised, and put on display at the National Museum of Naval Aviation at Pensacola, Florida.[104] Peter Smith also wrote widely on the Dauntless and its performance at Midway.[105] In 2011, Craig Symonds published a brilliant overview of the battle that incorporated all the new insights of the previous two decades. The author rightly stressed that the American victory "was less incredible and less miraculous than it has often been portrayed," though, for narrative reasons, he separated the final torpedo attack and that of the dive bombers, when the two were actually simultaneous.[106] Three years later, in 2014, Stephen Moore published *Pacific Payback*, a gripping account of the *Enterprise* dive bombers in the first half of 1942. The book, as its title suggests, placed particular emphasis on the desire for revenge after Pearl Harbor.[107]

Meanwhile, the commemoration of Midway continued to gather apace. The International Midway Memorial Foundation was established in 1992 to increase awareness of the battle through events and public access to the island itself. In 1999, as if to recognize these efforts, the US Navy established two annual holidays. The first, October 13, commemorates the birthday of the navy itself. The second, June 4, marks the "anniversary of the Battle of Midway . . . one of the most decisive sea battles in world history . . . won, not by superior numbers or daunting technology, but by the courage and tenacity of sailors who fought a vicious air and sea battle against overwhelming odds."[108]

✪

THE PASSAGE OF TIME also caused the battle to loom larger in the memory of its participants. Though he had so far remained silent, Kleiss began to share his perspective soon after the turn of the century. By this point, many other veterans of the battle had died. As he had at other moments during his life, Kleiss began to think that his survival was divinely ordained. Just after his ninetieth birthday, another significant change took place in his life: Jean, his wife of sixty-four years, died of pancreatic cancer in 2006. Kleiss found himself haunted by his memories. "Today," he said in his final years, "that day—Thursday, June 4, 1942—hovers over my shoulder like an annoying friend. . . . [I]t will not leave me alone."[109]

The idea of two worlds, of military and civilian, of battlefront and homefront, is an established theme in literature and history. Odysseus travels for a decade in order to cross the boundary between the killing fields of Troy and his hearth in Ithaca. The narrator of Rudyard Kipling's poem "The Return" juxtaposes the African "plains which the moonshine turns to sea" with the mean "putty, brass, an' paint" of England. In Kleiss's case these worlds were clearly defined by time. Midway was life in 1942; it was not his twilight in the aughts. Yet his memory of Midway challenged the division between these worlds. Memory caused his past to merge with the present, the battlefield to merge with his life in Texas. Like Odysseus, who returned home only to draw his sword again, and like Kipling's narrator, who christens London "Thamesfontein," in homage to the Boer town "Bloemfontein," Kleiss seemed to realize that the distinction between the two worlds was a false one. Midway happened in the same world in which his infant daughter nearly died, and in which his wife did die. Kleiss's letter on the eve of battle suggested that life was cold-blooded and ruthless in war alone. His memoir suggests that by the end he had changed his mind. "Nothing," he said when his wife was gone, "could fill the emptiness her death created."[110]

In 2005, Alvin Kernan published his account, a more comprehensive view than Lord's or Prange's, in which Midway was a culmination of events that preceded the day itself. "Fate," Kernan wrote, "began to weave its web long before the battle."[111] Kernan also sought to reveal what he called "the Unknown Battle of Midway," that is, the way in which the American victory contained within it the merciless death of the torpedo bombers. Parshall and Tully published *Shattered Sword* that same year. It, too, revealed a darker Midway, a battle of lies and blunders. And, because their story was told from the perspective of the Japanese, it was—like *Beyond Pearl Harbor*, Ron Werneth's remarkable collection of interviews, published in 2008—a monument of defeat.[112]

Some believed that systems or cultures superseded events. "The outcome of the battle was primarily the result of decisions made and taken by individuals," said Craig Symonds in his book *The Battle of Midway*. "Essential to understanding those decisions," he continued, "is an appreciation of the culture that informed these individuals, for while they were free agents, they were also products of their society."[113] Cathal Nolan advanced a similar argument in his book *The Allure of Battle*. In his view, war is a question of attrition, not decisive battles; of the common man, not senior officers. Midway, from the perspective of Symonds and Nolan, was a victory that said more about America and Japan than it did about Heinemann, Nimitz, or Kleiss.

Kleiss's memoir, *Never Call Me a Hero* (2017), which he wrote with the help of historians Timothy and Laura Orr, was a remarkable work. Much of the narrative is fortified by Kleiss's fascinating personal letters, which, unlike many other sources relating to the battle, were written at the time rather than in retrospect. But it is hard to imagine him publishing *Never Call Me a Hero* in the 1950s or 1960s, or indeed, at any point before Clarence Dickinson's death in 1984, or, more critically, before Jean's death in 2006. "After Jean died," Kleiss wrote in the memoir, "the memory of the battle flowed out of me like a broken dam."[114]

Never Call Me a Hero was a long time in coming, but it was worth the wait. First, it was a work of authentic Americana. Kleiss described his odyssey from small-town obscurity to war and back again. Second, his story took spirituality and romance seriously. Third, he embraced Kernan's comprehensive view—seeking to describe the battle as the result of earlier events. The difference was that for Kleiss, Midway's lessons lay not in the flaws of the Devastator but in the virtues of the Dauntless. The story was a cause for celebration, not mourning. Fourth, Kleiss was forensic in a style reminiscent of Parshall and Tully. His narrative named heroes (Earl Gallaher, John Snowden) as well as villains (Clarence Dickinson and, to a certain extent, Wade McClusky); it settled scores. Fifth, Kleiss moved against the trend of describing the battle as a clash of cultures or civilizations. In his account, it was the result of actions taken by specific individuals. The morning of June 4 received special attention. To be precise, it was the moment of the strike, the moment that the flight deck erupted in flames.[115] Sixth, Kleiss "disagree[d]" with the "luck theory." Instead, he argued that "we won the battle because we knew our stuff just a little bit better than our foes knew theirs." It was like the tennis analogy from the dive-bomber instructional film: slight differences in skill resulted in dramatic differences in outcome.

Then, in April 2016, before his memoir was published, Dusty Kleiss, the last surviving Midway dive-bomber pilot, at the age of one hundred, died. With him, the battle finally passed into history.

✪

THE FIRES OF THE battle have been most recently tended by Roland Emmerich with his 2019 blockbuster film *Midway*. Perhaps motivated by the interest in the battle that has developed since the turn of the twenty-first century, Emmerich wanted it to be as historically accurate as possible. Each character corresponds to a real figure, each action to a documented event. Even the dialogue matches up with various memoirs and firsthand accounts of the battle. The strongest historical aspect is the attention given to the Dauntless. The morning dive-bombing attack on the *Kido Butai* is the climax of the film. It is one of the most important truths about the battle and one that is communicated very well.

The story focuses on the pilots of the *Enterprise* Air Group, including Dick Best and Clarence Dickinson, as they struggle to perform under the stress of combat. On the morning of June 4, 1942, when a nervous rear-seat gunner asks to stay behind rather than participate in the battle, Best tells him, "You should get back in that plane. For *yourself.*" He is not reminded of General Douglas MacArthur's hallowed words, of duty, honor, or country; nor is he reminded of the remorseless enemy. Instead, there is a warning about the power of his own memory: "You'll remember this moment for the rest of your life," says Best. "And if you know that you came through when people were counting on you . . . well, you'll be a different man. You'll be able to face anything." The lesson is that combat, if endured successfully, becomes a talisman that guarantees success in the civilian afterlife; it is a past event that blesses the future. Cowardice, or failure, by contrast, leaves one bereft. In this sense, the uncertain American aviator is not fighting the Japanese but himself.

The attack on Pearl Harbor is the inciting incident that sets the story in motion. War comes from elsewhere and it provides its own justification. "We have awakened a sleeping giant and filled him with resolve," confesses Yamamoto with foreboding.[116] American power, if one can speak of such a thing, is provoked and prodded into life. The giant, presumably, wants nothing more than to return to sleep. As an American intelligence officer promises a Japanese friend at the start of the film, "Nobody wants a war." Once again, the fighting seems to be imposed from above rather than sought out by those involved. As if to finally recognize that the world has been put back to rights, at the end of the film, when the drama has concluded, a dedication appears on the screen: "To the Americans and Japanese who fought at Midway." Whatever differences these men had when they were killing each other, all has been forgotten. In a BBC interview about the making of the film, commenting on the joint dedication, Emmerich invoked his German heritage and the fact that his father was an unwilling soldier in World War II. The experience showed him that "people do their duty and do what they have to do but it's the politicians who screw up . . . and start wars." The lesson is a timely one, from Emmerich's perspective. In his view, one must remember "these amazing characters who risked their lives to fight for democracy," because today is a "time of . . . more nationalism wherever you look."[117]

As a work of political advocacy, the film raises many questions, however. More than half its $98 million budget came from two Chinese investment firms, Starlight and Shanghai RuYi Entertainment.[118] China took an interest in the battle because it commemorates the defeat of the Japanese, a long-standing rival. The film also featured the Doolittle Raiders' escape into China, an event that culminated in the killing of hundreds of thousands of Chinese civilians as the Imperial Japanese Army hunted for the American aircrews. There is no mention of the American internment of Japanese civilians, a minor theme of the 1976 film. In this sense the contemporary portrayal of the battle is one of unadulterated triumph. Even the defeated Japanese are better off having lost to such a virtuous America.

Perhaps inspired by Emmerich, there is Kevin Miller's recent novel on the battle. Drawing on his experience as a naval aviator, Miller portrays the drama of life aboard ship alongside the major events of the *Kido Butai*'s destruction. His story begins with the attack on Pearl Harbor, what one naval aviator calls "the unreality of a fairytale," and then focuses on the first two weeks of June 1942. The novel concludes with two brothers who survive the battle—Lloyd Childers, a tail-gunner in Torpedo Squadron Three, and Wayne Childers, a sailor aboard the *Yorktown*—embracing each other, astounded that "God took the others and not them."[119]

Much in life is beyond our control. One's birth, for example, is entirely the result of providence. It is a gift that cannot be earned or exchanged. One's battles are often similar: they are like war in Emmerich's film or Miller's novel—a storm that arrives from somewhere else, an unreality. In this sense those who attribute the outcome of Midway to luck are not entirely mistaken. Man is small and war only makes him seem smaller. Niccolò Machiavelli recognized this problem in *The Prince*. "I compare fortune," he wrote, "to one of those violent rivers which, when they are enraged, flood the plains, tear down trees and buildings, wash soil from one place to deposit it in another. Everyone flees before them, everybody yields to their impetus, there is no possibility of resistance."

World War II was a river of this kind. It was a moment of enormous force when events swept people along from one place to deposit them in another. But Machiavelli did not believe that such a disaster was cause for resignation. On the contrary, he suggested the opposite. To control a violent river, he said, one prepares when it is "flowing quietly." That is the time to "take precautions, constructing dykes and embankments so that when the river is in flood they would keep to one channel or their impetus be less wild and dangerous." And "so it is with fortune," he added. "She shows her potency when there is no well-regulated power to resist her, and her impetus is felt where she knows there are no embankments and dykes built to restrain her."[120] The destruction of war, in other words, is related to the preparation that takes place in advance of any open hostilities. Contemporary accounts of the Battle of Midway often focus on the former, on the momentary spectacle, rather than the latter, on the years of training, graft, and contemplation.

✪

JAPAN, NOW A CLOSE ally of the United States, has wrestled with the legacy of Midway and the Pacific War. Long ambivalent about the Imperial Navy's history, because of the brutal war that so harmed Japan's reputation, and constrained by their pacifist postwar constitution, the Japanese have become increasingly assertive. The new millennium saw the commissioning of the *Soryu*-class attack submarines, which shared a name with the vanquished Midway carrier. Admiral Yamamoto was the subject of another remarkably positive biopic in 2011, demonstrating the latent power of nationalist nostalgia, though not necessarily a growing military confidence.[121] Meanwhile, the Japanese "Self-Defense Forces" now boast vessels that are aircraft carriers in all but name. In 2018 it was announced that two "helicopter destroyers" would be modified to carry vertical take-off and landing jets. One of them was named the *Kaga*.[122]

The legacy of Midway also resonates with the changing balance of power in East Asia. For the first time since World War II, the West faces a serious naval challenge in the Pacific.[123] The People's

Republic of China—a communist dictatorship—poses both an ideological threat and a strategic one. It has built a large ocean-going navy with a growing carrier capability; the first domestically built aircraft carrier is expected to enter service in 2023. In fact, according to a US Department of Defense report in 2020, the PRC now boasts "the largest navy in the world with an overall battle force of approximately 350 ships."[124] It menaces Taiwan directly and has established a massive military presence in the contested South China Sea. Beyond this, Beijing's "Belt and Road Initiative," which seeks to transform the whole of Eurasia, and the maritime "String of Pearls" concept, which attempts something similar in the Indo-Pacific, shows the PRC's vaulting ambition.[125]

Over the past few years, the United States and the rest of the Western world generally have slowly been waking up to all of this. In February 2016, Admiral Harry Harris, chief of US Pacific Command, warned Congress, saying he believed that "China seeks hegemony in East Asia." In April 2021, the Australian secretary for home affairs, Michael Pezzullo, announced that the "drums of war" were beating in the Pacific and that the nation needed to prepare accordingly. As for the PRC, leader Xi Xinping has warned advisers to "prepare for war" in the South China Sea.[126]

In fact, the People's Republic of China poses some of the same problems for the United States as Imperial Japan did in World War II, but on a much larger scale. Like Imperial Japan, the PRC's leaders believe that the current order in the region is illegitimate and stacked against their interests. Whatever one thinks of these claims and demands, they are not simply to be mocked or disregarded. If we don't deal with them, or prepare to counter them, then we may suffer another Pearl Harbor—but there is no guarantee that we have done the necessary preparation to earn another Midway.

There are two principal reasons to be concerned. First, the US Navy is, as former navy secretary John Lehman has written, "stretched too thin and woefully underfunded."[127] Its ship and dockyards are in crisis. Furthermore, as James Holmes, professor of maritime strategy at the Naval War College, has pointed out, the United States cannot expect to outbuild the PRC in any naval war of attrition.[128] The fighting navy, as Seth Cropsey, the director of the Center for American Seapower, lamented, is now only 297 ships strong, fewer than half the number during the Reagan administration, and is tasked with deterring not only the PRC but also Russia, Iran, and North Korea.[129] Second, the PRC is unlikely to oblige the United States by walking into a trap in the middle of the Pacific Ocean, as the Japanese did at Midway. It is more likely to inflict a surprise defeat in the narrow waters of the South China Sea comparable to the sinking of the *Prince of Wales* and the *Repulse* in December 1941.[130]

The new reality is reflected in the changing visions of how a conflict between the United States and the PRC—which have been circulating for nearly three decades—might evolve. Early scenarios described since the 1990s, such as Humphrey Hawksley and Simon Holberton's *Dragon Strike*, imagined that Beijing might inflict some initial shocks, but that it would eventually be crushed by the might of American power.[131] Over the past few years, though, a much darker prospect has emerged. In his 2020 book *Asia's New Geopolitics*, Michael Auslin imagines a scenario that he calls "the Sino-American littoral war of 2025." In this "future history," the United States comes off worse in the end than the PRC, and its entire East Asian security architecture begins to unravel.[132] In the terrifying novel *2034* by Elliot Ackerman and Admiral James Stavridis, the former supreme allied commander of the North Atlantic Treaty Organization, the US Navy is completely outclassed by the PRC in the South China Sea.[133]

In these circumstances, as Elbridge Colby, former deputy assistant secretary for defense and the lead author of the 2018 National Defense Strategy, has argued, Washington must prepare to win a war with China—one which it cannot afford to lose—precisely in order to prevent that war from happening.[134] In the Pacific, as David Zikusoka of the Center for a New American Security wrote, the United States' best hope may be to draw the PRC into a complex struggle on many fronts far from home. America, he argued, has learned "how to fight away games," whereas the PRC has not, or at least not yet. Ultimately, this is about deterrence.

"The defense establishment," Zikusoka said, "needs to start thinking about how it would fight a Second Battle of Midway to ensure it never has to fight at all."[135]

When a military confrontation arises between the West and the People's Republic of China, it will consist in large part of a contest for the sea. In some respects, this will take the form of a battle for the control of islands, many of them obscure outposts such as Midway, that govern access to the continents of Asia and North America. But in other respects this will be a battle between naval resources, between carriers that attack one another from beyond the horizon with aircraft or missiles. It is understandable, then, that the Battle of Midway, which bears strategic and tactical similarities to a likely future scenario, has been the focus of renewed attention. The battle also offers important lessons about the value of fundamentals, such as intelligence and reconnaissance, or the principles of surprise and simplicity, as well as outright aggression. There is also the obvious lesson of the Dauntless, a sturdy and powerful weapon, built in adequate numbers in advance of the war.

Unsurprisingly, the PRC has taken a keen interest in the Battle of Midway and its lessons. "China," as Lyle Goldstein wrote in the *National Interest* in 2017, "hopes to get right what Imperial Japan got wrong." Tactically, they have criticized the submarine and carrier deployment and the immense risk of exposing the *Kido Butai* so far from home. Strategically, they have noted the failure to prepare the economy for a long war, so that battlefield losses could be replaced. A more cautious approach, they have concluded, might well have "caused the Americans to bleed heavily" and seek a negotiated solution.[136]

After a detailed analysis of Japanese military records, the PRC published a report in 2016 that made several important observations. Overall, the report attributed the Japanese failure to industrial weakness relative to the United States. Because Japan had less manufacturing power, it needed to force an early confrontation with the United States, and this necessitated an attack on Midway. The suggestion here is that even if Japan had won, it would have been in a difficult position: unable to successfully invade Hawaii and unable to prevent the United States from developing more ships to continue its war effort. The lesson that China has learned from this is that outright confrontation with the United States is a challenging strategy to carry out.[137]

Worryingly, all of this suggests that PRC strategists think that a war with the United States might be winnable, or survivable, even if China was to lose an opening Midway-style clash. This may also help to explain why Chinese funders backed Emmerich's *Midway* movie—actually making its completion possible after he was unable to secure the backing necessary in the United States.[138] "Don't push us into war," Emmerich's Yamamoto tells the Americans. "You must give the chance to us who are the more reasonable to own the day." The message that the aspiring power in Asia should not be boxed into a corner by the United States may have been Tokyo's message then, but it is Beijing's warning now.

Our own lessons from Midway are somewhat different. First of all, the battle shows that procurement wins wars. "You have two kinds of equipment," said George Gay at the end of his book *Sole Survivor*. "Experimental and obsolete."[139] His point was that the military was in continual need of improving its equipment. The same is true of doctrine, a set of beliefs that tends to ossify around certain leaders or conventions.

Second, the Battle of Midway teaches us that war takes place not in some other world but in our own world. The danger of interpreting World War II as a reaction to the attack on Pearl Harbor is that it causes one to believe that the problems of war are solved during wartime. But Heinemann and the Dauntless demonstrate that peacetime is when one prepares for the violent river of war. Moreover, there is the example of Nimitz and Kleiss, officers who entered war as the product of decades of peace, though both men had lived through—and in Nimitz's case served in—World War I. The point is that they believed certain things about life and death, about God and country, that sustained them in battle.

Finally, luck and the possibility of miracles are not a good basis for policy or historical inquiry. These forces are unknown to us and cannot be controlled, and we must not rely upon them for the protection of our way of life. It is much the same with history, which seeks to explain and understand, not to dismiss or obscure. In the case of the Battle of Midway, the enormous number of variables that were beyond Nimitz's or Kleiss's control should not prevent us from examining what they could control. Nowhere is this more evident than in the moment of Kleiss's dive, when—adjusting his plane through the use of his split flaps, control stick, trim tab, and rudder—he delivered his ordnance on target. All this skill was the result of an immense amount of preparation. This is why we must prepare for the moment when the river of fortune overflows, and recognize the importance of preparation, both in our personal lives and in the life of the nation.

✪

IT HAS NOW BEEN eighty years since the Battle of Midway. It would appear that much has changed. Doris Miller, once seen as fit only to serve as a mess steward, will give his name to a new US aircraft carrier. Modern weapons systems have a lethality and complexity unimaginable in Heinemann's time. The strategic situation is also different: the United States and Japan, for example, are now allies.

One thing, though, remains the same. East Asia is still the site of a furious contestation, at the heart of which lies the Indo-Pacific. The job that McClusky, Kleiss, and their comrades did may soon have to be done all over again. But America is now less prepared than it was when it was surprised at Pearl Harbor. Despite the loss of the battle fleet, and even before the great engine of American industry began its relentless production, the US carrier force of December 1941 was strong enough to stem and then turn the tide. Today, the US Navy is a formidable force, but it possesses only a proportion of its former dominance. Its real quality will be demonstrated only when it is put to the test—that is when we will know which of its systems are the Devastators and which are the Dauntlesses of our time. It is no wonder that the scenarios envisaged by analysts have darkened, going from assumptions of triumph, perhaps following early setbacks, to worries of stalemate and even defeat. Of course, it may be that the next war-winning platform has already been developed—whether on the West Coast, on the East Coast, or somewhere in between—and its crew already trained. Let us hope so, and even more, that they are never needed.

As conflict between the United States and the People's Republic of China looms in the Pacific, there is still a critical lesson in Midway for our time. We have seen that the devastatingly effective attack of the dive bombers was not a fluke. They did exactly what they had been trained to do. Equally important was the fact that their equipment, and especially the Douglas Dauntless bomber itself, did exactly what it had been designed to do. The peacetime American taxpayers got excellent value for their money. Even if the United States had not built a single new ship after Pearl Harbor or trained a single new pilot, it would still have won the Battle at Midway. This means that the United States today should not trust to luck or amateur genius, but to military preparedness in times of relative peace. The question Midway poses is not whether we were lucky then but whether we want to trust to luck today.

Machiavelli's lesson was that good princes prepare. In times of peace, they set to work, hoping not to avoid danger entirely but to mitigate it. Heinemann, continually drafting automobiles, boats, whatever he could find, in hopes of landing a job designing aircraft, prepared. Nimitz, sailing from Batangas to Pearl Harbor and elsewhere, experimenting with the circular formation, launching daring raids, prepared. Kleiss, practicing his carrier take-offs and landings, his dive-bombing runs and his navigational skills, prepared. While hunting for the *Kido Butai*, low on fuel, uncertain whether he would manage the return flight home, he later said, he realized "we had trained too long and too hard to back out now."[140] By that point, he was swept up in the force of a violent river. Yet because of so much preparation, because strong embankments had been built up, when the destruction of the war came, it kept to one channel. From this channel flowed "a beautiful silver waterfall."[141]

ACKNOWLEDGMENTS

Mark Aldrich, Janice Anderson-Gram, Zach Anderson-Gram, Michael Auslin, Duane Bourne, Vance Breese Jr., Thomas Burchill, Tony diGiulian, Carl Dobson, Norman Friedman, Jared Galloway, Mary Hall, Bill Hamilton, Mike Hart, Keith Hedley, John Hemmings, James Holmes, Will Inboden, John Lehman, Kelly Lenkevich, Marc Levitt, Michael Lombardi, Mina Markovic, Celina McGregor, Russell Moore, Chuck Myers, Nancy Dobson Napier, Chris Nations, Grace Neie, Charles Nevius, Bill Norberg, Richard Nowatzki, Timothy and Laura Orr, Chris Parry, Jon Parshall, Clive Priddle, Anupama Roy-Chaudhury, Klaus Schmider, Katherine A. Scott, Debbie Seracini, Ciaran Simms, Constance Simms, Daniel Simms, Clara Snyder, Jay Spenser, Gabriel Spiers, Katherine Streckfus, James Talbot, Charlotte Tan, Yukako Taniguchi, Barrett Tillman, Tom Trombley, Katsuya Tsukamoto, Bob van der Linden, Liz Wake, David Williams, Sandra Wilson, Jonathan Yeung, Karl Zingheim.

LOSSES

Ships	United States	Japan
Carriers	1	4
Cruisers	0	1
Destroyers	1	0
Aircraft	148	248
Officers and Men	362	3,057

NOTE ON SOURCES

The Silver Waterfall relies on three kinds of source material: memoirs and biographies, archives, and personal visits to important locations. The wealth of material from the first category by or about participants of the battle and others who contributed to its outcome includes, most notably, Dusty Kleiss's *Never Call Me a Hero* (2017) and Ed Heinemann's *Combat Aircraft Designer* (1980), the latter coauthored by Rosario Rausa. Also included in this category are Japanese accounts that have not yet been presented in English, including Teiichi Makishima's *Midway kaisen—Hokyu tsuzukazu* (The Battle of Midway: Supplies Dwindle), first published in 1967. The second category includes material from the Operational Archives, Naval History and Heritage Command, Washington Navy Yard, Washington DC; the National Museum of the Pacific War, Fredericksburg, Texas; the US Naval Institute Oral History Collection and the Nimitz Library, United States Naval Academy, Annapolis, Maryland; and Edward Henry Heinemann Personal Papers, San Diego Air and Space Museum Library and Archives, San Diego, California. The third category includes our visits to the museum on the descendant of the one surviving US aircraft carrier from the battle, the USS *Hornet*, now at Alameda, California, which contains oral and written histories from men who served on the original ship, and the USS *Midway* Museum in San Diego, California. The *Midway* did not serve in World War II, of course, but it is named for the famous battle.

Also, a note on Japanese transliterations. For ease of reading we have omitted accent marks on Japanese words except when they appear in the endnotes. For the same reason we have followed the convention of listing all names as first name, then family name, similar to Mitsuo Fuchida. Finally, we also refer to Japanese aircraft by the Western nicknames that became common later in the war.

NOTES

Chapter 1: The Engineer

1. Brendan Simms, *Hitler: Only the World Was Enough* (London, 2019), 514–515.

2. Edward H. Heinemann and Rosario Rausa, *Combat Aircraft Designer: The Ed Heinemann Story* (London, 1980), 2.

3. Russell A. Kazal, *Becoming Old Stock: The Paradox of German-American Identity* (Princeton, NJ, 2004), 1.

4. Heinemann and Rausa, *Combat Aircraft Designer*, 4 (mistranslated there as "magician").

5. See Jay Spenser, *The Airplane: How Ideas Gave Us Wings* (New York, 2008), 16–36.

6. Heinemann and Rausa, *Combat Aircraft Designer*, 3.

7. Heinemann and Rausa, *Combat Aircraft Designer*, 5.

8. Patti Marshall, "Neta Snook," *Aviation History* 17 (2007); Neta Snook Southern, *I Taught Amelia to Fly* (New York, 1974).

9. Heinemann and Rausa, *Combat Aircraft Designer*, 2.

10. Heinemann and Rausa, *Combat Aircraft Designer*, 6–7.

11. "Introduction," Edward Henry Heinemann Personal Papers, San Diego Air and Space Museum Library and Archives (Heinemann Papers hereafter), Box 4/8.

12. Barrett Tillman, "Heinemann: Before the Beginning," Heinemann Papers, Box 4/16, pp. 5–6.

13. Heinemann and Rausa, *Combat Aircraft Designer*, 14; Kenneth C. Carter to Ed Heinemann, Long Beach, California, May 17, 1987, Heinemann Papers, Box 3/17.

14. Tillman, "Heinemann," 7, 10; Heinemann and Rausa, *Combat Aircraft Designer*, 6–7, 13, 14, 17.

15. Heinemann and Rausa, *Combat Aircraft Designer*, 8, 35.

16. Jay P. Spenser to Ed Heinemann, National Air and Space Museum, Washington, DC, May 9, 1983, Heinemann Papers, Box 3/9; personal correspondence between the authors and Jay Spenser.

17. Close examination of correspondence between Heinemann and his sister suggests that while there were severe tensions between them about money, her husband's race does not appear to have played any role.

18. W. A. Mankey, testimonial for E. Heineman [sic], Santa Monica, California, February 25, 1927, Heinemann Papers, Box 2/2.

19. E. M. Fisk, testimonial for E. H. Heineman [sic], Long Beach, California, December 12, 1927, Heinemann Papers, Box 2/2.

20. G. E. Moreland, testimonial for E. H. Heineman [sic], Los Angeles, California, October 23, 1929, Heinemann Papers, Box 2/2.

21. Interview with Edward H. Heinemann, conducted by Daniel R. Mortensen, Office of Air Force History, Rancho Santa Fe, California, April 5, 1984, Heinemann Papers, Box 4/9, p. 2.

22. Heinemann and Rausa, *Combat Aircraft Designer*, 10–12.

23. Karl Peter Grube to Joseph Holty, Aurora, Illinois, June 27, 1986, Heinemann Papers, Box 3/15.

24. Heinemann and Rausa, *Combat Aircraft Designer*, 17.

25. "Moreland Monoplane," *Aero Digest*, September 1929, 146–147.

26. Edward H. Heinemann, "Aircraft Design Then and Now," lecture text, February 1981, Heinemann Papers, Box 2/1, p. 1.

27. Andrew Hamilton, "Ed Heinemann: Naval Aviation's Secret Weapon" (Los Angeles, no date), Heinemann Papers, Box 6/16.

28. John K. Northrop, testimonial for E. H. Heineman [sic], Burbank, California, October 13, 1931, Heinemann Papers, Box 2/2.

29. See biographical sketch, no author, no place, no date, Heinemann Papers, Box 4/16.

30. Peter C. Smith, *The History of Dive-Bombing* (Barnsley, UK, 2007), first published as *Impact!* (1981), 12–13.

31. E. R. Johnson, *United States Naval Aviation, 1919–1941* (Jefferson, NC, 2011), 8–10; Peter C. Smith, *Midway: Dauntless Victory* (Barnsley, UK, 2007), 168; Barrett Tillman, *The Dauntless Dive Bomber of World War II* (Annapolis, MD, 1976); Thomas Wildenberg, *Destined for Glory* (Annapolis, MD, 1998), 10. A US Navy dive-bombing video from 1942 claims the technique was "first devised by the United States Navy several years ago." See "Dive Bombing in a World War 2 Aircraft U.S. Navy Training Film—1943," YouTube, posted October 2, 2012, by Zeno's Warbird Videos, www.youtube.com/watch?v=lOz_i_2USkY.

32. Authors' interview with Richard Nowatzki, Rosemont, California, January 11, 2020. Not all pilots describe dive recovery as stressful. See Robert Winston, *Dive Bomber* (London, 1940), 80–81.

33. David Rigby, *Wade McClusky and the Battle of Midway* (Oxford, 2019), 21, 51, 55, 83, 85.

34. Wildenberg, *Destined for Glory*, 73–74.

35. Interview with Heinemann by Mortensen, April 5, 1984.

36. Wildenberg, *Destined for Glory*, 95.

37. Planes in the 1920s could carry more than 1,000 pounds of ordnance, but they couldn't controllably dive straight down with it. These included, for instance, the Naval Aircraft Factory TN (1927) and the Martin T4M (1927).

38. Malcolm Gladwell, *The Bomber Mafia: A Story Set in War* (London, 2021), 25–29 (quotation p. 29). See also Tami Davis Biddle, *Rhetoric and Reality in Air Warfare: The Evolution of British and American Ideas About Strategic Bombing, 1914–1945* (Princeton, NJ, 2002).

39. See Naoko Shimazu, *Japan, Race and Equality: The Racial Equality Proposal of 1919* (London, 1998).

40. Limitation of Naval Armament (Five-Power Treaty or Washington Treaty), signed February 6, 1922, www.loc.gov/law/help/us-treaties/bevans/m-ust000002-0351.pdf.

41. Hiroyuki Agawa, *The Reluctant Admiral*, trans. John Bester (Tokyo, 1979 [1969]), 27–33.

42. Eric Bergerud, *Fire in the Sky* (Boulder, 2000), 191; David C. Evans and Mark R. Peattie, *Kaigun: Strategy, Tactics, and Technology in the Imperial Japanese Navy, 1887–1941* (Annapolis, MD, 1997), 308.

43. Mark R. Peattie, *Sunburst: The Rise of Japanese Naval Air Power, 1909–1941* (Annapolis, MD, 2001), 80–83; Agawa, *Reluctant Admiral*, 79, 92.

44. Peattie, *Sunburst*, 26.

45. J. Francillon, *Japanese Aircraft of the Pacific War* (London, 1970), 2–3.

46. Bergerud, *Fire in the Sky*, 193.

47. By this point, the Japanese air arm numbered some 3,000 planes to the US Navy's 5,479. See Francillon, *Japanese Aircraft of the Pacific War*, 41; Johnson, *United States Naval Aviation*, 322.

48. Evans and Peattie, *Kaigun*, 307.

49. Heinemann and Rausa, *Combat Aircraft Designer*, 34; Edward Heinemann and Glenn E. Smith Jr., "Sugar Baker Dog: The Victor at Midway" (unpublished manuscript, 1987, copy in H. Paul Whittier Historical Aviation Library, San Diego Aerospace Museum), pp. 5a–6. "Sugar Baker Dog" contains many details not in Heinemann and Rausa.

50. Ed Heinemann to "Bill" [last name unknown], July 4, 1973, Heinemann Papers, Box 2/15.

51. Wing area is calculated by measuring the surface area of the wing. The larger the wing, the greater the amount of lift it can generate. The wing area of the F2F was 203 square feet, the SBC's was 317 square feet, and the SBD's was 325 square feet.

52. John Anderson, *The Grand Designers* (Cambridge, 2018), 68–115.

53. Heinemann and Smith, "Sugar Baker Dog," 11–12.

54. Thus the recollection of David McCampbell, who was then working as a riveter: see David McCampbell to Ed Heinemann, Lake Worth, Florida, February 4, 1981, Heinemann Papers, Box 3/4.

55. Heinemann and Rausa, *Combat Aircraft Designer*, 35.

56. Heinemann and Smith, "Sugar Baker Dog," 13; Israel Taback, *The NACA Oil-Damped V-G Recorder* (Washington, DC, 1950), 1–2.

57. Heinemann and Rausa, *Combat Aircraft Designer*, 35. See also "I think I have made more 9G pullups than anybody on earth—from the rear seat," in interview with Heinemann by Mortensen, April 5, 1984, p. 28.

58. Heinemann and Smith, "Sugar Baker Dog," 13.

59. Heinemann and Smith, "Sugar Baker Dog," 18–19.

60. Heinemann and Rausa, *Combat Aircraft Designer*, 37.

61. Heinemann and Smith, "Sugar Baker Dog," 14.

62. See Heinemann and Smith, "Sugar Baker Dog," 17a, 17b.

63. Heinemann and Rausa, *Combat Aircraft Designer*, 39.

64. Heinemann and Smith, "Sugar Baker Dog," 18.

65. Heinemann and Smith, "Sugar Baker Dog," 14.

66. David Brazelton, *The Douglas SBD Dauntless* (no place, 1967), unpaginated.

67. Heinemann and Rausa, *Combat Aircraft Designer*, 44. In a letter to Barrett Tillman, Athena, Oregon, November 6, 1976, Heinemann Papers, Box 2/20, Heinemann recalls that Clexton "helped me make the SBD right."

68. Heinemann and Rausa, *Combat Aircraft Designer*, 43; Heinemann and Smith, "Sugar Baker Dog," 26.

69. Heinemann, untitled draft article for *Foundation* magazine, Heinemann Papers, Box 4/8, p. 2.

70. Heinemann and Smith, "Sugar Baker Dog," 27.

71. Heinemann and Rausa, *Combat Aircraft Designer*, 46–48.

72. George Kernahan, "Douglas SBD-2 Dauntless," 42.

73. Tillman, *Dauntless Dive Bomber*, 12.

74. Quoted in Heinemann and Rausa, *Combat Aircraft Designer*, 42.

75. John Ward, *Hitler's Stuka Squadrons* (Staplehurst, UK, 2004), 48.

76. Brazelton, *Douglas SBD Dauntless*, 9; Peter Smith, *Douglas SBD Dauntless* (Ramsbury, UK, 1997), 148–155.

77. Smith, *Douglas SBD Dauntless*, 149–150.

78. Heinemann and Smith, "Sugar Baker Dog," 30–31. On the wider question of "technology transfer" to Japan at this time, see pp. 183–186.

79. See Katherine Scott, "A Safety Valve: The Truman Committee's Oversight During World War II," in *Congress and Civil-Military Relations*, ed. Colton C. Campbell and David P. Auerswald (Washington, DC, 2015); Alonzo L. Hamby, *Man of the People: A Life of Harry S. Truman* (New York, 1995), 248–260.

80. Brazelton, *Douglas SBD Dauntless*, 5–6.

81. Heinemann and Rausa, *Combat Aircraft Designer*, 54; Karl Peter Grube to Joseph Holty, Aurora, Illinois, June 27, 1986, Heinemann Papers, Box 3/15.

82. Frank N. Fleming memorandum, "Commendation of El Segundo Personnel," Washington, DC, August 25, 1941, Heinemann Papers, Box 2/2.

83. Colonel Carl F. Greene to Ed Heinemann, Langley Field, October 3, 1941, Heinemann Papers, Box 2/2.

84. "Tripolitis" to Ed Heinemann, San Diego, November 10, 1941, Heinemann Papers, Box 2/2. ("The only deficiency mentioned was that certain standard drawings called for on some of the assemblies were not provided with the set. I hope you will take some action and aim for a perfect score next time.")

85. Ed Heinemann to New Employees, Douglas Aircraft Company, no date, Heinemann Papers, Box 4/8.

86. Tillman, *Dauntless Dive Bomber*, 10. On production at El Segundo, see also Bill Yenne, *The American Aircraft Factory in World War II* (Minneapolis, 2006), 76–80.

87. Ed Heinemann speech, "Our War Effort," [El Segundo], March 20, 1942, Heinemann Papers, Box 4/8.

88. "BuAer had originally contemplated terminating SBD production in early 1942 at 174 (i.e. 57 SBD-1s, 87 SBD-2s, and 30 SBD-3s) but the intervention of World War II kept the assembly line moving until mid-1944, resulting in a further 470 SBD-3s, 780 SBD-4s, 3,025 SBD-5s, and finally 450 SBD-6s. Another 953 were completed for the AAR as the A-24 (SBD-3), A-24A (SBD-4), and A-24B (SBD-5)," in Johnson, *United States Naval Aviation*, 51; René Francillon, "Le SBD, Scout Bomber Douglas, 'Dauntless': Lambin mais venimeux," *Le Fana de l'Aviation* 427 (June 2005), 25.

Chapter 2: The Strategist

1. E. B. Potter, *Nimitz* (Annapolis, MD, 1976), 9; Chester W. Nimitz to Chester B. Nimitz, 1905, National Museum of the Pacific War, https://digitalarchive .pacificwarmuseum.org/digital/collection/p16769coll4.

2. Dede W. Casad and Frank A. Driscoll, *Chester W. Nimitz: Admiral of the Hills* (Fort Worth, Texas, 1983), 3–34 (quotation, p. 4).

3. Robert A. Caro, *The Years of Lyndon Johnson*, vol. 1, *The Path to Power* (London, 2019 [1981]), 56, 58, 60–61 (with quotation).

4. Potter, *Nimitz*, 116.

5. T. R. Fehrenbach, *Lone Star* (New York, 2000 [1968]); Casad and Driscoll, *Chester Nimitz*, 33.

6. Potter, *Nimitz*, 49. On the influence of Mahan, see Ian Toll, *Pacific Crucible* (New York, 2011), 14–18.

7. Potter, *Nimitz*, 29.

8. Chester Nimitz to Charles Henry Nimitz, April 18, 1900, National Museum of the Pacific War, https://digitalarchive.pacificwarmuseum.org/digital/collection /p16769coll4.

9. Chester Nimitz to Charles Henry Nimitz, April 18, 1900.

10. Chester Nimitz to Charles Henry Nimitz, January 23, 1900, and June 4, 1900, National Museum of the Pacific War, https://digitalarchive.pacificwarmuseum.org /digital/collection/p16769coll4.

11. Chester Nimitz to Charles Henry Nimitz, April 18, 1900.

12. Potter, *Nimitz*, 30.

13. Chester W. Nimitz to Chester B. Nimitz, September 14, 1901, National Museum of the Pacific War, https://digitalarchive.pacificwarmuseum.org/digital /collection/p16769coll4.

14. Chester Nimitz to Charles Henry Nimitz, October 3, 1901, National Museum of the Pacific War, https://digitalarchive.pacificwarmuseum.org/digital /collection/p16769coll4.

15. Chester W. Nimitz to Chester B. Nimitz, September 14, 1901.

16. Chester W. Nimitz to Chester B. Nimitz, November 1901, November 5, 1902, and Chester Nimitz to Charles Henry Nimitz, December 1902, National Museum of the Pacific War, https://digitalarchive.pacificwarmuseum.org/digital/collection /p16769coll4.

17. Potter, *Nimitz*, 472.

18. Chester W. Nimitz to Charles Henry Nimitz, January 31, 1902, National Museum of the Pacific War, https://digitalarchive.pacificwarmuseum.org/digital /collection/p16769coll4.

19. Potter, *Nimitz*, 51.

20. Quoted in Craig Symonds, *The Battle of Midway* (Oxford, 2011), 7.

21. Quoted in Casad and Driscoll, *Chester W. Nimitz*, 74.

22. Chester Nimitz to Charles Henry Nimitz, June 4, 1905.

23. *Los Angeles Herald*, March 2, 1905.

24. *San Francisco Call*, March 2, 1905.

25. Resolved by the board on May 5, 1905. John Young, "The Support of the Anti-Oriental Movement," *Annals of the American Academy of Political and Social Science* 34, no. 2 (September 1909): 16.

26. Remarks of President John Willis Baer at his inauguration at Occidental, He quotes Maltbie Babcock, "Baer Inaugurated as the President of Occidental College," *Los Angeles Herald*, October 27, 1906.

27. "Clash with Dai Nippon Must Come in Time: Supremacy of Pacific at Stake," *San Francisco Call*, February 1, 1907.

28. Chester W. Nimitz to Chester B. Nimitz, December 11, 1907, National Museum of the Pacific War, https://digitalarchive.pacificwarmuseum.org/digital /collection/p16769coll4.

29. Potter, *Nimitz*, 61.

30. Potter, *Nimitz*, 116, 122–124.

31. For a text of the Plan of San Diego, see "Investigation of Mexican Affairs," vol. 1, Committee on Foreign Relations, United States Senate, Document No. 285 (Washington, DC, 1920), 1205–1207.

32. James Sandos, *Rebellion in the Borderlands: Anarchism and the Plan of San Diego, 1904–1923* (Norman, OK, 1992).

33. "Maumee II (Fuel Ship No. 14), 1916–1948," *Dictionary of American Naval Fighting Ships*, www.history.navy.mil/research/histories/ship-histories/danfs/m/maumee -ii.html.

34. Caro, *Years of Lyndon Johnson*, 1:80–81.

35. James H. Belote and William M. Belote, *Titans of the Seas: The Development and Operations of Japanese and American Carrier Task Forces During World War II* (New York, 1975), 23.

36. Walter Borneman, *The Admirals* (New York, 2012), 131–133.

37. Quoted in Potter, *Nimitz*, 139, 141.

38. James Cook, *Carl Vinson: Patriarch of the Armed Forces* (Macon, GA, 2004), 102–103, 146, 151–153.

39. Lisle Rose, *The Ship That Held the Line: The U.S.S.* Hornet *and the First Year of the Pacific War* (Annapolis, MD, 1995), 4.

40. David Rigby, *Wade McClusky and the Battle of Midway* (Oxford, 2019), 71.

41. Mitsuo Fuchida's first flight while a cadet at Etajima occurs by happenstance. See Mitsuo Fuchida, *For That One Day*, trans. Douglas T. Shinsato and Tadanori Urabe (Kamuela, HI, 2011), 29.

42. Thomas Wildenberg, *All the Factors of Victory: Admiral Joseph Mason Reeves and the Origins of Carrier Airpower* (Dallas, VA, 2003).

43. For a detailed study, see Katsuya Tsukamoto, "Japan's 'Carrier Revolution' in the Interwar Period," (PhD diss., Fletcher School of Law and Diplomacy, 2016).

44. Fuchida, *For That One Day*, 46.

45. David Evans and Mark Peattie, *Kaigun: Strategy, Tactics, and Technology in the Imperial Japanese Navy, 1887–1941* (Annapolis, MD, 1997), 338–339.

46. Evans and Peattie, *Kaigun*, 379; Jim Sawruk, Anthony Tully, and Sander Kingsepp, "Carrier Aviation Meets the Leviathan, Part One," *The Hook* 48, no. 3 (2020): 27–32.

47. See Fleet Problem IX, Albert Nofi, *To Train a Fleet for War* (Annapolis, MD, 2010), 119.

48. Nofi, *To Train a Fleet*, 36, 113, 124.

49. Nofi, *To Train a Fleet*, 123, 124.

50. Symonds, *Battle of Midway*, 314; Edward P. Stafford, *The Big E: The Story of the USS* Enterprise (Annapolis, MD, 2002 [1962]), 307; Rose, *Ship That Held the Line*, 176, 198, 208.

51. Nofi, *To Train a Fleet*, 35, 36.

52. Joseph F. Underwood, *The Eight Said No: A Personal History of the Pacific War* (Paducah, KY, 1998), 63–64.

53. Minoru Genda, "Tactical Planning in the Imperial Japanese Navy," lecture delivered at the Naval War College, March 7, 1969, *Naval War College Review* 22, no. 8 (1969): 3–4.

54. Fuchida, *For That One Day*, 47.

55. Cathal Nolan, *The Allure of Battle* (Oxford, 2017), 491–502.

56. Mark R. Peattie, *Sunburst: The Rise of Japanese Naval Air Power, 1909–1941* (Annapolis, MD, 2001), 75, 147.

57. Hansgeorg Jentschura, Dieter Jung, and Peter Mickel, *Warships of the Imperial Japanese Navy, 1869–1945* (Annapolis, MD, 1977), 42–44.

58. Quoted in Ron Werneth, *Beyond Pearl Harbor: The Untold Stories of Japan's Naval Airmen* (Atglen, PA, 2008), 192.

59. Evans and Peattie, *Kaigun*, 315.

60. Dallas Isom, *Midway Inquest: Why the Japanese Lost the Battle of Midway* (Bloomington, IN, 2007), 356.

61. Mark Stille, *Midway 1942: Turning Point in the Pacific* (Oxford, 2010), 20; Mark Stille, *Imperial Japanese Navy Aircraft Carriers, 1921–1945* (Oxford, 2006), 9. Radar allowed US ships to detect planes "more than 50 nautical miles" away, whereas the Japanese relied on visual sighting, possible only "out to about 20 miles." Malcolm LeCompte, "Radar and the Air Battles of Midway," *Naval History* (Summer 1992): 29.

62. Evans and Peattie, *Kaigun*, 329, 346–347.

63. Mitsuo Fuchida and Masatake Okumiya, *Midway: The Battle That Doomed Japan in Five Fateful Minutes* (London, 1961), 41.

64. John Campbell, *Naval Weapons of World War Two* (Annapolis, MD, 1985), 110, 200; Stille, *Imperial Japanese Navy Aircraft Carriers*, 7–8.

65. Stille, *Midway 1942*, 20.

66. Peattie, *Sunburst*, 155–156.

67. Peter C. Smith, *Midway: Dauntless Victory* (Barnsley, UK, 2007), 149–151.

68. Fuchida and Okumiya, *Midway*, 240.

69. Quoted in Werneth, *Beyond Pearl Harbor*, 208.

70. Toshiyuki Yokoi, "Thoughts on Japan's Naval Defeat," in *The Japanese Navy in World War II*, ed. David C. Evans (Annapolis, MD, 1969), 508–510.

71. Barrett Tillman, *Enterprise: America's Fightingest Ship and the Men Who Helped Win World War II* (New York, 2012), 23.

72. Jeremy A. Yellen, "Into the Tiger's Den: Japan and the Tripartite Pact," *Journal of Contemporary History* 5 (2016): 555–576.

73. See Theo Sommer, *Deutschland und Japan zwischen den Maechten, 1935–1940. Vom Antikominternpakt zum Dreimaechtepakt* (Tübingen, Germany, 1962).

74. Quoted in Cameron Forbes, *Hellfire: The Story of Australia, Japan and the Prisoners of War* (Sydney, 2005), 118.

75. *Papers Relating to the Foreign Relations of the United States: Japan, 1931–1941*, vol. 2 (Washington, DC, 1943), 373–375.

76. Gordon Prange said that "the Hull note was not an ultimatum," in *At Dawn We Slept* (New York, 1981), but Benn Steil called it an "austere ultimatum," in *The Battle of Bretton Woods* (Princeton, NJ, 2013), 55.

77. Quoted in Eri Hotta, *Japan 1941: Countdown to Infamy* (New York, 2013), 20, 192.

78. Naoko Shimazu, *Japan, Race and Equality: The Racial Equality Proposal of 1919* (London, 1998).

79. Genda, "Tactical Planning," 5.

80. Nobutaka Ike, *Japan's Decision for War* (Stanford, CA, 1967), 248.

81. Ike, *Japan's Decision for War*, 247–249.

82. Potter, *Nimitz*, 169.

83. Potter, *Nimitz*, 6; Halina Rodzinski, *Our Two Lives* (New York, 1976), 211–212.

84. Fuchida, *For That One Day*, 89.

85. See Robert K. Chester, "'Negroes' Number One Hero': Doris Miller, Pearl Harbor, and Retroactive Multiculturalism in World War II Remembrance," *American Quarterly* 65, no. 1 (2013): 31–61.

86. Belote and Belote, *Titans of the Seas*, 3.

87. Roger Chesneau, *King George V Class Battleships* (London, 2004), 13; William Garzke and Robert Dulin, *Battleships of World War II* (London, 1980), 195–207.

88. Fuchida, *For That One Day*, 117–119.

89. William Leahy, *And I Was There* (London, 1950), 82.

90. *Sunday Star* (Washington, DC), December 14, 1941.

91. Potter, *Nimitz*, 10, 172.

92. Casad and Driscoll, *Chester Nimitz*, 133.

93. Orders from King, December 30, 1941, CINCPAC Files, US Navy Gray Book, vol. 1, p. 121.

94. Chester W. Nimitz to Catherine Nimitz, December 21, 1942, Nimitz Papers, Naval Heritage Command.

95. John Lundstrom, *Black Shoe Carrier Admiral* (Annapolis, MD, 2006), 11.

96. Potter, *Nimitz*, 33–38.

97. Symonds, *Battle of Midway*, 99.

98. Quoted in Hiroyuki Agawa, *The Reluctant Admiral*, trans. John Bester (Tokyo, 1979 [1969]), 299.

99. Agawa, *Reluctant Admiral*, 300–301.

100. Fuchida, *For That One Day*, 127.

101. Quoted in Werneth, *Beyond Pearl Harbor*, 163, 192.

102. Fuchida and Okumiya, *Midway*, 239.

103. Masanori Ito, *The End of the Imperial Japanese Navy: A Japanese Account of the Rise and Fall of Japan's Seapower, with Emphasis on World War II*, trans. Roger Pineau (New York, 1962 [1956]), 62.

104. Authors' interview with Richard Nowatzki, Rosemont, California, January 11, 2020.

105. Agawa, *Reluctant Admiral*, 300.

106. Ito, *End of the Imperial Japanese Navy*, 55.

107. Juzo Mori, *The Miraculous Torpedo Squadron*, trans. Nick Voge (2015 [1952]), 184. (Our page numbers have been auto-generated by the printout of the Kindle version.)

108. Symonds, *Battle of Midway*, 108–110, 131; Ito, *End of the Imperial Japanese Navy*, 57; Yokoi, "Thoughts on Japan's Naval Defeat," 507; Cathal Nolan, *The Allure of Battle* (Oxford, 2017), 491.

109. Fuchida and Okumiya, *Midway*, 114.

110. Matome Ugaki, *Fading Victory* (Annapolis, MD, 2008), 141–142.

111. Peattie, *Sunburst*, 75, 147.

112. Edwin Layton, *And I Was There* (New York, 1985), 56–57, 356–357, 361. For Nimitz's use of intelligence before Midway, see also Erik J. Dahl, "Why Won't They Listen? Comparing Receptivity Toward Intelligence at Pearl Harbor and Midway," *Intelligence and National Security* (2013): 83–90.

113. Layton, *And I Was There*, 369.

114. Layton, *And I Was There*, 390.

115. Ed Heinemann, untitled note, "To: Engineering Personnel," March 25, 1942, Heinemann Papers, Box 4/8.

116. Symonds, *Battle of Midway*, 156 ff.

117. John Lundstrom, *First Team* (Annapolis, MD, 1984), 302; Barrett Tillman, *The Dauntless Dive Bomber of World War II* (Annapolis, MD, 1976), 52–53.

118. Peter C. Smith, *The Dauntless in Battle: The Douglas SBD Dive-Bomber in the Pacific, 1941–1945* (Lawrence, PA, 2019), 33–38. See also Belote and Belote, *Titans of the Seas*, 85–93.

119. Quoted in Werneth, *Beyond Pearl Harbor*, 80.

120. Rose McDermott and Uri Bar-Joseph, "Pearl Harbor and Midway: The Decisive Influence of Two Men on the Outcomes," *Intelligence and National Security* 31, no. 7 (2016): 949–962 (esp. p. 960); Dahl, "Why Won't They Listen?"

121. Griffith Bailey Coale, *Victory at Midway* (New York, 1944), 66.

122. McDermott and Bar-Joseph, "Pearl Harbor and Midway," 959.

123. Potter, *Nimitz*, 78.

124. Symonds, *Battle of Midway*, 191–192.

125. Mark Harris, *Five Came Back: A Story of Hollywood and the Second World War* (London, 2014), 144–145 (with quotations).

126. Quoted in Werneth, *Beyond Pearl Harbor*, 117, 192.

127. For the importance of the Japanese intelligence failures to the course of the battle, see Anthony Tully and Lu Yu, "How Faulty Intelligence Drove Scouting at the Battle of Midway," *Naval War College Review* 68 (2015): 85–99.

128. Mori, *Miraculous Torpedo Squadron*, 185–188.

Chapter 3: The Pilot

1. Dusty Kleiss to Jean Mochon, June 3, 1942, Personal Papers of Jack "Dusty" Kleiss (Kleiss Papers hereafter), shared by Timothy and Laura Orr.

2. N. Jack "Dusty" Kleiss, with Timothy and Laura Orr, *Never Call Me a Hero: A Legendary American Dive-Bomber Pilot Remembers the Battle of Midway* (New York, 2017), 1–10 (quotations, pp. 5, 9).

3. Kleiss, *Never Call Me a Hero*, 11.

4. Kleiss, *Never Call Me a Hero*, 16.

5. Kleiss, *Never Call Me a Hero*, 13–17.

6. Carroll Storrs Alden, "The Changing Naval Academy: A Retrospect of Twenty-Five Years," *United States Naval Institute Proceedings* 55, no. 316 (June 1929), reprinted in *The U.S. Naval Institute on the U.S. Naval Academy: The History*, ed. Thomas J. Cutler, U.S. Naval Institute Chronicles (Annapolis, MD, 2015), Kindle loc. 919.

7. Thomas H. Moorer, in Jeremiah Denton, James L. Holloway III, Charles R. Larson, James A. Lovell, John J. McMullen, Thomas H. Moorer, Oliver L. North, et al., "Naval Academy Memories," *Naval History*, October 1995, reprinted in Cutler, *U.S. Naval Institute on the U.S. Naval Academy: The History*, Kindle loc. 2175.

8. Alden, "The Changing Naval Academy," Kindle loc. 1037.

9. Kleiss, *Never Call Me a Hero*, 29–31.

10. Kleiss, *Never Call Me a Hero*, 34–35.

11. Kleiss, *Never Call Me a Hero*, 38–39.

12. David Rigby, *Wade McClusky and the Battle of Midway* (Oxford, 2019), 51.

13. Kleiss, *Never Call Me a Hero*, 72.

14. Kleiss, *Never Call Me a Hero*, 60.

15. Kleiss, *Never Call Me a Hero*, 33, 39, 65.

16. Kleiss, *Never Call Me a Hero*, 63.

17. Kleiss, *Never Call Me a Hero*, 69–70.

18. Kleiss, *Never Call Me a Hero*, 72.

19. See Craig Symonds, *The Battle of Midway* (Oxford, 2011), 61.

20. Edward P. Stafford, *The Big E: The Story of the USS* Enterprise (Annapolis, MD, 2002 [1962]); Barrett Tillman, *Enterprise: America's Fightingest Ship and the Men Who Helped Win World War II* (New York, 2012).

21. Kleiss, *Never Call Me a Hero*, 73.

22. Kleiss, *Never Call Me a Hero*, 72.

23. George Gay, *Sole Survivor: The Battle of Midway and Its Effect on His Life* (Naples, FL, 1979), 24, 29, 30, 33–39.

24. Tillman, *Enterprise*, 12.

25. Kleiss, *Never Call Me a Hero*, 293.

26. Tillman, *Enterprise*, 23–24.

27. Kleiss, *Never Call Me a Hero*, 76.

28. Dave Hirschman, "Flying a National Treasure," *Aircraft Owners and Pilots Association Magazine*, January 5, 2011.

29. Kleiss, *Never Call Me a Hero*, 122.

30. Peter C. Smith, *Midway: Dauntless Victory* (Barnsley, UK, 2007), 133.

31. Harold L. Buell, *Dauntless Helldivers: A Dive-Bomber Pilot's Epic Story of the Carrier Battle* (New York, 1991), 42.

32. "Interview with Earl Gallaher," conducted by Jim Bresnahan, June 4, 1992, World War II Database, https://ww2db.com/doc.php?q=403.

33. Kleiss, *Never Call Me a Hero*, 98.

34. Buell, *Dauntless Helldivers*, 40, 53, 70; "Mark Twain Whittier," United States Navy Memorial, accessed July 2, 2021, http://navylog.navymemorial.org /whittier-mark.

35. Kleiss to Jean Mochon, November 14, 1941, Kleiss Papers.

36. Clarence Dickinson, with Boyden Sparkes, *The Flying Guns: Cockpit Record of a Naval Pilot from Pearl Harbor Through Midway* (New York, 1942), 84.

37. Kleiss, *Never Call Me a Hero*, 79.

38. Buell, *Dauntless Helldivers*, 69.

39. Kleiss, *Never Call Me a Hero*, 83, 101.

40. Alvin Kernan, *The Unknown Battle of Midway: The Destruction of the American Torpedo Squadrons* (New Haven, CT, 2005), 43.

41. Quoted in Stephen L. Moore, *Pacific Payback: The Carrier Aviators Who Avenged Pearl Harbor at the Battle of Midway* (New York, 2014), 142.

42. Kleiss, *Never Call Me a Hero*, 101–103, 241.

43. Gay, *Sole Survivor*, 50, 93–95.

44. Gay, *Sole Survivor*, 50, 58.

45. Gay, *Sole Survivor*, 60.

46. Moore, *Pacific Payback*, 143.

47. James S. Gray Jr., "Decision at Midway," Battle of Midway Roundtable, 2009 [1963], www.midway42.org/Midway_AAR/VF-6-1.aspx, p. 3.

48. Moore, *Pacific Payback*, 179, 99. Kernan, in *Unknown Battle*, 55, said that gunners were allowed to sit at the back of the ready room.

49. Kernan, *Unknown Battle*, 56–58.

50. One notable exception was a gun team aboard the *Hornet*. See Lisle Rose, *The Ship That Held the Line: The U.S.S.* Hornet *and the First Year of the Pacific War* (Annapolis, MD, 1995), 25.

51. See Morris J. MacGregor and Bernard C. Nalty, eds., *Blacks in the United States Armed Forces: Basic Documents*, vol. 6, *Blacks in the World War II Naval Establishment* (Wilmington, DE, 1977), 12–14, 69, 109–117; Chris Dixon, *African Americans and the Pacific War, 1941–1945: Race, Nationality, and the Fight for Freedom* (Cambridge, 2018).

52. Alvin Kernan, *Crossing the Line: A Bluejacket's Odyssey in World War II* (New Haven, CT, 2007), 98.

53. Bill Norberg to Steven McGregor, email, June 13, 2020.

54. Joseph F. Underwood, *The Eight Said No: A Personal History of the Pacific War* (Paducah, KY, 1998), 54. See also Kernan, *Unknown Battle*, 54; Authors' interview with Richard Nowatzki, Rosemont, California, January 11, 2020 (on airdales).

55. The authors are grateful to Timothy Orr for sharing a photo from Kleiss's personal papers that shows him having a beer with Myers in 1941. Papers of Dusty Kleiss, August 16, 2021.

56. Kernan, *Unknown Battle*, 54.

57. Rose, *Ship That Held the Line*, 28, 91, 215. See also Kernan, *Crossing the Line*, 50.

58. Moore, *Pacific Payback*, 69.

59. Kleiss, *Never Call Me a Hero*, 157, 160, 171–172.

60. Moore, *Pacific Payback*, 115.

61. Moore, *Pacific Payback*, 120.

62. Kleiss, *Never Call Me a Hero*, 238.

63. Kleiss, *Never Call Me a Hero*, 90.

64. Joe Taylor of VT-5, as quoted in Stuart D. Ludlum, *They Turned the War Around at Coral Sea and Midway: Going to War with* Yorktown's *Air Group Five* (Bennington, VT, 2011), 13–14.

65. Kernan, *Unknown Battle*, 18.

66. Stanford E. Linzey, *USS* Yorktown *at Midway: The Sinking of the USS* Yorktown *(CV-5) and the Battles of the Coral Sea and Midway* (Fairfax, VA, 2004), 40–41.

67. Kernan, *Crossing the Line*, 37.

68. Linzey, *USS* Yorktown *at Midway*, 78.

69. Rose, *Ship That Held the Line*, 217.

70. Steven McGregor, phone interview with Bill Norberg, June 18, 2020.

71. Linzey, *USS* Yorktown *at Midway*, 48–49.

72. Rose, *Ship That Held the Line*, 145; Clifford Merrill Drury, *The History of the Chaplain Corps, United States Navy*, vol. 2 (Philadelphia, 1994), 172.

73. Quoted in Ron Werneth, *Beyond Pearl Harbor: The Untold Stories of Japan's Naval Airmen* (Atglen, PA, 2008), 45, 79, 111.

74. Makishima Teiichi, *Midway kaisen—Hokyu tsuzukazu* (Battle of Midway—Supplies Dwindle) (2020 [1967]), Kindle loc. 251. We are grateful to Jonathan Yeung for help with this source.

75. Mitsuo Fuchida and Masatake Okumiya, *Midway: The Battle That Doomed Japan in Five Fateful Minutes* (London, 1961), 44.

76. Andrieu d'Albas, *Death of a Navy* (New York, 1957), 127–128.

77. Robert Barde, "The Battle of Midway: A Study in Command" (PhD diss., University of Maryland, 1971), 120.

78. Quoted in Werneth, *Beyond Pearl Harbor*, 137–138.

79. Quoted in Werneth, *Beyond Pearl Harbor*, 18, 80.

80. Kernan, *Unknown Battle*, 57.

81. Dickinson, *Flying Guns*, 13–14.

82. Tillman, *Enterprise*, 36.

83. Kleiss, *Never Call Me a Hero*, 114–116.

84. Dickinson, *Flying Guns*, 24–25.

85. H. L. Hopping, "Report of Action with Japanese at Oahu on December 7, 1941," Scouting Squadron Six Action Report, filed December 15, 1941, USS Enterprise CV-6 Association, Action Reports and Logs, www.cv6.org/ship/logs/ph/vs6-action19411207.htm.

86. Kleiss, *Never Call Me a Hero*, 121.

87. Norberg interview, June 18, 2020.

88. John Hancock, "The Battle of Midway, 75th Anniversary Recollections," hosted by the American Veterans Center Conference, October 27, 2017, C-SPAN, www.c-span.org/video/?436377-2/battle-midway-75th-anniversary-recollections.

89. Kleiss, *Never Call Me a Hero*, 131.

90. Kleiss to Jean Mochon, December 31, 1941, Kleiss Papers.

91. Kleiss to Jean Mochon, February 10, 1942, Kleiss Papers.

92. Presidential Proclamation, Aliens, No. 2526, December 8, 1941.

93. Kleiss, *Never Call Me a Hero*, 165–166. See, generally, Eric T. Gunderson, "American Volksdeutsche: An Analysis of the Nazi Penetration of the German-American Community in the United States," *American Intelligence Journal* 33 (2016): 68–77.

94. Cleo J. Dobson, *Cleo J. Dobson: U.S. Navy Carrier Pilot, World War II, a Personal Account* (2018), 8, 25.

95. Kleiss, *Never Call Me a Hero*, 85.

96. US Navy, Pacific Fleet, *Current Tactical Orders and Doctrine, US Fleet Aircraft*, vol. 1, *Carrier Aircraft* (USF-74) (Washington, DC, 1941), 100.

97. US Navy, Pacific Fleet, USF-74, 74, 122.

98. US Navy, Pacific Fleet, USF-74, 105, 143–144.

99. Interview with Dick Best, Carlton Productions (2001), 23716, Reel 1, Imperial War Museum; Dusty Kleiss, Flight Log Book, March 1942, provided by Timothy and Laura Orr.

100. Quoted in Kernan, *Unknown Battle*, 68. In the same vein, see "war was . . . a serious business," in Buell, *Dauntless Helldivers*, 99.

101. Moore, *Pacific Payback*, 73.

102. Kleiss, *Never Call Me a Hero*, xvii.

103. Rigby, *Wade McClusky*, 10, 21, 85–86, 146–147, et passim.

104. Barrett Tillman, "Dick Best," *The Hook* (Spring 1996): 14–17 (quotation, p. 15).

105. Dickinson, *Flying Guns*, 40.

106. Dobson, *Cleo J. Dobson*, 21.

107. Norman Jack Kleiss, *VS-6 Log of the War: Personal Diary and USS Enterprise Orders of a Scouting Six SBD Dive Bomber Pilot* (San Antonio, TX); Kleiss, *Never Call Me a Hero*, 104.

108. Dickinson, *Flying Guns*, 95.

109. Kleiss, *Never Call Me a Hero*, 55–56 (Winn), 79 (Gallaher).

110. Kleiss, *Never Call Me a Hero*, 127.

111. Norman Vandivier to family, February 12, 1941, Vandivier Family Papers, William Henry Smith Memorial Library, Indiana Historical Society, Series 2, Box 1.

112. Norman Vandivier to family, June 2, 1941, Vandivier Family Papers, Series 2, Box 1.

113. Quoted in Moore, *Pacific Payback*, 52–53.

114. Kleiss, *Never Call Me a Hero*, 85, 119.

115. Kleiss, *Never Call Me a Hero*, 142–143.

116. Kernan, *Unknown Battle*, 40–48.

117. Lloyd Childers, "Midway from the Backseat of a TBD," *The Hook* 18 (1990): 36.

118. Quoted in Kernan, *Unknown Battle*, 62.

119. Kleiss, *Never Call Me a Hero*, 168.

120. Quoted in Kleiss, *Never Call Me a Hero*, 174–175.

121. Fuchida and Okumiya, *Midway*, 114.

122. Fuchida and Okumiya, *Midway*, 130.

123. Quoted in Fuchida and Okumiya, *Midway*, 115.

124. Fuchida and Okumiya, *Midway*, 145.

125. Symonds, *Battle of Midway*, 209–210.

126. Rose, *Ship That Held the Line*, 107.

127. Dickinson, *Flying Guns*, 136.

128. Kleiss, *Never Call Me a Hero*, 176.

129. Dobson, *Cleo J. Dobson*, 38–44.

130. Norman Vandivier to family, February 7 and May 27, 1942, Vandivier Family Papers, Series 2, Box 1; Moore, *Pacific Payback*.

131. Rose, *Ship That Held the Line*, 107–108.

132. Moore, *Pacific Payback*, 163.

133. Symonds, *Battle of Midway*, 190.

134. Gay, *Sole Survivor*, 17–18.

135. Moore, *Pacific Payback*, 168.

136. Robert Cressman, *That Gallant Ship: USS* Yorktown *(CV5)* (Missoula, MT, 2000), 124.

137. Moore, *Pacific Payback*, 169. See also Buell, *Dauntless Helldivers*, 95.

138. Linzey, *USS* Yorktown *at Midway*, 103.

139. Earl Gallaher, "Report of Action, June 4–6, 1942," Scouting Squadron Six Action Report, filed June 20, 1942, USS Enterprise CV-6 Association, Action Reports and Logs, www.cv6.org/ship/logs/action19420604-vs6.htm.

140. Dickinson, *Flying Guns*, 151.

141. Kleiss, *Never Call Me a Hero*, 178.

142. Chester Nimitz to Catherine Nimitz, Pearl Harbor, June 2, 1942, Nimitz Papers, Naval Heritage Command.

143. Dickinson, *Flying Guns*, 138.

144. E. B. Potter, *Nimitz* (Annapolis, MD, 1976), 92.

145. Rose, *Ship That Held the Line*, 116–117.

146. This at any rate is the recollection of George Gay several decades after the battle, in Gay, *Sole Survivor*, 108.

147. Rigby, *Wade McClusky*, 153–154.

148. Operation Plan No. 29-42, May 27, 1942.

149. Dickinson, *Flying Guns*, 139.

150. Kernan, *Crossing the Line*, 57.

151. John Thach, "A Beautiful Silver Waterfall," in *Carrier Warfare in the Pacific: An Oral History Collection*, ed. E. T. Wooldridge, Smithsonian History of Aviation and Spaceflight Series (Washington, DC, 1993), 51–52.

152. Pat Frank and Joseph Harrington, *Rendezvous at Midway:* USS Yorktown *and the Japanese Carrier Fleet* (New York, 1967), 153–154.

153. Ludlum, *They Turned the War Around*, 199, 212.

154. Linzey, *USS* Yorktown *at Midway*, 106.

155. Gray, "Decision at Midway."

156. Gay, *Sole Survivor*, 109.

157. Juzo Mori, *The Miraculous Torpedo Squadron*, trans. Nick Voge (2015 [1952]), 190–191 (quotation, p. 191).

Chapter 4: The Approach

1. See Juzo Mori, *The Miraculous Torpedo Squadron*, trans. Nick Voge (2015 [1952]), 196.

2. See the eyewitness description in Mitsuo Fuchida and Masatake Okumiya, *Midway: The Battle That Doomed Japan in Five Fateful Minutes* (London, 1961), 159–160.

3. Fuchida and Okumiya, *Midway*, 155, 162.

4. Jonathan B. Parshall and Anthony P. Tully, *Shattered Sword: The Untold Story of the Battle of Midway* (Washington, DC, 2005), 80.

5. Kaname Harada, quoted in Dan King, "Survivors of Midway Share Memories," *Orange County Register*, September 4, 2010, www.ocregister.com/2010/09/04 /dan-king-survivors-of-midway-share-memories.

6. Quoted in Ron Werneth, *Beyond Pearl Harbor: The Untold Stories of Japan's Naval Airmen* (Atglen, PA, 2008), 219.

7. Fuchida and Okumiya, *Midway*, 162–163.

8. George Gay, *Sole Survivor: The Battle of Midway and Its Effect on His Life* (Naples, FL, 1979), 112–113; Lisle Rose, *The Ship That Held the Line: The U.S.S.* Hornet *and the First Year of the Pacific War* (Annapolis, MD, 1995), 120.

9. Lewis R. Hopkins, *Dive Bomber Operations in World War II: Battle of Midway* (Fredericksburg, TX, 2004), 9.

10. Clarence Dickinson, with Boyden Sparkes, *The Flying Guns: Cockpit Record of a Naval Pilot from Pearl Harbor Through Midway* (New York, 1942), 140.

11. Interview with Earl Gallaher, conducted by Jim Bresnahan, June 4, 1992, World War II Database, https://ww2db.com/doc.php?q=403.

12. James F. Murray, "Midway: The View from a Bombing Six Rear Seat," *The Hook* 17, no. 1 (Spring 1989): 41.

13. N. Jack "Dusty" Kleiss, with Timothy and Laura Orr, *Never Call Me a Hero: A Legendary American Dive-Bomber Pilot Remembers the Battle of Midway* (New York, 2017), 184.

14. Planes were usually loaded on the flight deck. Hence, the Devastators must have been loaded below in order to expedite departure once the first deck load was airborne.

15. Kleiss, *Never Call Me a Hero*, 185–186.

16. Gordon W. Prange, with Donald M. Goldstein and Katherine V. Dillon, *Miracle at Midway* (New York, 1982), 238.

17. Fuchida and Okumiya, *Midway*, 165–166.

18. Ira L. Kimes, "Report of Battle of Midway Islands," June 7, 1942, accessed online June 29, 2021, Battle of Midway Roundtable, www.midway42.org/ShowPDF .aspx?Page=Midway_AAR/mag22co.pdf.

19. Prange, *Miracle at Midway*, 239.

20. Stuart D. Ludlum, *They Turned the War Around at Coral Sea and Midway: Going to War with* Yorktown's *Air Group Five* (Bennington, VT, 2011), 203.

21. Parshall and Tully, *Shattered Sword*, 200.

22. See R. D. Heinl Jr., *Marines at Midway*, Historical Section, Division of Public Information, US Marine Corps, 1948, 30–32.

23. Mori, *Miraculous Torpedo Squadron*, 196.

24. John Ford, *The Battle of Midway* (1942), YouTube, posted by Zeno's Warbird Videos, www.youtube.com/watch?v=MW8tQ_6dqS8.

25. Pat Frank and Joseph Harrington, *Rendezvous at Midway: USS Yorktown and the Japanese Carrier Fleet* (New York, 1967), 158.

26. Parshall and Tully, *Shattered Sword*, 149.

27. Interview with Gallaher by Bresnahan, June 4, 1992.

28. David Rigby, *Wade McClusky and the Battle of Midway* (Oxford, 2019), 156, 218.

29. Hopkins, *Dive Bomber Operations*, 11.

30. See the description in Seth Paridon, "First Strike at Midway: Attacking and Discovering IJN *Kaga*," National WWII Museum, October 22, 2019, www.national ww2museum.org/war/articles/first-strike-midway-attacking-and-discovering-ijn-kaga.

31. Murray, "Midway," 42.

32. Alvin Kernan, *Crossing the Line: A Bluejacket's Odyssey in World War II* (New Haven, CT, 2007), 66–67.

33. Kernan, *Crossing the Line*, 40.

34. Barrett Tillman, *The Dauntless Dive Bomber of World War II* (Annapolis, MD, 1976), 65.

35. See Hopkins, *Dive Bomber Operations*, 11.

36. Kleiss, *Never Call Me a Hero*, 191.

37. Murray, "Midway," 41.

38. Hopkins, *Dive Bomber Operations*, 11.

39. Earl Gallaher, "Report of Action, June 4–6, 1942," Scouting Squadron Six Action Report, filed June 20, 1942, USS Enterprise CV-6 Association, Action Reports and Logs, www.cv6.org/ship/logs/action19420604-vs6.htm.

40. Kleiss, *Never Call Me a Hero*, 191.

41. Accounts vary. In *Pacific Payback: The Carrier Aviators Who Avenged Pearl Harbor at the Battle of Midway* (New York, 2014), Stephen L. Moore says 12,000 feet (p. 192). Richard Best said 14,000 in "In His Own Words: A Narrative from Battle of Midway Veteran, LCDR Richard H. Best, USN (Ret.)," International Midway Memorial Foundation, accessed June 29, 2021, www.immf-midway.com/midway_itow_best .html. In *Wade McClusky*, Rigby reported that they reached 19,000 feet (p. 177).

42. Quoted in Moore, *Pacific Payback*, 192; Best, "In His Own Words."

43. Quoted in Moore, *Pacific Payback*, 187.

44. C. Wade McClusky, "Accounts: C. Wade McClusky. LCDR C. Wade McClusky: Battle of Midway," USS Enterprise CV-6 Association, accessed June 29, 2021, www.cv6.org/company/accounts/wmcclusky.

45. See the description in Murray, "Midway," 42, and Dickinson, *Flying Guns*, 147–148.

46. Barrett Tillman, *Enterprise: America's Fightingest Ship and the Men Who Helped Win World War II* (New York, 2012), 69.

47. Gay, *Sole Survivor*, 115; Rose, *The Ship That Held the Line*, 127.

48. Gay, *Sole Survivor*, 116–117.

49. Quoted in Werneth, *Beyond Pearl Harbor*, 91.

50. Albert K. Earnest and Harry Ferrier, "Avengers at Midway," *Foundation* 17, no. 2 (Spring 1996), 1–7.

51. Fuchida and Okumiya, *Midway*, 166–167; Parshall and Tully, *Shattered Sword*, 151.

52. Parshall and Tully, *Shattered Sword*, 151–152, 156, 157; quoted in Werneth, *Beyond Pearl Harbor*, 23, 119.

53. Quoted in Werneth, *Beyond Pearl Harbor*, 219–220.

54. Parshall and Tully, *Shattered Sword*, 159.

55. For an account of the attack, see Heinl, *Marines at Midway*, 32–35.

56. V. J. McCaul, "Executive Officer's Report of the Battle of Midway," Annex D, June 7, 1942, Battle of Midway Roundtable, accessed April 10, 2019, www .midway42.org/ShowPDF.aspx?Page=Midway_AAR/mag22xo.pdf.

57. Robert J. Cressman, "Dauntless in War: Douglas SBD-2 BuNo 2106," *Naval Aviation News* 76, no. 5 (July/August 1994).

58. Fuchida and Okumiya, *Midway*, 168–169.

59. Quoted in Werneth, *Beyond Pearl Harbor*, 92.

60. Quoted in Werneth, *Beyond Pearl Harbor*, 92.

61. Parshall and Tully, *Shattered Sword*, 183.

62. Parshall and Tully, *Shattered Sword*, 165–166; Dallas Isom, *Midway Inquest: Why the Japanese Lost the Battle of Midway* (Bloomington, IN, 2007), 160–164.

63. "USS Nautilus, Narrative of June 4, 1942," Action Reports, reel 3 ("Nautilus Report" hereafter), ISSUU, https://issuu.com/hnsa/docs/ss-168_nautilus.

64. Parshall and Tully, *Shattered Sword*, 184–185.

65. Craig Symonds, *The Battle of Midway* (Oxford, 2011), 242; Ira L. Kimes, "Report of Battle of Midway Islands," June 12, 1942, 5.

66. Thaddeus V. Tuleja, *Climax at Midway*, 116; Symonds, *Battle of Midway*, 218; Fuchida himself used "Nagumo's dilemma." Fuchida and Okumiya, *Midway*, 174.

67. Quoted in Prange, *Miracle at Midway*, 231, 232.

68. Prange said that Nagumo made this decision "a minute or two after receipt of the Tone scout's radio" message. Prange, *Miracle at Midway*, chap. 26 (p. 233). *Senshi Sōsho*, the official Japanese history of the war, seems to suggest that Nagumo expected at least one carrier as soon as American ships were sighted. Parshall and Tully, *Shattered Sword*, 164.

69. Paul Holmberg to Walter Lord, June 9, 1958, Walter Lord Interviews, Naval Heritage Command, p. 2. In *Black Shoe Carrier Admiral* (Annapolis, MD, 2006), John Lundstrom writes that Fletcher "desired a force in hand to commit when necessary" (p. 251).

70. John Thach, "A Beautiful Silver Waterfall," in *Carrier Warfare in the Pacific: An Oral History Collection*, ed. E. T. Wooldridge, Smithsonian History of Aviation and Spaceflight Series (Washington, DC, 1993), 52–53.

71. Moore, *Pacific Payback*, 198.

72. Alvin Kernan, *The Unknown Battle of Midway: The Destruction of the American Torpedo Squadrons* (New Haven, CT, 2005), 115.

73. Tillman, *Dauntless Dive Bomber*, 65–67.

74. Kleiss, *Never Call Me a Hero*, 194.

75. Gay, *Sole Survivor*, 118–119.

76. Bowen Weisheit, *The Last Flight of Ensign C. Markland Kelly* (Baltimore, 1996).

77. Max Leslie to Walter Lord, March 8, 1966, Naval Heritage Command, p. 3.

78. DeWitt Shumway, Report of Action, Bombing Squadron Three, June 10, 1942; Tillman, *Dauntless Dive Bomber*, 72.

79. Thach, "Beautiful Silver Waterfall," 54.

80. Lloyd Childers, "Midway from the Backseat of a TBD," 36–37.

81. Paul Holmberg to Walter Lord, June 9, 1958, Naval Heritage Command, pp. 5–6.

82. Moore, *Pacific Payback*, 199; Thach, "Beautiful Silver Waterfall," 54.

83. "USS Nautilus Report," 2.

84. Mori, *Miraculous Torpedo Squadron*, 201.

85. Parshall and Tully, *Shattered Sword*, 205–207.

86. Robert J. A. Mrazek, *A Dawn Like Thunder: The True Story of Torpedo Eight* (Boston, 2008), 134–137; Kernan, *Unknown Battle*, 92.

87. Gay, *Sole Survivor*, 119–128.

88. McClusky, "Accounts: C. Wade McClusky"; Kleiss, *Never Call Me a Hero*, 95.

89. See Rigby, *Wade McClusky*, 162–163.

90. Kleiss, *Never Call Me a Hero*, 196.

91. Stuart J. Mason, "Accounts: John Doherty and Bombing Six. CDR Stuart J. Mason," USS Enterprise CV-6 Association, accessed June 29, 2021, www.cv6.org /company/accounts/jdoherty/jdoherty_2.htm.

92. Paridon, "First Strike at Midway."

93. Moore, *Pacific Payback*, 203–204.

94. Murray, "Midway," 42; Kleiss, *Never Call Me a Hero*, 196.

95. Fuchida and Okumiya, *Midway*, 180–181.

96. R. E. Laub, "Torpedo Squadron Six Action Report," June 4, 1942, USS Enterprise CV-6 Association, Action Reports and Logs, Battle of Midway Roundtable, http://midway42.org/Midway_AAR/VT-6.aspx.

97. Parshall and Tully, *Shattered Sword*, 213–214.

Chapter 5: The Attack

1. N. Jack "Dusty" Kleiss, with Timothy and Laura Orr, *Never Call Me a Hero: A Legendary American Dive-Bomber Pilot Remembers the Battle of Midway* (New York, 2017), 198.

2. James F. Murray, "Midway: The View from a Bombing Six Rear Seat," *The Hook* 17, no. 1 (Spring 1989): 42.

3. Kleiss, *Never Call Me a Hero*, 197; Stephen L. Moore, *Pacific Payback: The Carrier Aviators Who Avenged Pearl Harbor at the Battle of Midway* (New York, 2014), 214–215.

4. Dusty Kleiss, Flight Log Book, January to May 1942, provided by Timothy and Laura Orr.

5. Kleiss, *Never Call Me a Hero*, 198.

6. David Rigby, *Wade McClusky and the Battle of Midway* (Oxford, 2019), 170.

7. As heard by Clarence Dickinson, with Boyden Sparkes, *The Flying Guns: Cockpit Record of a Naval Pilot from Pearl Harbor Through Midway* (New York, 1942), 151. Like Best himself, he places the order as given shortly before the dive rather than on sighting the enemy fleet. Richard Best, "In His Own Words: A Narrative from Battle of Midway Veteran, LCDR Richard H. Best, USN (Ret.),"

International Midway Memorial Foundation, accessed June 29, 2021, www.immf -midway.com/midway_itow_best.html.

8. Lew Hopkins, in Jim Bresnahan, ed., *Refighting the Pacific War: An Alternative History of World War II* (Annapolis, MD, 2011), 148.

9. Rigby, *Wade McClusky*, 183–184.

10. Leslie's interview with Lord is more hectic at this point than his report filed after the battle. In the first he can't raise anyone; in the second he hears from VT-3. Max Leslie to Walter Lord, March 8, 1966, Naval Heritage Command, p. 3.

11. Paul Holmberg to Walter Lord, June 9, 1958, Naval Heritage Command, p. 7.

12. Paul Holmberg to Walter Lord, June 9, 1958, p. 2.

13. Kleiss, *Never Call Me a Hero*, 199.

14. Dickinson, *Flying Guns*, 150.

15. Interview with Earl Gallaher, conducted by Jim Bresnahan, June 4, 1992, World War II Database, https://ww2db.com/doc.php?q=403.

16. Dickinson, *Flying Guns*, 149.

17. Moore, *Pacific Payback*, 216 et passim.

18. Kleiss, *Never Call Me a Hero*, 199.

19. Toshio Hashimoto, *Shōgen Midowei Kaisen* (Witnesses to the Midway Sea Battle) (Tokyo, 1999), 212. We are grateful to Jon Parshall for sharing this source and to Jonathan Yeung for his help with it.

20. Mitsuo Fuchida and Masatake Okumiya, *Midway: The Battle That Doomed Japan in Five Fateful Minutes* (London, 1961), 181.

21. Quoted in Ron Werneth, *Beyond Pearl Harbor: The Untold Stories of Japan's Naval Airmen* (Atglen, PA, 2008), 140; Haruo Yoshino, John Bruning Collection, Hoover Institution, 2000C119.

22. Parshall and Tully, who have made a special study of the Japanese fleet at Midway, noted that the entire combat air patrol tended to attack the immediate enemy, with no one left to check for other threats. "The CAP behaved almost organically," they wrote, "like white blood cells swarming a toxin." Jonathan B. Parshall and Anthony P. Tully, *Shattered Sword: The Untold Story of the Battle of Midway* (Washington, DC, 2005), 215. As another expert, John B. Lundstrom, put it, the Americans drew the Zeros "like a magnet attracting iron filings." John Lundstrom, *First Team* (Annapolis, MD, 1984), 363.

23. Haruo Yoshino, John Bruning Collection, Hoover Institution, 2000C119.

24. See Parshall and Tully, *Shattered Sword*, 229–231 et passim. For a contrary view, see Fuchida and Okumiya, *Midway*, 181–182. The dust jacket shows a "Kate" torpedo bomber about to take off.

25. Parshall and Tully, *Shattered Sword*, 221, 240.

26. Quoted in Werneth, *Beyond Pearl Harbor*, 140.

27. R. E. Laub, "Torpedo Squadron Six Action Report," June 4, 1942, USS Enterprise CV-6 Association, www.cv6.org/ship/logs/action19420604-vt6.htm.

28. Established by Lundstrom, *First Team*, 351 et passim.

29. Lundstrom, *First Team*, 352–356; Parshall and Tully, *Shattered Sword*, 221.

30. John Thach, "A Beautiful Silver Waterfall," in *Carrier Warfare in the Pacific: An Oral History Collection*, ed. E. T. Wooldridge, Smithsonian History of Aviation and Spaceflight Series (Washington, DC, 1993), 55–56.

31. Lloyd Childers, "Midway from the Backseat of a TBD," *The Hook* 18 (1990): 37.

32. Thach, "Beautiful Silver Waterfall," 57.

33. Childers, "Midway from the Backseat of a TBD," 37.

34. Parshall and Tully, *Shattered Sword*, 232, 236; quoted in Werneth, *Beyond Pearl Harbor*, 194.

35. Maeda interview, John Bruning Collection, Hoover Institution.

36. Quoted in Werneth, *Beyond Pearl Harbor*, 140.

37. Quoted in Dan King, *The Last Zero Fighter: Firsthand Accounts from WWII Japanese Naval Pilots* (Irvine, CA, 2012), 164.

38. Maeda interview, John Bruning Collection, Hoover Institution.

39. C. Wade McClusky, "Accounts: C. Wade McClusky. LCDR C. Wade McClusky: Battle of Midway," USS Enterprise CV-6 Association, accessed June 29, 2021, www.cv6.org/company/accounts/wmcclusky.

40. Moore, *Pacific Payback*, 218.

41. See the description in Dickinson, *Flying Guns*, 159.

42. Best, "In His Own Words."

43. Quoted in Werneth, *Beyond Pearl Harbor*, 156, 163.

44. Parshall and Tully, *Shattered Sword*, 234; John Campbell, *Naval Weapons of World War Two* (Annapolis, MD, 1985), 192–193.

45. Noted by Kleiss, *Never Call Me a Hero*, 201.

46. McClusky, "Accounts: C. Wade McClusky"; Lewis R. Hopkins, *Dive Bomber Operations in World War II: Battle of Midway* (Fredericksburg, TX, 2004), 12.

47. Craig Symonds, *The Battle of Midway* (Oxford, 2011), 302; Rigby, *Wade McClusky*, 177.

48. Thach, "Beautiful Silver Waterfall," 58.

49. Dickinson, *Flying Guns*, 159; Moore, *Pacific Payback*, 219.

50. Dickinson, *Flying Guns*, 154.

51. Sesu Mitoya, "I Fought the Americans at Midway," in *Heroic Battles of WWII*, ed. Howard Oleck (New York, 1962), 155.

52. Interview of Gallaher by Bresnahan.

53. Kleiss, *Never Call Me a Hero*, 201.

54. Interview of Gallaher by Bresnahan.

55. Quoted in Moore, *Pacific Payback*, 220.

56. Quoted in Werneth, *Beyond Pearl Harbor*, 163.

57. Parshall and Tully, *Shattered Sword*, 234.

58. Quoted in Werneth, *Beyond Pearl Harbor*, 156.

59. Parshall and Tully, *Shattered Sword*, 234.

60. Murray, "Midway," 42.

61. Fuchida and Okumiya, *Midway*, 182.

62. Parshall and Tully, *Shattered Sword*, 241.

63. "Check-off List for Diving," Douglas SBD Dauntless, *Pilot's Flight Operating Instructions*, 57.

64. Kleiss, *Never Call Me a Hero*, 200; US Navy, Pacific Fleet, *Current Tactical Orders and Doctrine, US Fleet Aircraft*, vol. 1, *Carrier Aircraft* (USF-74) (Washington, DC, 1941), 3.

65. Norman Jack Kleiss, *VS-6 Log of the War: Personal Diary and USS* Enterprise *Orders of a Scouting Six SBD Dive Bomber Pilot* (San Antonio, TX), 88.

66. Kleiss, *Never Call Me a Hero*, 202–203.

67. Kleiss, *VS-6 Log of the War*, 88.

68. Note on the times: Assuming 1 G acceleration and an initial velocity of 276 miles per hour, if the bomb is released at 1,500 feet, it lands in 3 seconds. If at 2,000 feet, then 4 seconds. If 2,500 feet, then 5.13 seconds. See Free Fall Calculator, Omni Calculator, www.omnicalculator.com/physics/free-fall; "Aircraft Bombs," OP 1280, US Department of the Navy, August 30, 1955, https://bulletpicker.com/pdf /OP%201280,%20Aircraft%20Bombs.pdf, pp. 3–4, 62; "Bombs and Bomb Components," TM 9-1325-200, US Departments of the Army, the Navy, and the Air Force, April 1966, https://bulletpicker.com/pdf/TM%209-1325-200,%20Bombs %20and%20Bomb%20Components.pdf, pp. 1–6, 7; "US Navy Projectiles and Fuzes," US Department of the Navy, 1945, p. 237. We thank Norman Friedman and Tony diGiulian for their advice on American ordnance.

69. Kleiss, *VS-6 Log of the War*, 88.

70. Parshall and Tully, *Shattered Sword*, 234.

71. Kleiss, *VS-6 Log of the War*, 88.

72. Quoted in Mitoya, "I Fought the Americans at Midway," 155.

73. Seth Paridon, "First Strike at Midway: Attacking and Discovering IJN *Kaga*," National WWII Museum, October 22, 2019, www.nationalww2museum.org/war /articles/first-strike-midway-attacking-and-discovering-ijn-kaga. Paridon said that Dexter came two behind Kleiss, but if it was the right sequence he should have come immediately after.

74. Parshall and Tully, *Shattered Sword*, 235; Kamei Hiroshi, *Middouē Senki* (Record of the Battle of Midway) (Kōdansha, 2014), 611. We are grateful to Jonathan Yeung for help with this source.

75. Kleiss, *Never Call Me a Hero*, 203, 204.

76. Paridon, "First Strike at Midway."

77. Dickinson, *Flying Guns*, 152, 153.

78. Dickinson, *Flying Guns*, 156–157.

79. Kamei Hiroshi, *Middouē Senki*, 610–611.

80. Edward Rutledge Anderson, War Diary, June 8, 1942. We are grateful to Ian Toll, Janice Anderson-Gram, and Zach Anderson-Gram for making this source available.

81. Thach, "Beautiful Silver Waterfall," 58.

82. Mitoya, "I Fought the Americans at Midway," 154.

83. Symonds, *Battle of Midway*, 306; Parshall and Tully, *Shattered Sword*, 236.

84. Juzo Mori, *The Miraculous Torpedo Squadron*, trans. Nick Voge (2015 [1952]), 204–205.

85. King, *Last Zero Fighter*, 53.

86. Quoted in Parshall and Tully, *Shattered Sword*, 236.

87. Quoted in Werneth, *Beyond Pearl Harbor*, 23.

88. Parshall and Tully, *Shattered Sword*, 235.

89. Quoted in Parshall and Tully, *Shattered Sword*, 236.

90. DeWitt Shumway, Report of Action, Bombing Squadron Three, June 10, 1942.

91. Pat Frank and Joseph Harrington, *Rendezvous at Midway: USS* Yorktown *and the Japanese Carrier Fleet* (New York, 1967), 176.

92. Parshall and Tully, *Shattered Sword*, 237.

93. King, *Last Zero Fighter*, 54.

94. Quoted in Frank and Harrington, *Rendezvous at Midway*, 172.

95. *The Japanese Story of the Battle of Midway*, OPNAV P32-1002 (trans. of Nagumo Report), US Navy, Office of Naval Intelligence, 1947, p. 20.

96. Parshall and Tully, *Shattered Sword*, 237, 238.

97. Hopkins, *Dive Bomber Operations in World War II*, 13.

98. Dickinson, *Flying Guns*, 157–158. (He does not identify the planes, but from the context they are most likely Torpedo Three.)

99. Best, "In His Own Words." Murray says 15,000 feet in "Midway," 42.

100. Murray, "Midway," 42.

101. Fuchida and Okumiya, *Midway*, 182. Best, "In His Own Words," says 2,000 feet. Murray says 1,500 feet in "Midway," 43.

102. Murray, "Midway," 4; Best, "In His Own Words." See also Earl Gallaher, "Report of Action, June 4–6, 1942," Scouting Squadron Six Action Report, filed June 20, 1942, USS Enterprise CV-6 Association, Action Reports and Logs, www .cv6.org/ship/logs/action19420604-vs6.htm.

103. Fuchida and Okumiya, *Midway*, 182.

104. Tom Cheek, "Watching the Attack on the First Carrier Striking Force," Pacific War Historical Society, www.pacificwar.org.au/Midway/TomCheek/Ringof Coral/WatchingAttack.html. Also in Ronald W. Russell, *No Right to Win: A Continuing Dialogue with Veterans of the Battle of Midway* (New York, 2006), 102.

105. Quoted in Werneth, *Beyond Pearl Harbor*, 23, 194.

106. Fuchida and Okumiya, *Midway*, 182.

107. Kamei Hiroshi, *Middoue Senki*, 598.

108. Quoted in Werneth, *Beyond Pearl Harbor*, 179.

109. Quoted in Walter Lord, *Incredible Victory* (Short Hills, NJ, 1967), 175.

110. Gallaher, "Report of Action, June 4–6, 1942," notes that seven of the nineteen pilots had joined the squadron in peacetime.

111. Quoted in Bresnahan, *Refighting the Pacific War*, 148.

112. Fuchida and Okumiya, *Midway*, 183.

113. Mitoya, "I Fought the Americans at Midway," 154.

114. Kleiss, *VS-6 Log of the War*, 88.

Chapter 6: The Inferno

1. Captain C. G. Grimes, chief, US Naval Technical Mission to Japan, "Target Report—Japanese Explosives," December 20, 1945, Fischer-Tropsch Archive, www .fischer-tropsch.org/primary_documents/gvt_reports/USNAVY/USNTMJ%20 Reports/USNTMJ-200E-0551-0578%20Report%200-25.pdf, p. 1.

2. Quoted in Ron Werneth, *Beyond Pearl Harbor: The Untold Stories of Japan's Naval Airmen* (Atglen, PA, 2008), 142.

3. Jonathan B. Parshall and Anthony P. Tully, *Shattered Sword: The Untold Story of the Battle of Midway* (Washington, DC, 2005), 255–256.

4. Quoted in Werneth, *Beyond Pearl Harbor*, 142.

5. Sesu Mitoya, "I Fought the Americans at Midway," in *Heroic Battles of WWII*, ed. Howard Oleck (New York, 1962), 154–155.

6. Quoted in Werneth, *Beyond Pearl Harbor*, 121, 142.

7. Parshall and Tully, *Shattered Sword*, 252.

8. Toshio Hashimoto, *Shōgen Midowei Kaisen* (Witnesses to the Midway Sea Battle) (Tokyo, 1999), 212.

9. See Walter Lord, *Incredible Victory* (Short Hills, NJ, 1967), 179.

10. Kamei Hiroshi, *Middouē Senki* (Record of the Battle of Midway) (Kōdansha, 2014), 621–622.

11. Juzo Mori, *The Miraculous Torpedo Squadron*, trans. Nick Voge (2015 [1952]), 206.

12. Parshall and Tully, *Shattered Sword*, 261.

13. Lord, *Incredible Victory*, 208–209.

14. Mitsuo Fuchida and Masatake Okumiya, *Midway: The Battle That Doomed Japan in Five Fateful Minutes* (London, 1961), 183.

15. Quoted in Fuchida and Okumiya, *Midway*, 184.

16. Makishima Teiichi, *Midway kaisen—Hokyu tsuzukazu* (Battle of Midway—Supplies Dwindle) (Tokyo:.2020 [1967]), Kindle loc. 1501.

17. Quoted in Werneth, *Beyond Pearl Harbor*, 194.

18. There is a detailed account in Captain C. G. Grimes, chief, US Naval Technical Mission to Japan, "Target Report—Japanese Damage Control," February 4, 1946, Fischer-Tropsch Archive, www.fischer-tropsch.org/primary_documents/gvt_reports/USNAVY/USNTMJ%20Reports/USNTMJ-200I-0718-0742%20Report%20S-84%20N.pdf: "Compared to American and British standards, Japanese damage control organization, training and equipment were inferior" (p. 1).

19. Captain C. G. Grimes, chief, US Naval Technical Mission to Japan, "Aeronautics Targets," February 4, 1946, Fischer-Tropsch Archive, www.fischer-tropsch.org/primary_documents/gvt_reports/USNAVY/USNTMJ%20Reports/USNTMJ-200A-0560-0608%20Report%20A-11.pdf, p. 20.

20. Mark R. Peattie, *Sunburst: The Rise of Japanese Naval Air Power, 1909–1941* (Annapolis, MD, 2001).

21. Parshall and Tully, *Shattered Sword*, 277; USS Franklin CV-13 War Damage Report, p. 4.

22. Parshall and Tully, *Shattered Sword*, 254.

23. N. Jack "Dusty" Kleiss, with Timothy and Laura Orr, *Never Call Me a Hero: A Legendary American Dive-Bomber Pilot Remembers the Battle of Midway* (New York, 2017), 205; Norman Jack Kleiss, *VS-6 Log of the War: Personal Diary and USS Enterprise Orders of a Scouting Six SBD Dive Bomber Pilot* (San Antonio, TX), 89; Stanley Culp, "Lieutenant Kleiss Has Had Enough Close Calls for Lifetime," Jax Air News, September 30, 1943, https://ufdc.ufl.edu/UF00028307/01521/3j.

24. Clarence Dickinson, with Boyden Sparkes, *The Flying Guns: Cockpit Record of a Naval Pilot from Pearl Harbor Through Midway* (New York, 1942), 160.

25. Earl Gallaher, "Report of Action, June 4–6, 1942," Scouting Squadron Six Action Report, filed June 20, 1942, USS Enterprise CV-6 Association, Action Reports and Logs, www.cv6.org/ship/logs/action19420604-vs6.htm, p. 2.

26. Kleiss, *Never Call Me a Hero*, 205–206.

27. Kleiss, *Never Call Me a Hero*, 205.

28. Lundstrom puts the start of Torpedo Three's final run at around 1030. John Lundstrom, *First Team* (Annapolis, MD, 1984), 362–363. Parshall and Tully place it about five minutes later. Parshall and Tully, *Shattered Sword*, 255.

29. Parshall and Tully, *Shattered Sword*, 219.

30. "Statement by Harry Corl," June 15, 1942, 2. See also Lloyd Childers, "Midway from the Backseat of a TBD," *The Hook* 18 (1990): 37. (As one would expect from two accounts written more than forty years apart, there are some differences in the details and sequencing.)

31. Lundstrom, *First Team*, 362.

32. Childers, "Midway from the Backseat of a TBD," 37.

33. Parshall and Tully, *Shattered Sword*, 155; Nagatomo Yasukuni, in Hashimoto, *Shōgen Midowei Kaisen*, 212.

34. Hashimoto, *Shōgen Midowei Kaisen*, 212.

35. "Statement by Harry Corl," 2.

36. John Thach, "A Beautiful Silver Waterfall," in *Carrier Warfare in the Pacific: An Oral History Collection*, ed. E. T. Wooldridge, Smithsonian History of Aviation and Spaceflight Series (Washington, DC, 1993), 57.

37. Childers, "Midway from the Backseat of a TBD," 37.

38. See *A Glorious Page in Our History* (Madison, WI, 1990), 100.

39. Lundstrom, *First Team*, 362–363.

40. See Lord, *Incredible Victory*, 181.

41. Lord, *Incredible Victory*, 180.

42. Hashimoto, *Shōgen Midowei Kaisen*, 212.

43. Mori, *Miraculous Torpedo Squadron*, 206–207.

44. Parshall and Tully, *Shattered Sword*, 261.

45. Mori, *Miraculous Torpedo Squadron*, 208; Parshall and Tully, *Shattered Sword*, 279.

46. Mori, *Miraculous Torpedo Squadron*, 209.

47. Lord, *Incredible Victory*, 208.

48. Makishima, *Midway kaisen*, loc. 1517.

49. Parshall and Tully, *Shattered Sword*, 257, 259.

50. Quoted in Werneth, *Beyond Pearl Harbor*, 92.

51. Fuchida and Okumiya, *Midway*, 184.

52. Fuchida and Okumiya, *Midway*, 184.

53. Fuchida and Okumiya, *Midway*, 184, 185.

54. Heijirō Ōmi, *Rengōkantai shireichōkan: Yamamoto Isoroku to sono sanbōtachi* (Tokyo, 2000), 105–106. We are grateful to Jonathan Yeung for help with this source.

55. Lord, *Incredible Victory*.

56. *The Japanese Story of the Battle of Midway*, OPNAV P32-1002 (trans. of Nagumo Report), US Navy, Office of Naval Intelligence, 1947, p. 21.

57. We have borrowed this apt phrase from the words put into the mouth of Tamon Yamaguchi in the film *Midway* (1976); numbers from Parshall and Tully, *Shattered Sword*, 262–263.

58. Parshall and Tully, *Shattered Sword*, 264.

59. Makishima, *Midway kaisen*, loc. 1559.

60. Hiroshi Suzuki, interviewed in Werneth, *Beyond Pearl Harbor*, 92; Parshall and Tully, *Shattered Sword*, 278; Grimes, "Target Report—Japanese Damage Control," 12.

61. Fuchida and Okumiya, *Midway*, 185.

62. Makishima, *Midway kaisen*, loc. 1617.

63. Makishima, *Midway kaisen*, loc. 1633.

64. See Lord, *Incredible Victory*, 209.

65. Parshall and Tully, *Shattered Sword*, 276.

66. Lord, *Incredible Victory*, 209.

67. Quoted in Werneth, *Beyond Pearl Harbor*, 24.

68. Parshall and Tully, *Shattered Sword*, 278–279.

69. Quoted in Werneth, *Beyond Pearl Harbor*, 121, 142.

70. Authors' interview with Richard Nowatzki, Rosemont, California, January 11, 2020.

71. See Craig Symonds, *The Battle of Midway* (Oxford, 2011), 346.

72. Kleiss, *Never Call Me a Hero*, 207.

73. Robert J. Cressman, "Blaze of Glory: Charlie Ware and the Battle of Midway," *The Hook* 24, no. 1 (1996): 24–29, esp. 28–29. See also the account by the pilot of the only Dauntless from Ware's group to make it back: "Accounts: John McCarthy. ENS John McCarthy: Scouting Six and Midway," letter from John McCarthy to Mark Horan, 1992, USS Enterprise CV-6 Association, www.cv6.org/company/accounts /jmccarthy.

74. Kleiss, *Never Call Me a Hero*, 209.

75. C. Wade McClusky, "Accounts: C. Wade McClusky. LCDR C. Wade McClusky: Battle of Midway," USS Enterprise CV-6 Association, accessed June 29, 2021, www.cv6.org/company/accounts/wmcclusky.

76. Edward Rutledge Anderson, War Diary, 44.

77. Elliott Buckmaster, "Report of Action," June 4–6, 1942, report filed June 18, 1942, Battle of Midway Roundtable, http://midway42.org/Midway_AAR /USSYorktown.aspx. See also David L. Bergeron, "Fighting for Survival: USS *Yorktown* (CV5). Damage Control Experiences in 1942" (MA thesis, University of New Orleans, 2016), https://scholarworks.uno.edu/td/2125.

78. Stanford E. Linzey, *USS* Yorktown *at Midway: The Sinking of the USS* Yorktown *(CV-5) and the Battles of the Coral Sea and Midway* (Fairfax, VA, 2004), 86–87, 112.

79. William Ward Smith, *Midway: Turning Point of the Pacific* (New York, 1966), 114–116.

80. Recollection of Richard Nowatzki from the time the *Hornet* was hit in the Solomons a few months later from Nowatzki interview, January 11, 2020.

81. Linzey, *USS* Yorktown *at Midway*, 86, 112–113.

82. Elliott Buckmaster, "Report of Action"; Symonds, *Battle of Midway*, 349.

83. See Alvin Kernan, *Crossing the Line: A Bluejacket's Odyssey in World War II* (New Haven, CT, 2007), 62.

84. Parshall and Tully, *Shattered Sword*, 265–269.

85. Parshall and Tully, *Shattered Sword*, 285.

86. Parshall and Tully, *Shattered Sword*, 288.

87. As recounted by Fuchida and Okumiya, *Midway*, 190, presumably drawing on survivor reports. Juzo Mori had a different account in *Miraculous Torpedo Squadron*, 212–213.

88. Makishima, *Midway kaisen*, loc. 1625.

89. Andrieu d'Albas, *Death of a Navy: Japanese Naval Action in World War II* (New York, 1957), 128. The author, who was married to the daughter of a Japanese admiral, knew many of the protagonists personally.

90. Linzey, *USS* Yorktown *at Midway*, 113–115.

91. Linzey, *USS* Yorktown *at Midway*, 118–119.

92. Quoted in Werneth, *Beyond Pearl Harbor*, 186.

93. Mori, *Miraculous Torpedo Squadron*, 208–217; Parshall and Tully, *Shattered Sword*, 336.

94. Quoted in Werneth, *Beyond Pearl Harbor*, 121.

95. Mitoya, "I Fought the Americans at Midway," 156.

96. Parshall and Tully, *Shattered Sword*, 338–339.

97. Fuchida and Okumiya, *Midway*, 186.

98. Quoted in Werneth, *Beyond Pearl Harbor*, 92.

99. Fuchida and Okumiya, *Midway*, 186.

100. Fuchida and Okumiya, *Midway*, 187.

101. Quoted in Werneth, *Beyond Pearl Harbor*, 92.

102. Stephen L. Moore, *Pacific Payback: The Carrier Aviators Who Avenged Pearl Harbor at the Battle of Midway* (New York, 2014).

103. Symonds, *Battle of Midway*, 313, 320.

104. Symonds, *Battle of Midway*, 349.

105. Mitoya, "I Fought the Americans at Midway," 157.

106. Cleo J. Dobson, *Cleo J. Dobson, U.S. Navy Carrier Pilot, World War I., a Personal Account* (2018), 47.

Chapter 7: The Legacy

1. Geoffrey Till, "Midway: The Decisive Battle?," *Naval History* 19, no. 5 (October 2005): 32–36. See, more generally, Phillips Payson O'Brien, *How the War Was Won: Air-Sea Power and Allied Victory in World War II* (Cambridge, 2015).

2. Eric Hotta, *Japan 1941: Countdown to Infamy* (New York, 2013).

3. Cathal J. Nolan, *The Allure of Battle: A History of How Wars Have Been Won and Lost* (Oxford, 2017), 3, 502 et passim.

4. David C. Evans and Mark R. Peattie, *Kaigun: Strategy, Tactics, and Technology in the Imperial Japanese Navy, 1887–1941* (Annapolis, MD, 1997); Toshiyuki Yokoi, "Thoughts on Japan's Naval Defeat," in *The Japanese Navy in World War II*, ed. David C. Evans (Annapolis, MD, 1969), 514.

5. The counterfactual is explored in Dallas Isom, *Midway Inquest: Why the Japanese Lost the Battle of Midway* (Bloomington, IN, 2007), 278–293; George Friedman, "Midway: The Battle That Almost Lost the War," *Geopolitical Futures*, June 7, 2017, https://geopoliticalfutures.com/midway-battle-almost-lost-war; Ben David Baker, "What If Japan Had Won the Battle of Midway," *The Diplomat*, January 8, 2016, https://thediplomat.com/2016/01/what-if-japan-had-won-the-battle-of-midway. Two chapters of Jim Bresnahan, ed., *Refighting the Pacific War: An Alternative History of World War II* (Annapolis, MD, 2011), 104–168, are devoted to Midway.

6. For Hawaii, see J. J. Stephan, *Hawaii Under the Rising Sun: Japan's Plans for Conquest After Pearl Harbor* (Honolulu, 1984), 109–134.

7. See Jeremy Black, "Midway and the Indian Ocean," *Naval College War Review* 62, no. 4 (2009): 131–140.

8. Craig Symonds, *The Battle of Midway* (Oxford, 2011), 3–4; Andrew Roberts, *The Storm of War* (New York, 2011), 256.

9. George Gay, *Sole Survivor: The Battle of Midway and Its Effect on His Life* (Naples, FL, 1979), 108; Cleo J. Dobson, *Cleo J. Dobson: U.S. Navy Carrier Pilot, World War II, a Personal Account* (2018), 46–47; Edward Rutledge Anderson, War Diary, 50. Though he was an artist, Griffith Bailey Coale personally visited the Pacific during the period and agreed. Griffith Bailey Coale, *Victory at Midway* (New York, 1944), 151.

10. Stephen L. Moore, *Pacific Payback: The Carrier Aviators Who Avenged Pearl Harbor at the Battle of Midway* (New York, 2014), 360.

11. Robert M. Morgenthau and Frank M. Tuerkheimer, "From Midway to Mideast: How a Victory in the Pacific 65 Years Ago Helped Defeat Hitler and Found Israel," *Newsweek* 149 (June 18, 2007).

12. Authors' interview with Karl Zingheim, USS Midway Museum, January 7, 2020.

13. Alvin Kernan, *The Unknown Battle of Midway: The Destruction of the American Torpedo Squadrons* (New Haven, CT, 2005), 8.

14. Christopher Parry, "Do Norman Dixon's Theories About Incompetence Apply to Senior Naval Commanders?" (PhD diss., University of Reading, 2017), 251.

15. Clarence Dickinson and Boyden Sparkes, "Pearl Harbor Remembered: I Fly for Vengeance," *Saturday Evening Post*, October 10–24, 1942.

16. F. C. Hadden, *Midway Islands* (Honolulu, 1943), reprinted from *The Hawaiian Planters' Record* 45, no. 3 (1941): 1.

17. Michael Medved, *God's Hand on America* (New York, 2019), 281.

18. Gay, *Sole Survivor*, 108.

19. Mitsuo Fuchida and Masatake Okumiya, *Midway: The Battle That Doomed Japan in Five Fateful Minutes* (London, 1961), 181.

20. Kernan, *Unknown Battle*, 105.

21. Gay, *Sole Survivor*, 120.

22. Clarence Dickinson, *The Flying Guns: Cockpit Record of a Naval Pilot from Pearl Harbor Through Midway* (New York, 1942), 161.

23. N. Jack "Dusty" Kleiss, with Timothy and Laura Orr, *Never Call Me a Hero: A Legendary American Dive-Bomber Pilot Remembers the Battle of Midway* (New York, 2017), 222.

24. John Lundstrom, *First Team* (Annapolis, MD, 1984), 362, puts one down to antiaircraft fire and one or two down to Zeros.

25. As noted by R. A. Spruance, Task Force 16 Action Report, June 16, 1942, Battle of Midway Roundtable, http://midway42.org/Midway_AAR/RAdmiral _Spruance.aspx, p. 2.

26. Anthony P. Tully, in Bresnahan, *Refighting the Pacific War*, 151; Peter C. Smith, *Midway: Dauntless Victory* (Barnsley, UK, 2007), 165; Peter C. Smith, *The Dauntless in Battle: The Douglas SBD Dive-Bomber in the Pacific, 1941–1945* (Lawrence, PA, 2019), 115, 117, 123–124; Tillman to Heinemann, November 2, 1977, Heinemann Papers, Box 2/22.

27. *Interrogations of Japanese Officials*, vols. 1 and 2, *United States Strategic Bombing Survey [Pacific]*, October 6, 1945, p. 11, Naval History and Heritage Command, www.history.navy.mil/research/library/online-reading-room/title-list-alphabetically/i/interrogations-japanese-officials-voli.html.

28. *Interrogations of Japanese Officials*, October 10, 1945, p. 23.

29. *Interrogations of Japanese Officials*, October 9, 1945, p. 29.

30. *Interrogations of Japanese Officials*, October 25, 1945, p. 40.

31. Clark Lee, "Story of Midway," *Evening Star*, June 11, 1942, A1, A6.

32. Kleiss, *Never Call Me a Hero*, 238–239 (with quotations).

33. "Awakening of Air Power," *Aviation* 41, no. 9 (September 1942): 102–103.

34. See Malcolm Gladwell, *The Bomber Mafia: A Story Set in War* (London, 2021).

35. Spruance, Task Force 16 Action Report, June 16, 1942, p. 2.

36. Edward H. Heinemann and Rosario Rausa, *Combat Aircraft Designer: The Ed Heinemann Story* (London, 1980), 256.

37. Gay, *Sole Survivor*, 158.

38. "State of Affairs in the Pacific Decisively Determined by This Operation," *Tokyo Asahi Shimbun*, June 11, 1942. We are grateful to Jonathan Yeung for bringing this article to our attention.

39. See Gerhard Krebs, *Japan im pazifischen Krieg* (Munich, 2010), 297.

40. Masanori Ito, with Roger Pineau, *The End of the Imperial Japanese Navy: A Japanese Account of the Rise and Fall of Japan's Seapower, with Emphasis on World War II*, trans. Roger Pineau (New York, 1962 [1956]), 68.

41. Quoted in Ron Werneth, *Beyond Pearl Harbor: The Untold Stories of Japan's Naval Airmen* (Atglen, PA, 2008), 92, 121, 142, 163, 196, 220.

42. Kamei Hiroshi, *Middoue Senki* (Record of the Battle of Midway) (Kōdansha, 2014), 624.

43. Lea Jacobs, "December 7th, the Battle of Midway, and John Ford's Career in the OSS," *Film History* 32, no. 1 (2020): 1–39.

44. Mark Harris, *Five Came Back: A Story of Hollywood and the Second World War* (London, 2014), 153, 158. Harris is skeptical that James Roosevelt was actually at Midway (p. 155), although Nimitz mentions meeting him there prior to the battle. Nimitz to Catherine, May 4, 1942, Nimitz Papers, Naval Heritage Command.

45. Harris, *Five Came Back*, 150, 158–159.

46. Dickinson, *Flying Guns*, 52.

47. Lloyd Addison Smith to Fred Vandivier, June 18, 1942; Fred Vandivier to Lloyd Smith, June 29, 1942; Tony Schneider to Fred Vandivier, October 22, 1942, Vandivier Family Papers.

48. "Welcome Aboard . . . ," *Sun Line* 4, no. 1 (November 1, 1965).

49. Kleiss, *Never Call Me a Hero*, 252.

50. Kleiss, *Never Call Me a Hero*, 241, 242–243.

51. E. B. Potter, *Nimitz* (Annapolis, MD, 1976), 398.

52. This is credibly disputed by Jonathan Parshall in "Fuchida's Whoppers," *Naval War College Review* 66, no. 2 (Spring 2013): 137.

53. Kamei Hiroshi, *Middoue Senki*, 625.

54. Heinemann and Rausa, *Combat Aircraft Designer*, 110–124.

55. Quoted in "The Dauntless Story," Heinemann Papers.

56. Barrett Tillman to Heinemann, Heinemann Papers, Box 2/22. See also figures in Barrett Tillman, *The Dauntless Dive Bomber of World War II* (Annapolis, MD, 1976), ix (300,000 tons in 1942).

57. "Design and Operation of United States Combat Aircraft," Office of War Information, January 1942, 23.

58. "Douglas Dauntless SBD Dive Bomber," no date (but clearly during the war), Douglas SBD General, San Diego Air and Space Museum Aircraft Files.

59. Kleiss, *Never Call Me a Hero*, 281.

60. Barrett Tillman, *Enterprise: America's Fightingest Ship and the Men Who Helped Win World War II* (New York, 2012).

61. Potter, *Nimitz*, 400.

62. Kleiss, *Never Call Me a Hero*, 260–263.

63. David Rigby, *Wade McClusky and the Battle of Midway* (Oxford, 2019), 323.

64. Quoted in Martin Fackler, "Retired Fighter Pilot Sees an Old Danger on the Horizon," *New York Times*, April 3, 2015.

65. See Douglas "Interoffice Memorandum: Japanese Market Position," by W. A. Sipprell, February 5, 1962 (copied to Heinemann), Heinemann Papers, Box 2/7.

66. Lecture by Ed Heinemann, July 10, 1953, San Francisco, Heinemann Papers, Box 4/8.

67. Heinemann to Zip Rausa, November 21, 1977, Heinemann Papers, Box 2/22. For similar sentiments expressed in a milder manner, see Heinemann and Rausa, *Combat Aircraft Designer*, 256.

68. Heinemann to Enrique Candioti, Rancho Santa Fe, California, August 2, 1987, Heinemann Papers, Box 3/18.

69. Heinemann to Brigadier-General Tomas A. Rodriguez, Rancho Santa Fe, California, November 4, 1987, Heinemann Papers, Box 3/18.

70. Moore, *Pacific Payback*, 360.

71. Jeffrey Meyer, *Gary Cooper: American Hero* (New York, 1998), 236–238; James H. Farmer, "Hollywood Goes to North Island NAS," *Air Classics* 259 (September 1989).

72. Sandra Wilson, "Film and Soldier: Japanese War Movies in the 1950s," *Journal of Contemporary History* 48, no. 3 (July 2013): 540.

73. See Harold Salomon, "Japan's Longest Days: Toho and the Politics of War Memory, 1967–1972," in *Chinese and Japanese Films on the Second World War*, ed. King-fai Tam, Timothy Y. Tsu, and Sandra Wilson (London, 2015), 126.

74. Fuchida and Okumiya, *Midway*, 181, 239–241. In the same vein, see Masanori and Pineau, *The End of the Imperial Japanese Navy*, 54, 61, 63, 69.

75. Masataka Chihaya, "An Intimate Look at the Japanese Navy," in *The Pearl Harbor Papers*, ed. Donald Goldstein and Katherine Dillon (Dulles, VA, 1993), 314, 317, 328, 360. We are grateful to Katsuya Tsukamoto for sharing this source.

76. *Sensi Sosho*, 102 vols. (Tokyo, 1966–1980), 587–589.

77. Walter Lord, *Incredible Victory* (Short Hills, NJ, 1967), ix–x.

78. Gordon W. Prange, with Donald M. Goldstein and Katherine V. Dillon, *Miracle at Midway* (New York, 1982), viii, 383, xii. The first book titled *Miracle at Midway* was by Charles Mercer and published by Putnam in 1977.

79. Ronald W. Russell, *No Right to Win: A Continuing Dialogue with Veterans of the Battle of Midway* (New York, 2006), 318.

80. J. K. Yamamoto, "A Tale of Two Midways: Comparing the 1976 and 2019 Iterations of the World War II Drama," *Rafu Shimpo Daily News*, November 22, 2019, www.rafu.com/2019/11/a-tale-of-two-midways.

81. Vincent Canby, "On Film, the Battle of 'Midway' Is Lost," *New York Times*, June 19, 1976.

82. See Chris Klimek, "Midway vs. Midway vs. The Battle of Midway: How the New Movie Stacks Up to Past Film Versions," *Air and Space Magazine*, November 15, 2019, www.airspacemag.com/daily-planet/emmidwayem-versus-emmidwayem-versus-emmidwayem-how-latest-movie-about-battle-different-and-how-its-still-same-180973493.

83. Gay, *Sole Survivor*, 311.

84. Gay, *Sole Survivor*, 315.

85. See Guy Vander Jagt to Heinemann, Washington, DC, January 20, 1976, Heinemann Papers, Box 2/19. Vander Jagt was chairman of the fund.

86. Certificate of Appreciation, July 4, 1977, Heinemann Papers, Box 2/22.

87. Reagan to Heinemann, Washington, DC, January 13, 1984, and March 27, 1984, Heinemann Papers, Box 3/11.

88. Robert De Haven to Leon DeLisle, February 28, 1989, Heinemann Papers, Box 4.

89. Gay, *Sole Survivor*, 288.

90. Mitsuo Fuchida, *For That One Day*, trans. Douglas T. Shinsato and Tadanori Urabe (Kamuela, HI, 2011), 15.

91. Feng Shao-Zhu to Heinemann, Beijing, March 8, 1983, Heinemann Papers, Box 3/9 (also contains some undated notes by Heinemann on his trip to Beijing). Feng Shao-Zhou was deputy chief representative for China National Aero Technology Import and Export Corporation.

92. Heinemann to David Lewis, December 5, 1984, Heinemann Papers, Box 3/12.

93. Heinemann to "Joe" [Surname Omitted], April 3, 1988, Heinemann Papers, Box 4/1.

94. Heinemann to Sun Fang and Huang Peicheng, January 16, 1987, Heinemann Papers, Box 3/17.

95. Heinemann to Gao Zhong Tong (China Yanshan Science and Technology Corporation, Beijing), Rancho Santa Fe, California, August 23, 1984, Heinemann Papers, Box 3/12.

96. Heinemann to David Lewis, August 23, 1984 ("Dave" appears to be David Lewis, chairman of the board at General Dynamics), Heinemann Papers, Box 3/12.

97. John Lehman, *Oceans Ventured: Winning the Cold War at Sea* (New York, 2018), 156.

98. Details kindly supplied in Bob van der Linden to Steven McGregor, email, October 1, 2020.

99. Prange, *Miracle at Midway*, xiii.

100. John Lundstrom, *First Team* (Annapolis, MD, 1984), 351–364.

101. Thomas Wildenberg, "Midway: Sheer Luck or Better Doctrine," Naval History and Heritage Command, 2004, www.history.navy.mil/research/library/online-reading-room/title-list-alphabetically/m/midway-sheer-luck-or-better-doctrine.html.

102. Isom, *Midway Inquest*.

103. Russell, *No Right to Win*, 59–61.

104. Robert J. Cressman, "Dauntless in War: Douglas SBD-2 BuNo 2106," *Naval Aviation News* 76, no. 5 (July/August 1994): 24–26.

105. Smith, *Midway: Dauntless Victory*.

106. Symonds, *Battle of Midway*, 5.

107. Moore, *Pacific Payback*, 1–3.

108. Admiral Jay Johnson, Administrative Message, June 4, 1999, Naval History and Heritage Command, www.history.navy.mil/browse-by-topic/commemorations-toolkits/wwii-75/battle-of-midway/why-we-celebrate.html#99.

109. Kleiss, *Never Call Me a Hero*, xiv.

110. Kleiss, *Never Call Me a Hero*, 279.

111. Kernan, *Unknown Battle*, 107.

112. Werneth, *Beyond Pearl Harbor*.

113. Symonds, *Battle of Midway*, 5.

114. Kleiss, *Never Call Me a Hero*, 279.

115. Kleiss, *Never Call Me a Hero*, 270–271.

116. There is, in fact, no evidence that Yamamoto ever used this famous phrase, but it certainly reflects his thinking at the time.

117. Roland Emmerich, "Midway: The Pacific War On Screen," *BBC History Extra Podcast*, November 11, 2019.

118. Forty-five percent of the budget was covered by distribution deals and 55 percent came from the investment firms. Erich Schwartzel, "Hollywood Revisits Battle of Midway—with Backing from China," *Wall Street Journal*, November 8, 2019, www.wsj.com/articles/hollywood-revisits-battle-of-midwaywith-backing-from-china-11573214401.

119. Kevin Miller, *Silver Waterfall* (Pensacola, FL, 2020), Kindle loc. 5760.

120. Niccolò Machiavelli, *The Prince*, chap. 25.

121. Marco del Bene, "Past to Be Ashamed Of or Proud Of? Echoes of the Fifteen-Year War in Japanese Film," in King-fai Tam et al., *Chinese and Japanese Films*, 171–172.

122. Greg Waldron, "Analysis: Izumo and Kaga, Aircraft Carriers in All But Name," *Flight Global*, April 23, 2019, www.flightglobal.com/analysis/analysis-izumo-and-kaga-aircraft-carriers-in-all-but-name/132356.article.

123. Toshi Yoshihara and James Holmes, *Red Star over the Pacific: China's Rise and the Challenge to US Maritime Strategy* (Annapolis, MD, 2020).

124. Quoted in Harry Lye, "China Boasts World's Largest Navy, US DoD Report," Naval Technology, September 2, 2020, www.naval-technology.com/features/china-boasts-worlds-largest-navy-us-dod-report.

125. Bruno Macaes, *Belt and Road: A Chinese World Order* (London, 2018), 33–34.

126. Quoted in Michael Auslin, *Asia's New Geopolitics: Essays on Reshaping the Indo-Pacific* (Stanford, CA, 2020), 5, 226.

127. Lehman, *Oceans Ventured*, 283. See also Roger Thompson, *Lessons Not Learned: The US Navy's Status Quo Culture* (Annapolis, MD, 2007).

128. James Holmes, "Can the Navy Fix Its Shipyard Problem?," 19FortyFive, May 9, 2021, www.19fortyfive.com/2021/05/can-the-u-s-navy-fix-its-shipyard-problem.

129. Seth Cropsey, "US Naval Strategy Is at Sea," *Wall Street Journal*, April 27, 2021, www.wsj.com/articles/americas-naval-strategy-is-at-sea-11619543738.

130. See, generally, Auslin, *Asia's New Geopolitics*, xi et passim.

131. Humphrey Hawksley and Simon Holberton, *Dragon Strike: The Millennium War* (Basingstoke, UK, 1997).

132. Auslin, *Asia's New Geopolitics*, 185–228.

133. Elliot Ackerman and Admiral James Stavridis, *2034: A Novel of the Next World War* (New York, 2021).

134. Elbridge A. Colby, *The Strategy of Denial: American Defense in an Age of Great Power Conflict* (New Haven, CT, 2021).

135. David Zikusoka, "The Second Battle of Midway," Center for a New American Security, July 18, 2019, www.cnas.org/publications/commentary/the -second-battle-of-midway.

136. Lyle J. Goldstein, "What Do China's Military Strategists Think of the Battle of Midway?," *The National Interest*, June 4, 2017, https://nationalinterest.org /feature/what-do-chinas-military-strategists-think-the-battle-midway-20990. A revised version of this article was published due to "reader interest" after the Emmerich film as "Forget the Movie: China Is Studying the Battle of Midway," *The National Interest*, November 8, 2019, https://nationalinterest.org/blog/buzz /forget-movie-china-studying-battle-midway-95331.

137. Goldstein, "What Do China's Military Strategists Think?"

138. Xu Fan, "China's Role in Midway's Success," *China Daily*, November 13, 2019, www.chinadaily.com.cn/a/201911/13/WS5dcb9b9da310cf3e35577187.html.

139. Gay, *Sole Survivor*, 308.

140. Kleiss, *Never Call Me a Hero*, 198.

141. John Thach, "A Beautiful Silver Waterfall," in *Carrier Warfare in the Pacific: An Oral History Collection*, ed. E. T. Wooldridge, Smithsonian History of Aviation and Spaceflight Series (Washington, DC, 1993), 58.

INDEX

interpretation in Japan, 207–208,
219–220, 225–227
interpretation in US, 206–207,
208–209, 220, 229–230, 233
junior officers' role, 201–202
legacy, 234–235
lessons from, 237–238, 240
losses, 202, 242
memory of, 214–215, 229, 232
movie by Ford, 70–71, 127, 208–209
and outcome of war in the Pacific,
199–201
personal accounts, 229–231
in popular culture, 218–222, 228,
231–233
preparations by Japanese, 71–72,
107–110, 118, 121–122
preparations by US, 69–71, 72, 73,
112–118, 124–125, 129, 189
return of US planes, 177, 179, 187, 188
scouting and reconnaissance, 112–113,
114, 125–126, 133, 134, 136
secondary explosions in carriers,
171–174, 175, 181–182
sighting of Japanese by US, 114
sinking of Japanese carriers, 171
survivors at sea, 196–197
tension building, 114–118, 124–125
as turning point in World War II, 3–4,
115, 198, 200, 201
victory as luck, 3–4, 220, 222
Midway (film, 1976), 3, 221–222
Midway (film, 2019), 231–233, 238
Midway (ship), 214
Mikasa (battleship), 212
Miller, Doris, 57, 107, 239
Miller, Kevin, 233
Mines Field airport, 25
Miracle at Midway (Prange), 3, 220, 225
Mitchell, Samuel G. "Pat," 138
Mitoya, Sesu
in Battle of Midway, 155, 157, 159,
161–162, 167, 172, 195
on Battle of Midway, 198
Mitscher, Pete (Mark Andrew), 63, 131,
187
Miura, Gishiro, 196
Mochon, Eunice. *See* Jean
monoplane, development of, 24–25
Moore, Stephen, 228
Moreland Aircraft, 13
Moreland M-1, 14

Morgenthau, Robert M., 201
Mori, Juzo
after Battle of Midway, 212, 216
in Battle of Midway, 126–127, 132,
140, 162, 163, 173–174, 180–181,
194–195
to Battle of Midway, 72, 118, 122
and defense of Japan, 64
Morinaga, Takayoshi, 155, 157, 180, 208
Morita, Chisato, 185
Motoki, Shigeo, 208, 213
Murray, George, 115
Murray, James, 128, 129, 146, 157,
164–165
Myers, Curtis, 93

Nagara (cruiser), 174, 182, 185, 191, 192
Nagumo, Chuichi
after Battle of Midway, 212
attack on Midway, 123
for Battle of Midway, 121
in Battle of Midway, 132, 133,
134–136, 140, 143, 144, 150, 174,
182, 185–186, 191, 195, 196
intelligence for Battle of Midway, 72,
121
over-confidence, 63, 109
personality, 108–109
plans for Battle of Midway, 108–109
in revisions of history, 226
and scouting, 126, 133, 134, 136
"Nagumo's dilemma" or "Nagumo's
ordeal," 135–136
National Advisory Committee for
Aeronautics (NACA, now NASA),
26
Nautilus (submarine), 126, 135, 140
Naval Academy (Annapolis), 36–37
Naval Air Station Pensacola, 80
naval aviation
advances in 1930s, 25
debates on bombing types, 206–207
as field in US and first examples, 15
Japanese in, 20, 21–22, 200
See also seaplanes
naval warfare, and gunpower *vs.* airpower
debate, 42, 43, 45–46, 52–53, 58,
103–104
navy of Japan. *See* Japanese Navy
navy of US. *See* US Navy
Nelson, Donald, 67
Never Call Me a Hero (Kleiss), 230–231

285

Brendan Simms is author of *The Longest Afternoon* (2014), a dramatic description of the defense of the farm of La Haye Sainte during the Battle of Waterloo in 1815. In 2019 he published the acclaimed biography *Hitler*. His most recent book, cowritten with Charlie Laderman, is *Hitler's American Gamble: Pearl Harbor and Germany's March to Global War* (2020).

Steven McGregor deployed to the Sunni Triangle of Death as an infantry officer in the 101st Airborne Division. There he was awarded the Combat Infantryman's Badge and the Purple Heart. After his military service he moved to England and completed postgraduate studies in history. This is his first book.

PublicAffairs is a publishing house founded in 1997. It is a tribute to the standards, values, and flair of three persons who have served as mentors to countless reporters, writers, editors, and book people of all kinds, including me.

I. F. Stone, proprietor of *I. F. Stone's Weekly*, combined a commitment to the First Amendment with entrepreneurial zeal and reporting skill and became one of the great independent journalists in American history. At the age of eighty, Izzy published *The Trial of Socrates*, which was a national bestseller. He wrote the book after he taught himself ancient Greek.

Benjamin C. Bradlee was for nearly thirty years the charismatic editorial leader of *The Washington Post*. It was Ben who gave the *Post* the range and courage to pursue such historic issues as Watergate. He supported his reporters with a tenacity that made them fearless and it is no accident that so many became authors of influential, best-selling books.

Robert L. Bernstein, the chief executive of Random House for more than a quarter century, guided one of the nation's premier publishing houses. Bob was personally responsible for many books of political dissent and argument that challenged tyranny around the globe. He is also the founder and longtime chair of Human Rights Watch, one of the most respected human rights organizations in the world.

∙ ∙ ∙

For fifty years, the banner of Public Affairs Press was carried by its owner Morris B. Schnapper, who published Gandhi, Nasser, Toynbee, Truman, and about 1,500 other authors. In 1983, Schnapper was described by *The Washington Post* as "a redoubtable gadfly." His legacy will endure in the books to come.

Peter Osnos, *Founder*